JUL 3 0 2013

D. R. Toi
PO Box 1698
Newport News, VA 23601

July 31-2013 TO

PRANIC NOURISHMENT

NUTRITION FOR THE NEW MILLENIUM

by

JASMUHEEN

This book is
Book 1 of the Divine Nutrition Series
Book 2 – Ambassadors of Light
Book 3 – The Prana Program
Book 4 – The Law of Love
Book 5 – Memories & Motivations – Breatharian Pathways
Book 6 – Being Essence

Pranic Nourishment – Nutrition for the New Millennium
Book 1 of the Divine Nutrition : Living on Light Series by Jasmuheen
2012 edition

Published by the
Self Empowerment Academy
P.O. Box 1754, Buderim, 4556, Australia
Fax: +61 7 5445 6075

Published February 1996
Updated June 1996; October 1997
April 1997; April 2001; April 2002 &
March 2006 & August 2012
2nd Edition November 1996

3rd Edition January 1997 additions for German
Translation and European distribution called
"Lichtnahrung"
4th Edition and name change from
Prana & Immortality to Pranic Nourishment
October 1997

5th Edition – 2012 –
ISBN 978-1-84753-407-1

E-book produced October 2002
Re-edited & re-released August 2006 & August 2012

DEDICATION

For all those
interested in tuning to their highest
maximum potential.

To those who then have the courage to allow the
Divine spark within
to sustain them
and …

To those who can give themselves
permission to be all that they can.

"The Divine, decrees rules.
These are the natural laws of energy.
When we understand and apply these,
magic and order are brought in to play within the chaos.
We begin to comprehend our limitless nature
and our abilities as creative beings,
here, quite simply to create,
to be, to know joy, to love unconditionally
and to honour."

Jasmuheen

FOREWORD

It's funny when you are really meant to do something it never goes away! It's like a jack-in-a-box that keeps popping its lid and saying 'hi' or 'boo' as the case may be. You shut the lid and then up it pops again!

I guess that's the way it's been with this book and the whole process that myself, and now many others, have undergone to allow the physical body to be sustained and nourished purely by Light.

Although my guidance, received in September 1995, was to produce a booklet of information on Being sustained by Prana, I have never held the desire to either 'market' the idea or my experience 'en mass' or to physically help anyone through this process. Neither has been part of my service here at this time.

After undergoing the 'process' (detailed in the later chapters) in June 1993 I went into a period of nearly six months solitude. I meditated, many days for nearly 3 hours, I wrote in my journal and generally sought to open up the channels of communication for my own inner guidance to clearly and strongly flow through.

During this time, I began to channel and received very clear instructions from my Divine Self as to what my purpose and 'mission' was in this embodiment. I established the Self Empowerment Academy and began teaching the Art of Resonance classes and holding seminars on all I had come to understand. I travelled to where I was invited.

In mid 1995, I was invited to attend the International Gathering of the Masters at Lake Taupo in New Zealand. The invitation was issued specifically for me to share about being sustained by Prana. This is something I had not thought about for some time and more has transpired since I wrote the notes that formed chapter 27 in the book *In Resonance* that feels appropriate to share here. (Some of the more relevant information on my personal journey, living on prana and physical immortality I have also taken from my book *In Resonance*).

I do not think any of the dozen of us who underwent the 21-day process in that June of 1993 had any idea of the division that would befall not only our community of Lightworkers but also all communities from Melbourne, Adelaide, Perth and Tasmania, and probably others that I am not aware of, as a consequence of our choices.

Many reacted to this process with the idea that you cannot 'fast your way to Ascension', many responded that they could not possibly give up their food, some offered money to follow me around to prove I was not a 'closet eater'. This process has triggered much doubt and fear, much criticism and judgment.

Many have undergone the 21 days and then returned to a lighter diet of fresh fruit and vegetables; some have resumed their regular eating patterns. All realities and understanding serve each individual but, regardless of personal understanding, beings that stay with this process are definitely being sustained by Light.

It is not about fasting, it is about allowing, trusting, clicking into an energy pattern of knowing that our true sustenance is provided by Cosmic Light, which sustains many beings from many Universes, and is a possibility offered to us here and now. Nor is it a process of denial. During the last 2 years I have often been guided by the Masters to even stop having fluid, they have assured me that the body needs only 'Liquid Light' but I like a cup of tea, I like socialising over a 'cuppa' with friends and – at the time of writing this – I have not conquered my intermittent interest in flavour. When I can embrace that without denial, I will do so for every step of the way is one I wish to do in joy and comfort with ease and grace.

After the initial excitement of discovering, that Prana can sustain us waned, and due to some intense negative reactions by many, I stopped sharing or even mentioning about this aspect of my journey. It suited me, so I stayed with it but I could see that for the majority of people it was not even a remote possibility, as the pleasure gained from food is quiet immense in our Western society. Many, I have found, do not eat to live but actually live to eat.

They (the Ascended Masters) show me visions of a world without hunger, no food outlets or farming except to grow for the sake of beauty not need. Imagine how many billions of dollars could be diverted to other things if everyone trusted they could be fed by Universal substance, by God's Light alone?

Personal and social change comes from people's dreams and visions, from daring to explore other possibilities. For me this journey has been one requiring great discipline and trust, as there has been no reference manual to read, no healers to inform me of bodily changes based on their previous exposure. Due to the reactions of fear, judgment etc. just mentioned I found myself silently continuing my path only sharing when sincerely asked to do so. As I travelled with my seminars etc. rumour spread and by mid 1995, I found that approximately 50% of those attending workshops sincerely wanted more information.

I also have found that either during or shortly after my seminars many, under their own volition began the process I described – usually with very little information. Information gives not only power but also choice. The purpose of this book is to give as much information as possible to help to make this journey as easy as possible. This is a journey only for any whose hearts guide them to undertake it in this particular manner.

One of the things that I have come to understand is the only thing we are truly limited by is our beliefs. That we have the ability, and the opportunity, to create a reality that allows us to live our life to our fullest potential. If our life is not operating at maximum potential and fulfilling our personal standards and expectations then maybe we can look at our belief systems and broaden or change our model of understanding.

The model I have created embraces a reality of Universal Laws, energy bands of Consciousness, Beings of Light and ascension and it changes as I grow and reawaken to my own Divinity. The understanding that I have gained from my model is that this is a journey of wonder and joy, that when we truly recognise that which we are then it does not matter where we are, or on what plane of expression we focus for all is interconnected and all is One. There is no separation except that which we choose to create. The ability to live on light also adds another band of freedom to existence, which is incredibly empowering.

In my journey, I have found many individuals who are interested in pranic nourishment from a dietary point of view and are not particularly tuned to the Ascended Master paradigm. Others, though understanding various energy bands and the 'other life forms' reality, have felt that undergoing a 21-day process either time consuming or too extreme and also have expressed interest in a more 'gentle way'. For them, we include the chapter "Other Ways".

In this revised edition we have also included more information on tuning, the four body system and vibrational frequencies as I had originally thought that beings drawn to this book would naturally be tuned instruments and have the type of understanding covered in my book *In Resonance* yet I have since found this is not always so.

So ... if the information and content of this book has appeal to you then ask in your meditation and times of contemplation for guidance for your next step – for only the Divine One Within you can provide what you need.

October 1997:

This is just our story and research, the decision to undergo the process mentioned here must come from your own heart simply because it feels right for you. Realise that this is potentially one of the most powerful things you may ever do, that if you prepare for this properly, you will never be the same afterwards. Your life will change, your perspective will change and much more ... so ...

Again, we update this journal. Firstly to change the name from *Prana & Immortality* to *Pranic Nourishment* as it reflects more accurately our work, and secondly to include the article of 'Self Healing' to tune yourself pre-process and 'Transmutation' and 'Being in Balance', to advise you on things post process. As with anything, we encourage you to use your discernment and absorb what feels right within your heart, at this time it may not be in your blueprint to be part of this but it is in mine to let you know of its possibility!

April 2002:

Over the last decade of researching this subject and sharing this with the world, we have come to understand many more things since this book was first written. The most important thing is that no initiation can guarantee a person's ability to live free from the need from physical food. The secret to this is in the individual's personal frequency or keynote. The more they anchor themselves into the Theta and Delta fields, the easier this becomes.

While our personal research with this still continues, the medical aspects we now leave to Dr. Sudhir Shah and his team in India and a synopsis of his findings with being nourished by prana is now in the back of this book. More research can be found in my follow-up book to this *Ambassadors of Light — World Health, World Hunger Project*.

The main point I would like to make in this update is that it is unnecessary to do the 21-day initiation that is outlined in this book. Due to shifts over the last decade within the morphogenetic field, many are now moving into the living on light reality with joy, ease, and Grace and as a natural consequence of their daily lifestyle choice, which keeps them tuned to the right channel to do this successfully. Further tools to do this are outlined in what I hope to be my final book on the subject *The Food of Gods*.

March 2006:

The Food of Gods manual of research was completed in 2003 and was followed by the book *The Law of Love & Its Fabulous Frequency of Freedom*. In 2005, I completed the book *The Prana Program* that offers a simplistic program for Third World feeding using prana — or micro food — as an internal nourishment source.

If what is written in the following pages touches your heart, then I recommend that you read all follow-up manuals on this topic before proceeding with your personal journey with this. As this book you are about to read was written over a decade ago, and so much more has come to light, re the ability we all have to receive perfect nourishment from the Divine One Within us.

An Internet search using www.google.com recently revealed over 4.35 million listings for prana, 124 million listings for chi and 48 million listings for the universal life force. Hence, while it may still be unusual for Westerners to increase the pranic flow to the degree that it can healthily nourish them on all levels, this force has been accessible for eons of time and can now be utilised to free our Western World and Third World countries from all health and hunger challenges. This is the reason that I have become public with the journey, for the Divine One Within has so many gifts to nourish us and the following journey is one. While this book primarily deals with the 21-day process - which I no longer recommend - there are many ways to move into the prana only nourishment reality. While the 21-day process that we discuss from Chapters 9 to 14 will give a gift to the one undergoing this initiation, it may not be the gift of living purely on pranic light.

August 2012 Update:
It is hard to believe that it is nearly twenty years since I underwent the controversial 21-day process that we outline in this book, a sacred initiation that works so beautifully for some yet has proven dangerous for the unprepared. Nonetheless, the 'being nourished by prana as cosmic micro food reality' has continued to spread itself around the world.

In 2006, I began to film the documentary *In The Beginning There Was Light* with Austrian film critic P.A. Straubinger. Six years in the making, Peter filmed over 200 hours of footage as he interviewed countless of people about their experiences of being able to be physically nourished by prana. For me it was wonderful to be able to share about these ones with him during this interview, as in 1993, when I underwent this initiation there were no books of reference and virtually no one that was in the public eye who did this and who was also involved in positive global education about this phenomena. To arrive in 2006 and be able to talk of all the others I had discovered who were now also active was wonderful!

Released at the Cannes film festival in 2010, the movie invites a sceptical viewer to understand a little more regarding the power of our mind, using the examples of people living on prana as a physical body nourishment source and it has been instrumental in educating many about this field of possibility.

So, we hope you enjoy this new 2012 version of this book and all that it contains; as what we share here has many benefits on health, hunger and environmental levels in our world. It is also part of human evolution.

NAMASTE – Jasmuheen

CONTENTS

DEDICATION 5
FOREWORD 7
- Chapter 1 13
  - ENERGY – 13
  - the Four Body System, Photon Energy 13
  - and the Body as an Energy System 13
- Chapter 2 17
  - Understanding & Working 17
  - with Vibrational Frequencies 17
- Chapter 3 22
  - 33 – The Universal Beat 22
- Chapter 4 28
  - The Sustaining Force of Prana 28
- Chapter 5 33
  - The Story of Giri Bala 33
  - The Story of Teresa Neumann 34
- Chapter 6 35
  - Physical Immortality 35
- Chapter 7 40
  - The Great Immortalists 40
    - Babaji 40
    - Comte de Saint Germain 41
    - The Yoga of Everlasting Life 42
  - Vrishvahan Samadhi (Soruba) 43
  - written by Leonard Orr 43
    - Prana & Interdimensional Life – 46
    - plus message from Arcturius 46
    - The Arcturians – Message 48
- Chapter 8 58
  - One Way 58
- Chapter 9 60
  - Being Sustained by Prana 60
  - A Personal Journey 60
- Chapter 10 65
  - Questions and Answers 65
- Chapter 11 73
  - Spirituality and Sexuality 73
    - Sexuality & Spirituality – Male Potency 73
  - by Eltrayan 74
    - Sexuality & Spirituality – Female Potency 76
- Chapter 12 78

- The Journeys of Others 78
- **Chapter 13** 86
  - A Sacred Initiation 86
- **Chapter 14** 89
  - Guidelines for the 21-day process 89
  - by Charmaine Harley 89
    - Questionnaire 92
    - The 21-day Day Procedure - Converting the Physical Body 103
- **Chapter 15** 111
  - Other Ways 111
- **Chapter 16** 113
  - Future Potential – World Hunger 113
- **Chapter 17** 116
  - Paradigms – Kuthumi 116
    - Received through Jasmuheen 2nd September 1996 116
- **Chapter 18** 121
  - Programming – Mind Power 121
    - NEW MILLENIUM GUIDELINES 124
    - the Ascended Ones 125
- **Chapter 19** 126
  - Self Healing 126
- **Chapter 20** 131
  - Postscript end May 1996 – 131
  - Press Reaction 131
    - 2nd Postscript – Social Reaction 133
- **Chapter 21** 136
  - "To Eat or not to Eat" 136
- **Chapter 22** 143
  - The Balance of Being 143
    - Update April 2001: 145
    - Get Fit for Prana 147
    - The Hypothesis: on Prolonged Fasting 149
    - with Dr. Sudhir Shah 149
    - Additions March 2006: 155
    - A THREE LEVEL CONFIRMATION SYSTEM 156
    - Q & A's on the 21-day process, ... 161
    - 2012 Update 167
    - Jasmuheen's Background 177

Chapter 1

ENERGY –
the Four Body System, Photon Energy and the Body as an Energy System

February 1996:
I have come to understand that the process that I – and many others – have undergone to allow the body to be sustained by light; is about utilising photon energy to sustain us via a process like photosynthesis. Rather than take the energy from the sun as plants do we have developed the ability to tap into and absorb the Universal Life force or 'chi' energy directly into our cells. This occurs via mind mastery where command and expectation utilizes the Universal Law of Resonance where like attracts like. Because I expect the pranic forces to nourish and sustain me having undergone the 21-day process as outlined in the latter chapters, it does.

The ability to be sustained by prana is a natural consequence of being a tuned instrument. Research into holistic medicine shares that human beings exist within physical reality in what is termed a four-body system. This consists of the physical, emotional, mental and spiritual or etheric bodies. Simplistically these can be likened to a four-string guitar. When they are out of tune, we can experience various degrees of physical, emotional or mental illness or dissatisfaction with life. When they are tuned, life becomes magical.

When these lower bodies (termed lower due to their slower rate of vibration) are tuned to the frequency of the higher bodies then human beings can live life to their highest maximum potential. Telepathy, clairvoyance and being able to exist without food or even sleep, are just natural by-products of being a tuned instrument.

To elaborate further on the concept of energy ...

Energy – according to the Oxford dictionary, is the "ability of matter or radiation to do work". According to Stephen Hawking in *A Brief History of Time*, the term 'conservation of energy' is the Law of Science that states that energy (or its equivalent in mass) can neither be created nor destroyed – but it can and does, change form.

According to Dr. Deepak Chopra in his book *Ageless Body, Timeless Mind*, every atom is more than 99.9% empty space and the subatomic particles moving at great speed through this space are bundles of vibrating energy which carry information and unique codings. He calls this "thinking non-stuff" as it cannot be seen by physical eyes.

In order to build life from lifeless matter, energy and information have to be exchanged through the RNA and DNA to create cellular structure. The flow of this Intelligence is what sustains us and is what Dr. Chopra calls the Universal Field. He states that the physical world is just a mirror of deeper Intelligence organizing matter and energy that also resides in us. We are part of all so we need to take care of all lovingly. Even though we are unique in our individuality we are all bound together by a common thread of pure energy that sustains each cell in our being and all life as a whole.

Religions call this energy God or super consciousness and consider it to be Omnipresent, Omnipotent and Omniscient. Quantum physics call this energy the 'grand unification energy' and also consider it to be everywhere, all powerful and all knowing. New Agers call this energy by other labels – the All That Is, Divine Intelligence etc. They are all just labels describing the same force or power. Energy is just energy – its gradation factor is the purity of consciousness that is attached to it.

Joseph Cater's *The Awesome Life Force* actually describes this energy as consisting of ethers and more complex "soft particles". Combinations of ethers produce photons of light, which in turn produce electrons and protons of atoms. This is how thought can materialize solid objects out of apparently nothing.

Our body's composition is of ethers, atoms and cells which hold this energy and information. So it stands to reason that if 'God' is everywhere and is actually, according to science, a pure intelligent energy field that sustains all life, we can then go within, if we desire, and contact this energy or our own 'inner God'.

Thoughts, words and actions are also energy. Energy expands, contracts and changes form, so that what we send out comes back to us. This is covered in more detail in other chapters of our book *In Resonance*. In religious terms it is, as you sow, so shall you reap. In energy terms all is governed by the Universal Law of Resonance and the Law of Attraction, where like attracts like.

As mentioned earlier, human Beings have four 'lower' bodies of energy, which resonate at different frequencies - the physical (the only one visible or appearing solid to our physical eyes); the emotional, the mental and the spiritual. We also have higher energy bodies; termed higher because they resonate at higher frequency pitches. Barbara Ann Brennan's book *Hands of Light – A Guide to Healing Through the Human Energy Field* covers these bodies and energy fields in great detail and is recommended reading for those interested.

When we bring these bodies of energy into perfect alignment or harmony with each other, we achieve higher 'knowing' and experience higher purpose to our existence as everything just clicks into place.

This state of enlightenment, so keenly sought by Eastern Esoteric students, is achieved by fine tuning the four lower bodies not only in perfect resonance with each other but to a pitch that allows the Higher Self or Soul and then the I Am Presence, Inner God or Christ Consciousness to take full residence within the physical body.

So in summary: - We are energy systems, we transmit and emit signals. If we send random signals, we get random or haphazard life experiences. If we control our signals we can then gain a large measure of control of our life. Taken one step further, if we tune our bodies and realign our frequencies (the energy signals we transmit) to a purer, more harmonious pitch, we can then control the quality and quantity of our life and life experiences."

As this book also encompasses information on physical immortality, I would like to include the following information ...

On Reincarnation:- having been established scientifically that energy cannot be created or destroyed but it can change form; and having understood that human beings are systems of energy, I would like to make the logical statement that reincarnation simply allows for the indestructibility of energy and while matter such as our physical bodies can decay and die, the energy within – that sustains the body – simply changes form and moves on. Anyone interested in exploring the concept of reincarnation may care to research the Edgar Cayce material, known to be the most widely documented of all case studies on this topic.

There is a Universal Law called the Law of Evolution and Rebirth that states that humankind go "through a slow process of development carried on with unwavering persistence through repeated embodiment in forms, of increasing efficiency, whereby all are in time, bought to a height of spiritual splendour in recognition of Source and true identity. This Law is also known as the Law of Periodicity" – quote from *The Vision of Ramala*.

From my detailed research and personal experience of this research into past and future life regression where one re-accesses cellular memory under the simultaneous timeframe, reincarnation is factual and may be referred to sporadically through the rest of the book. A simplistic understanding is as follows ... life in embodiment is a school, a process of growth and learning. When we die, we drop the energy field of the physical body but for awhile retain the energy fields of the emotional, mental and spiritual bodies. These are integrated into one conscious energy field and we are literally on holiday.

Holiday is a time of reflection, where we look at the past school term, see what we learnt, how well we have passed or have not passed our tests. Tests not passed must be re-sat next term and so we then plan for the next school term and select the 'curriculum' and subjects we wish to study.

This learning and testing is to do with our growth as beings and lessons generally are about intangible things like empathy, love, compassion, service etc. School time is also a period of learning from relationships and life in a dense, material plane generally. Why sparks of the Divine (us) have chosen to be in the school of life on planet Earth is another story.

So when we have learnt all there is for us to learn at this school and have passed all our exams, we move on to another learning institution thus breaking the cycle of reincarnation on this plane of Earth.

Our energy fields continue to change form just as energy itself does as per the Universal Law of Change and Transmutation which states that the only constant thing is the changing form of, and the indestructible nature of energy. This has been referred to as the Immortality of the 'soul'. Physical Immortality is also possible and allows us to continue in the same physical form to not only complete this learning, but stay and improve the curriculum, if we desire. This is covered in the chapter on "Immortality."

For many pranic nourishers and 'liquidarians' physical immortality is also a natural consequence of allowing the Divine spark within to both sustain and regenerate them if they desire.

Yoga students often ask me if one needs to do specific Kria yoga techniques to bring the pranic forces into the body, others ask if we need to spend time in the sun each day. The process of being sustained by prana that is described in this text is one that will automatically sustain us if we expect it to. After the 21 days the process is natural and requires no further focus. Just to expect then allow, however how much pranic food we can attract or make within the body is a reflection of our own consciousness and our personal frequency field emanations are what guarantee our success with this.

Our bodies breathe for us without our conscious command. Similarly when reprogrammed, the body will absorb the pranic forces directly and sustain us and nourish us completely once we eliminate all other belief systems to the contrary. This is a process of mind mastery, a sacred initiation, a natural by-product of which is that one no longer needs to eat food. It is a journey of refinement, of powerful yet subtle forces.

To gain a greater understanding of the more refined aspects of our being we need to explore further the idea of vibrations and frequencies.

Chapter 2

Understanding & Working with Vibrational Frequencies

February 1996:
I remember standing on the sidewalk one sunny Brisbane spring in the mid eighties and intuitively realising that I needed to understand about vibrations and frequencies. At that time I had been regularly meditating for 15 years and while I experienced many powerful benefits from this practice, from somewhere deep inside came a knowing that the next important step in my 'spiritual' journey involved understanding energy bands. It was at this time in my research that I had understood that our four lower bodies – physical, emotional, mental and spiritual could be likened to a four string guitar. When each body or energy field was tuned our life flowed harmoniously and when any were 'out of tune' life was not as harmonious. I realised also that we have the free will to consciously tune ourselves or not. Being aware of the bodies as systems of energy simply gave us choice to be tuned instruments and create life as we wished rather than events in life happening randomly.

As Annalee Skarin shares in her book *Ye Are Gods* – "Learn to control vibrations by controlling thoughts and you will hold the keys of Eternal Life in your hands. The Eternal energy surging through all matter, the power of existence in atoms with their whirling molecules and electrons in all earthly substance are nothing more or less than vibrations condensed to the point of slow, heavy, mortal tangibility. Control the vibrations and the power to control substance and material energy will eventually be given, that is the keys of handling Eternal Life, for energy is life, and life and Light and Love and energy are the Eternal elements and are vibrations created by mental thinking.

Every thought sent forth is a never ending vibration winging its way across the Universe to bring us back just what we sent forth. We can control the vibrations that emanate from us – and we can thereby control our destinies. Thus, science and religion can at last join hands and step into the spiritual realms of eternal progress and happiness together. One reaches the Higher Knowledge through a complete understanding of the material elements which melt into Light and energy and vibration through investigation; the other through its direct search into the spiritual, for both are one, expressed in various degrees of intensity and vibration."

Further research provided me also with the following excerpt from *We the Arcturians* by Dr. Norma Milanovich, Betty Rice and Cynthia Ploski: - "We discovered that the frequency at which a Being vibrates is directly related to the command it has over its thoughts, words and emotions. When a Being is vibrating at a lower frequency, it permits many other forms of energies to mix and mingle with its pool of energy and its cycles. When this happens, the thoughts have a tendency to get confused which causes a being to experience frustration. In this state of BEingness, one who is operating at this frequency can get very discouraged and depressed which only has the tendency to keep the vibratory level at a constant lower level.

"When one increases one's frequency to that of the speed of Light, then the mastery of the process begins. This means that the Being now has access to more information in the Universal Consciousness, but that Being also has the command to dictate what will or will not come through the filter.

"The process actually becomes more complex as it becomes more simplified. When a Being does not understand this principle, that Being may go through cycles of high and low frequencies that direct its consciousness. This is because the frequencies are controlling it.

"When one discovers that he has command of thought within the frequency levels, then there are steps that he can follow to assure that these vibrations will be maintained. The reason a higher frequency protects a Being from receiving other, lower vibrations is that the Light consumed within the essence of that soul is impenetrable. When the Light within is deliberately changed by the Being who has assumed that consciousness pattern, then a transformation and stillness overtakes the body. In this transformation process, the Being becomes centred. When centred, the energy patterns are more logical, holistic and unrandomised.

"When we are centred, we are accessing the Universal code and when we tap into this frequency, we understand another's frequency patterns too. That is, again, because we are one. In the Oneness of this existence we are able to transmit and receive messages; and more importantly, we can become the sender and receiver of messages in perfect understanding."

In the information *Revelation from an Archangel – Ascension to the 12th Dimension*, Archangel Ariel states "matter, as you know it from the third dimension, is densification of Light ... When you have a process of densification such as your Universe, you reach a point when it's gone to maximum separation from the purest form of Light. At that point of maximum separation, a shift occurs, and the planet begins to reverse its process and start on what we would term a homeward route i.e. back to the One point." Each time a planet ascends it changes its vibratory rate to be less dense and more light and it undergoes this process in its own unique way.

In his book *Mahatma I & II*, Brian Grattan says that there are 352 initiations from Earth back to Source. Other research also confirms that there are seven bands with seven sublevels each, (seven to the power of seven). The first may be seen as seven planes of the Solar system plane with seven subplanes and is known as the cosmic physical plane. There are said to be seven cosmic planes – physical, astral, mental, Buddhic, atmic, monadic and Logoic. Our solar system planes belong in the cosmic physical. Once we complete these seven sublevels we move onto the bottom level of the next cosmic plane and so it continues, slowly evolving magnetically back to Source. It has been said that one day of God, which is an out breath and in breath, lasts 4 billion 320 million years and we still have 1.2 billion years left in our time until the in breath is complete and then the cycle starts again.

This is an interesting concept and one well explored by the Theosophists among others. The exact midpoint between the in and out breath is said to be in the year 2012, this date is the last date of the Mayan calendar and is foretold by the Hopi Indians and many other civilisations. This year marks a time of wondrous change with multitudes awakening to their true divinity. Regarding the in breath happening quicker than the out breath – a rubber band stretched tightly and slowly to its maximum capacity has tremendous tension and when released returns to its original condition incredibly quickly.

Due to the change in the vibrational frequency as we pull back in, our concept of time is also affected. Consequently, even though we have passed the mid way point in linear time (1.2 is not half of 4.3) the passage of time speeds up with the increase in the rate of oscillation. Similarly, as we 'get older' time seems to 'fly' because in comparison we actually have less time. If we were to live to 80, at eight we have 9/10 (90%) of our 'time' left. At 40 we have 50%. It has been said in channelled information that due to the change in frequency and faster rate of vibration, comparatively, our 24 hour days now are really 16 hour days.

Discussing the dimensions, or planes, as frequency bands, and dealing with the cosmic physical plane only the 'top' frequency band, the seventh is awareness as a multi dimensional experience of group matrix identity and social memory complex, a vibration of integration. Once a density reaches critical mass it then projects and progresses through a prism (or black hole exit point) and begins a new adventure into the next seven frequency band. It has been said that individual consciousness no longer exists at this point. It is the plane above the monad or I AM. The seventh dimension is pure light, pure tone, sacred geometry, pure expression and creativity. A plane of infinite refinement.

Communication with Beings of Light report our planet to be vibrating now at the top of the astral plane and that as it continues to shift and ascend, the lower dimensions will "be rolled up into the higher dimensions and cease to exist" – Archangel Ariel. The dimensions below the fifth are known as the "lower levels of creation", and from the 5th to the 9th, the Mid Creation realm.

The sixth is the Christ consciousness, or Buddhic, state of awareness where responsibility is taken for the whole rather than the self. It is where the monad is anchored. This is said to be the level of consciousness that existed in Jesus, as he became the Christed One. The sixth also holds the templates for the DNA pattern of all creation. It is made up of colour and sound (tone) and it holds all light languages. It is where consciousness creates thought and where one goes to work and learn while asleep. Beings here are energy but can create a body by choice if required as in the 5th.

The fifth is a plane of experimental awareness of "I" as a group identity and is not bound by linear time, it is about density of wisdom and a desire to share plus the merging of the oversoul as the Higher self. Beings on this plane may take physical form when and if they chose to. The fifth is the dimension of Light where all are Masters, are multi-dimensionally aware and are totally dedicated to Spirit and service to Divine Will.

The fourth is a state of super consciousness and the reintegration of group identity without the loss of the individual or ego identity. It brings the ability to interface with multi dimensional and multi density realities. It is the last density requiring a physical body. The fourth dimension is said to be emotion based and is also known as the astral world. As the planet and humanity evolves, it has been said that we have already entered into the energies of the fourth dimension and many have moved beyond the third dimensional consciousness. The Harmonic convergence brought a major energy alignment and shift in the vibrational frequency of both the planet and her beings. The 12:12 in 1994 opened the gateway to a further influx of energies for planetary realignment and these influxes of energies will continue in greater or lesser degrees.

The third is matter based and has a state of volumetric awareness, of ego and of individual, the vibration of this plane creates the illusion of separation and is thus a challenge to individual awakening. It presents humanity with the opportunity to discover that we are spiritual Beings trying to be human rather than human Beings trying to be spiritual.

The second plane is the density of the plant and animal kingdoms although these too have become more refined in frequency due to the changes in planetary vibrations, and are moving into the third. The second plane is usually absent of self awareness and ego. It is awareness as a line.

The first is mineral, water, atoms and molecules that make up the basic genetic codes and is awareness as a point. As a Being evolves spiritually, this is reflected in both his/her vibrational frequency and molecular structure. Regarding molecular density, the Ascended Masters have explained that the space between the electrons, neutrons and protons in atomic structure becomes greater as the 'light' expands within an atom. This 'light' is also a Being's conscious awareness of their inherent God nature or pure energy source. As this light or awareness grows, it expands to fill the space in each atom thereby changing the frequency or rate of oscillation of each atom. As a Being expands their awareness and increases the light quotient within their cellular structure they become multi dimensional i.e. able to move into other dimensions of reality. Again, it is simply shifting your point of conscious awareness and 'switching' channels.

Various reliable channelled sources report that as we evolve further into Light, our DNA changes to accommodate these changes and is in the process of becoming 12 strand. The influx of higher energies at this time will allow for humanity to evolve faster in the next 40 years than he/she has in the last 3 billion, these energies are also responsible for the speeding up of time as we know it.

Also, as our frequencies change abilities such as telepathy, healing by touch, clairvoyance, teleportation etc. become completely natural. As tuned instruments, operating at our highest maximum potential our life becomes harmonious, joyous and filled with synchronicity, grace and magic. Even though we cannot avoid this process of change – as due to the Earth's evolution, we must also change – we can consciously be aware and accelerate these changes if we wish to.

Well-researched information plus practical techniques for changing vibrational frequencies by conscious choice are outlined in full detail in my book *In Resonance*. Simplistically it can be achieved by the following: -

Most importantly and powerfully by meditation – breath work and light work – especially when meditation is used to increase the light quotient in our cellular structure;

By fuel chosen and maintenance of the physical body – treat the vehicle like a Porsche for peak performance or an 'old bomb' – we are always at choice;

Master the emotional body and cellular memory;

Master the mental body via intention, programming and accessing the four fifths of the brain that houses higher consciousness;

Mantras and toning using sonic waves.

The conscious process of tuning also brings strong feelings of empowerment as we literally understand the practical game of reality creation through signals we transmit as energy centres. Many now – having understood the laws that govern energy – are practically applying this understanding through mind mastery and being disciplined in their thinking then witnessing the practical change in events in their day-to-day reality. It is a time to bring the intellectual understanding from our research into cellular knowing which can only be achieved through the living of it practically. Living on light is one of the most practical ways to demonstrate this understanding as if beings do not eat then they will either live or die. Working with, understanding and applying the knowledge of the higher light science will guarantee that we will not die if we allow the Inner Teacher to sustain us fully. I call this inner teacher the Divine One Within or our DOW; our interdimensional Light Being friends call this our Essence.

Chapter 3

33 – The Universal Beat

February 1996:
Continuing from the understanding of vibrational frequencies and the power one can hook into when one is tuned, it is interesting to look then at what is termed beats and octaves …

Esoteric research shares that physical reality operates in bands of seven with seven sub-planes or sub-levels (octaves) in each band. Seven chakras, seven colours of refracted white light and so forth. So the beat of humanity in physicality on planet Earth can be labelled a resonance of seven. So we have a range of possibilities of physical reality creation of seven to the power of seven.

Further research shares that the beat of the solar system is 10 with 10 sub-levels in each energy band. The beat of the galaxy is 12 with 12 sub-levels. The highest and most refined beat one can obtain or tune to while still retaining physicality is 33 – the universal beat. Again, this beat fragments or refines into 33 sub-frequencies. 33 to the power of 33.

The journey of refinement brings the understanding of all the complexities of densities and parallel realities along the way. Simplistically this means that focusing on physical realities – the 'I'll believe it when I see it' school – will magnetize 7^7 variations into a being's field of reality and they will not be able to move beyond that field until they consciously refine themselves to the next beat.

This comes about as one undergoes the process of involution, inner reflection, contemplation and connection with the Divine One within. The beat of the Divine One is 33 as it is the creative spark and the essence of the unified field as determined by quantum physics and hence is the backdrop or blackboard upon which all creation is manifested in its various forms.

As a being consciously 'refines' and tunes themselves they can then access more possibilities, more realities. Hence we have many people now feeling expanded and multi-dimensional as the Inner Teacher begins to share the delights of all that we are – beyond just the more dense aspect of ourselves housed in a physical vehicle witnessing and enjoying physical reality of the 7^7 paradigm.

Conscious refinement brings great freedom and limitless being. Freedom from the need to eat. Freedom from the need to sleep. Freedom from utilising Gregorian time of 12:60 or Mayan time of 13:20 and moves us into the divine time flow where one finds themselves always in the perfect place at the perfect time and fully enjoying the now.

The subatomic particles or 'soft particle' of the quantum field, also known as prana, chi, the universal life force, or God, beat to the octave of 33^{33} in its most refined expression at least in this quadrant of this universe of expression.

When we tune to this beat, like we turn the dial of the radio to pick up a specific frequency, we literally move into the paradigm of oneness. We see the divine perfection of all. We lose all feelings or interpretations of separation. All is interconnected for that which is in us and in all has been consciously focused upon and thus by the Law of Resonance continually attracts like particles into your energy field to mirror your expanded state of consciousness.

It is a fascinating journey for me. As a metaphysical counsellor and facilitator and as I travel the world and people ask me questions, I now find I have to ask 'on what level do you want that information?' – depending on their beat and their ability to access various levels of reality. The simplest way to tune in is to ask that all our sharing with a being be for their highest good and our highest good, which then guarantees that the interaction is energetically matched and synchronized to the highest possible paradigm, that the two combined can possibly access.

Conscious tuning is like practicing scales on a piano. At first they are basic and then rhythm or beat combinations are introduced. Similarly as one expands their consciousness – through the desire in their heart to realise their full potential – we attract different levels of refinement which can be likened to refined note combinations.

Eventually one realizes that one has the power to create or access any level of reality they wish – and have been constantly creating to learn and evolve through all embodiments – even to the degree of creation of parallel realities. Logically Universal Mind – or intuition, instinct – will guide us to simplify the game and simply tune to the highest paradigm that is accessible which is God's beat. This is the symphony that is driving the unfoldment of the Divine Plan and when a being becomes part of the orchestra by aligning free will with the Divine Will of our Essence, all doors are guaranteed to open. The types of doors that open reflect our consciousness.

The only catch to this – as many have found – is divine time – being tuned further to the timing of it all. One can be an instrument in the divine orchestra and still be either out of step or synchronistic. The program of 'Dear Mother Father Creator God, I ask that the next perfect step of my piece in the Divine Blueprint clearly reveal itself to me and bring with it the perfect people required to make this piece manifest into physical reality NOW!' as many have now experienced, will guarantee alignment with divine time.

So one literally flows in a sea of Oneness. As Sai Baba says "For the individual and the Universal are One; the wave is the sea. Merging fulfils. When merged, the ego is dissolved; all symbols and signs of the particular, like name, form, caste, colour and creed, nationality, church, sect and the rights and duties consequent therein, will fade. For such individuals, who have liberated themselves from the narrowness of individuality, the only task is the uplifting of humanity, the welfare of the world and the showering of love. Even if they are quiet, the state of bliss in which they are will shower bliss on the world. Love is in all; love is of all; love is all".

The vibrational aspect of the feeling of this beat is pure love, divine love with variations of this from the $33^{\wedge}33$ to the coarser $7^{\wedge}7$ vibration and lower emotional body expression. Divine love is not only the source and building block of all creation energetically but also the most powerful transmutational force available. When tuned to, accessed and focused upon it absorbs, refines and realigns all lower emotions to the most refined beat possible while still retaining embodiment. Again, it brings freedom.

Commanding the Divine One to align our energy fields and express full embodiment in our physical reality automatically tunes us to the universal beat. All veils of illusion and separation fall away – like the peeling of layers of an onion until all that is, is the essence of All; perfectly tuned.

This is what I have come to term 'plugging in to the Cosmic Circuit Board'. This is where the discussion of pranic nourishment / liquidarianism leads us. For the ability to live on light is a natural by-product of giving ourselves permission to be sustained by the divinity within. Similarly, tuning beyond the need for sleep, or tuning so that one no longer feels temperature extremes but simply adjusts the body temperature to the comfort of the physical environment – is an ability I am still in training with.

All this is just raw human potential – to get to a point of expansion where there is no difference whether we are in physical embodiment or 'sitting on the lap of and wrapped in the arms of God' for all is one. We are one with all. This is what the Indian ascetics term 'Sat Chit Anand' – truth consciousness, bliss – I see myself in you. This is the paradigm of oneness and limitless being.

The Seven Elements and the
33 – the Universal Beat

The following information flows naturally on from the previous chapters. I had been programming that "the next piece of my part in the Divine Blueprint NOW CLEARLY reveal itself to me AND bring with it any beings who would aid in the physical manifestation of this part into physical reality NOW" when who should be magnetized to my field but Leonard Orr.

For those unfamiliar with Leonard's work, in 1974 he founded the Rebirthing Movement, now some 10 million strong worldwide. In Australia on tour, we managed to connect and discover each other's work. We swapped books and agreed to co-facilitate through Europe and part of South America. We now include some of his work on spiritual purification in the chapter on the Great Immortalists.

Reading Leonard's work has allowed me to understand another perspective of my own by recognising the connecting links. I have discovered that I am being intuitively guided to build bridges. I knew that I liked to network, to discover, share and enjoy brilliance and limitlessness. So adding a 're-birthing flavour' to our understanding, let us look now at effective bridge building via tuning. By this I mean tuning to the elements and also energy field purification utilising the elements.

What I may call tuning – usually the four body system – physical, emotional, mental, and spiritual; Leonard calls spiritual purification which is achieved by utilising the four elements. The following information continues on from our previous discussions on Vibrational Frequencies and the Universal Beat.

The first element is Fire – the 'learning to live with an open flame' practice – this is in the physical field of the 7^7 beat discussed in the article "33 – the Universal Beat" (TEV Vol. 2 Issue 3). Primarily fire also burns accumulated emotional dross from any energy field the mind intends.

The second element is Earth – tuning to the Earth element involves the practice of fasting, food mastery and exercise.

The third element is Air – tuning to this element is done through conscious energy breathing where each breath is connected, the inhale followed by the exhale and is deep and fine until one clicks into the experience of BEING BREATHED. In its finer expression, this is an experience of Akasa – the 6th element. Conscious connected breathing bridges the physical and etheric by bringing an experience of refinement into the physical vehicle.

The fourth element is Water. Bathing, long hot baths tune the sacral particularly powerfully and all the chakras. The sacral is the connecting link for the energy field of the emotional body to the physical – a bridge. Baths also realign and rebalance the bodies energy fields and dilutes, what Leonard terms, emotional 'energy pollution' accumulated by existing in the morphonogenic field of mass consciousness. Even long hot daily showers clean your auric field but, according to the rebirthers, not as powerfully as baths. They share that twice daily baths and rebirthing sessions can clear cellular memory on many levels within many time bands including simultaneous time.

The next, and fifth element, is the astral light which is of the Solar vibration 10^{10}. This is the vibration of living from the pranic field, and utilising photon energy through the body

After this is the sixth element, Akasa, the Galactic 12^{12} vibration – the quantum field. Akasa is the first element beyond the void – the Source – when creation first breathed expansively. It is semi manifest – the element in which everything occurs and also the essence within all that occurs.

Then as the seventh element with the 33^{33} Universal vibration we have Cosmic Fire, alternatively known as the Principle. In the expanding beat, cosmic fire is the first element and in the contracting beat, Cosmic Fire is the seventh element.

The five elements including astral light also correspond to our five senses. Fire = sight; earth = smell; air = touch; water = taste; astral light = hearing; also the sixth element – akasa = our 6th sense – intuition. The sense for Cosmic Fire element is yet to be revealed though I would share that perhaps it is the 7th sense of just KNOWING.

Bridging the worlds is discovering the 3 subtle elements, enjoying the exploration and experience of their power and then consciously directing their flow back into linear time and physical reality.

Tuning the four body system with the four elements empowers you in the physical plane provided mind mastery is adopted and demonstrated. It also brings into our cellular awareness a strong elemental force that will tune us to the heartbeat of the Mother Earth. The more tuned we are to the heartbeat of God, and the more we then allow the forces of the elements to tune us to the heartbeat of our planet, the stronger and more effective our bridge, between the differing vibrations of these worlds, will be.

Bridging the worlds occurs when the inner doorways have opened through the practice of 'spiritual purification' or through tuning the four body system to its synchronistic and 'Divine beat'. When these doorways are opened, pure consciousness can flow through directed by you, the Master. A strong bridge means more prana can flow into the physical system to sustain it with the nourishment it needs.

Masters are aware that only an aspect of their consciousness is expressed into physical reality. A Master is consciously familiar with all levels of creation, the microcosm, the macrocosm, as above so below.

Our physical body's atomic makeup is a microcosm of the macrocosm of Earth which is a microcosm of the macrocosm of the universe – which holds a keynote of 33. All hold mirror elements all in vibrations of various levels.

Utilising the Universal Law of Resonance, the "as you sow so shall you reap paradigm", we realise that the more we consciously tune to the Universal beat of 33^{33} – Oneness – the more we draw to us the mirror image of these elements. This is then what brings Oneness into evidence in the physical as it is mirroring our vibration and our creative power.

March 2006:
It is my understanding that our physical systems need to attract more astral light, akasa and particularly cosmic fire in order to be nourished without taking physical food. Cosmic fire is pure Divine Mother Love and the more we align with the Divine Love channel the more cosmic particles we attract to nourish us.

August 2012:
To help increase our prana divine love flow, we now offer the following meditations that can be downloaded from iTunes.

Love Breath Meditation:- The most significant meditation we can offer to increase your pranic flow and for the refinement of your personal rhythm into a more relaxed and peaceful state is the Love Breath Meditation. This meditation is designed to allow us to align more easily and powerfully to the divine essence within and thus increase our prana-chi flow. It also incorporates specific mantras to allow this pure energy force to rise and flood through us and out into the world, thus feeding everything and to also relax us. This meditation is also designed to stimulate group unification and feelings of Oneness. For more information on this meditation click here.

Pranic Nourishment Meditation:- A relaxing meditation with Jasmuheen on accessing alternate nourishment pranic flows from both the inner plane cosmic particle streams and from nature – connecting with Gaia's heart and the cosmic heart plus some additional programming. **NOTE:** It is recommended that you also apply the Etheric Pranic Feeding Devices Meditation with this to get the full benefit of etheric feeding PLUS live the lifestyle recommended in our *Food of Gods* research manual. For more information on this meditation click here.

Etheric Pranic Feeding Devices Meditation:- A detailed meditation using the Higher Light Science & Alchemical practices to create inner plane, etheric body feeding devices to increase and boost our chi flows which can in turn improve health, happiness and harmony levels. Also enhancing our telepathic abilities via pituitary and pineal gland fine-tunement. This meditation with Jasmuheen uses mind power, the Universal Law of Resonance, alchemical violet light transmissions and more. NOTE: It is recommended that you also apply the Pranic Nourishment Meditation with this to get the full benefit of etheric feeding PLUS live the lifestyle recommended in our *Food of Gods* research Manual. For more information on this meditation click here.

Chapter 4

The Sustaining Force of Prana

February 1996:
In order to understand how a Being can be sustained by only Light we need to understand that which is sustaining them i.e. prana – also known as the Universal life force energy or 'liquid light or cosmic particles'.

Prana is a subtle element which pervades each cell of every living tissue and fluid in an organism like electricity through atoms in a battery. Prana's biological counterpart, that Gopi Krishna terms apana, is a fine essence which resides in the brain and nervous system and is capable of generating a subtle radiation impossible to analyse in a laboratory. It circulates in the organism as motor impulse and sensation and conducts all the organic functions of the body, permeated and worked by the super intelligent cosmic life energy, prana, by which it is continually affected.

The term prana signifies both the cosmic life energy and its subtle biological conductor in the body and the two are inseparable. The extraction of prana to feed the brain is done by a limited group of nerves, operating in a certain bodily area. With the awakening of the kundalini, a radical alteration is made and other more extensive nerve groups are called into play and supply a more concentrated form of prana radiation into the brain from a vastly increased area of the body.

One could surmise that in order to be able to be sustained by prana or liquid light alone one must have a certain degree of spiritual awakening, that the full activation of the kundalini energy would also allow this process to operate at maximum efficiency.

There are three energy channels (nadis) in the spine that can carry the kundalini energy and intersect through the chakras:

Pingala – the solar nerve regulates the flow of heat and is on the right side of the *Susumna,* which flows inside the spinal cord.

Idakalai – is a cooling agent on the left side – it represents the moon.

All three lie within the astral body.

The medulla oblongata – is a brain centre at the base of the skull and is said to be a 'minor' chakra as it is an induction centre of spiritual energy from the higher bodies. Holding the head erect in meditation allows the medulla oblongata to receive this flow of pranic energy freely and unhindered. These spiritual or pranic energies flow into this centre through to the hypothalamus and, as it increases the Light quotient in our being, this increase allows us to be more telepathically receptive.

The Kundalini – prior to the activation of the kundalini energy I would recommend that the chakras be tuned and fully activated with Light and that the unified chakra meditation be done. (This meditation is included at the end of this chapter) I would also recommend that you instruct your I AM to switch on and connect the etheric and physical nervous systems so you are in complete alignment electromagnetically although this should happen by doing the unified chakra meditation.

It is also most important that you instruct your I AM to oversee the activation of the kundalini energy to avoid potential 'burn out'. It is well reported by Indian ascetics that if one has not prepared their consciousness and aligned their physical vehicle that awakening the 'sleeping serpent' (the kundalini) prematurely can create great damage or burn out in the body's electrical circuitry and even death. More information on this is covered in Gopi Krishna's book on kundalini. The awakening of the kundalini may occur quickly or slowly, as guided by your I AM, depending on each individual's instruction and desire.

To awaken the kundalini, simply program the following affirmation in meditation –
"I call forth and fully activate my kundalini energy as guided by my Monad and mighty I AM Presence".

If one increases the intake of pranic life force by drawing on the Cosmic Life Source, one can also conquer death. Slow rhythmic breathing absorbs more prana and allows it to be stored in the brain and nerve centres. Prana supplies electric force to the nerves, magnetizes the iron in the system and produces the aura as a natural emanation.

Excerpt from *Babaji and the 18 Siddha Kriya Yoga Tradition* by Marshall Govindan … "The secret to longevity lies in the technique of directing the breathing to subtle channels and centres. The secretion of nectar comes from the cerebral region through the opening behind the uvula and the mystic gland in the hypothalamus. This elixir of life will strengthen the human system and make it invulnerable to decay, degeneration, diseases and death."

In his book *Kundalini: the Evolutionary Energy in Man* – Gopi Krishna writes: "All systems of Yoga are based on the supposition that living bodies owe their existence to the agency of an extremely subtle immaterial substance pervading the universe and designated as prana, which is the cause of all organic phenomena, controlling the organisms by means of the nervous system and brain, manifesting itself as the vital energy. The prana, in modern terminology 'vital energy', assumes different aspects to discharge different functions in the body and circulates in the system in two separate streams, one with fervid and the other with frigid effect, clearly perceptible to yogis in the awakened condition".

He goes on to say "From my own experience, I can also confirm that there are certainly two main types of vital currents in the body, which have a cooling or heating affect on the system. Prana and apana exist side by side in the system in every tissue and every cell, the two flowing through the higher nerves and their tiny ramifications as two distinct currents though their passage is never felt in the normal state of consciousness, the nerves being accustomed to the flow from the very commencement of life".

Having understood prana as being the essence of life, we can then perhaps understand how an organism can be sustained by the etheric realms and by prana alone. Some individuals have achieved this through expanding their consciousness to higher vibrational frequencies that in turn, change the molecular structure of their physical, emotional and mental bodies and free them from the necessity of taking substance from the atmospheric realms. These beings are called breatharians. Others, I term liquidarians, may choose to exist purely on this liquid light but still drink for pleasure and for taste sensation.

Excerpt from *Seasons of the Spirit* by the Ascended Master Hilarion ... "It is incorrect to imagine that the energy that drives the physical body of man comes from the food he eats. This is one of the major misconceptions in the world today ... the energy of man's body must come from a far more subtle and refined source than that of carbohydrate molecules as is now believed. The life process in man does not exist at the mere chemical level, otherwise man would be nothing more than a beaker in which reactive chemicals were mixed, and with no more 'life' intelligence or spirit than would be found in such a beaker. When the chemical reaction has run its course, the beaker would be quiet still, lifeless, empty and the same in the case of the human being.

"No, the force that drives the human machine is not chemical but etheric. The ether is a form of all embracing substance more rarefied than the most subtle of man's chemicals, and indeed is the 'stuff' from which all the elements known to science are precipitated, just as water droplets can be precipitated from water vapour in the air. Mixed with the ether which fills all of man's three dimensional space (even between the protons and electrons of matter in what science considers to be 'empty' space) is a substance which we shall call prana, using the Eastern word for life energy. Indeed the Eastern religions know of this miraculous substance and understand quiet well its role in supporting the 'life' of man.

"When a human body breaths air into the lungs, the prana within the etheric counterpart of this air is taken into the etheric counterpart of the body and is then transformed into the various energies that one uses in everyday life; mental energy, emotional energy and physical energy. The oxygen which is taken into the blood via the lungs of course plays a part in metabolism, but it is only a minor role compared to the importance of the intake of prana."

Invocation to the Unified Chakra
from Tony Stubbs *An Ascension Handbook*

I breathe in Light through the centre of my heart
opening my heart into a beautiful ball of Light,
allowing myself to expand.

I breathe in Light through the centre of my heart
allowing the Light to expand,
encompassing my throat chakra
and my solar plexus chakra
in one unified field of Light within,
through and around my body.

I breathe in Light through the centre of my heart
allowing the Light to expand,

encompassing my brow chakra and my navel chakra
in one unified field of Light within,
through and around my body.

I breathe in Light through the centre of my heart
allowing the Light to expand,
encompassing my crown chakra and my base chakra
in one unified field of Light within,
through and around my body.

I breathe in Light through the centre of my heart
allowing the Light to expand,
encompassing my alpha chakra above my head,
and my omega chakra below my spine
in one unified field of Light within,
through and around my body.
I allow the wave of Metatron to resonate between them.
I am a unity of Light.

I breathe in Light through the centre of my heart
allowing the Light to expand,
encompassing my eighth chakra above my head,
and my thighs
in one unified field of Light within,
through and around my body.
I allow my emotional body to merge with my physical.
I am a unity of Light.

I breathe in Light through the centre of my heart
allowing the Light to expand,
encompassing my ninth chakra above my head,
and my calves
in one unified field of Light within,
through and around my body.
I allow my mental body to merge with my physical.
I am a unity of Light.

I breathe in Light through the centre of my heart
allowing the Light to expand,
encompassing my tenth chakra above my head,
and below my feet
in one unified field of Light within,
through and around my body.

I allow my spiritual body to merge with my physical.
I am a unity of Light.

I breathe in Light through the centre of my heart
allowing the Light to expand,
encompassing my eleventh chakra above my head,
and to below my feet
in one unified field of Light within,
through and around my body.
I allow my oversoul to merge with my physical.
I am a unity of Light.

I breathe in Light through the centre of my heart
allowing the Light to expand,
encompassing my twelfth chakra above my head,
and to below my feet
in one unified field of Light within,
through and around my body.
I allow my Christ oversoul to merge with my physical.
I am a unity of Light.

I breathe in Light through the centre of my heart
I ask that the highest level of my spirit radiate forth
from the centre of my heart,
filling this unified field completely.
I radiate forth throughout this day.
I am unity of spirit.

Chapter 5

The Story of Giri Bala

February 1996:
Many years ago, I read a wonderful book called *Autobiography of a Yogi*. It shares of the life of Paramahansa Yogananda and is the first book that I had read where I actually felt an energy of love and knowing just flow from the pages. It was also the first time that I had read of anyone simply living off the Light of Divinity.

The story of Giri Bala was told to Yogananda when he met with her when she was 68. At that time she had not eaten nor taken fluids for over 56 years. Still living the life of a humble and simple villager she had, in her early years as rumour spread, been taken to the palace of the leader of her province. There she was kept under strict observation and eventually 'released' with the sanction that yes she did exist purely on Light.

With Yogananda she shared how as a child she enjoyed a voracious appetite for which she was often chided and teased. At age nine she was betrothed and was soon ensconced in her husband's family abode. One day Giri suffered so greatly at her mother-in-law's tongue and teasing at her gluttony that she exclaimed "I shall soon prove to you that I shall never touch food again as long as I live". Teased further she then fled the village.

In great despair she cried from her very soul for God to send a Guru who could teach her to live by God's Light alone. At this time her Guru materialized in front of her and she was initiated into the art of a specific Kria Yoga technique to free the body of the need for physical sustenance.

The Guru shared "Dear little one, I am the guru sent here by God to fulfill your urgent prayer. He was deeply touched by its very unusual nature. From today you shall live by the astral light. Your bodily atoms shall be recharged by the infinite current."

Since that day she has neither eaten nor taken fluids and has no bodily excretions. Yogananda shared that "she is setting this example to prove that man is spirit in truth, and also to prove that man can live by the Eternal Light of God." (Quote from Dr. Stone's work *Forty of the World Great Saints and Spiritual Masters*).

> "Mankind is engaged in an eternal quest
> for that "something else"
> he hopes will bring him happiness,
> complete and unending,
> for those individual souls
> who have sought and found God,
> the search is over.

He is that something else."
Paramahansa Yogananda

The Story of Teresa Neumann

Again in his work *Autobiography of a Yogi*, Yogananda shares of his meeting with Teresa Neumann and Dr. Stone recounts this meeting in his book on the Masters.

"Teresa Neumann was born on good Friday in 1898 in Northern Bavaria. At the age of 20 she was in an accident and became blind and paralysed. She received a miraculous healing in 1923 through prayers to St. Therese of Lisieux. Since this time Teresa has not eaten any foods or liquids except for one small consecrated wafer a day.

"Stigmata, or sacred wounds of Christ, began to appear on her head, breast, hands and feet every Friday while she experiences the passion of Christ. Yogananda later said that in her past life she was Mary Magdalene. She is here to show (like Giri Bala) that it is possible to live on God's Light".

Throughout the 36 years that Teresa bore the stigmata, thousands of tourists would file into her small cottage to witness the miracle. Teresa died in 1962. Paola Giovetti's book *Teresa Neumann: The Stigmatist of Konnesreuth* covers her life in great detail for those interested.

The stories of Giri Bala and Teresa Neumann are easy to dismiss as experiences by 'saintly' people. Yet they were both simply individuals who had great trust and faith. From my research it appears that while Giri and Teresa were sustained purely by liquid light, neither embraced the tandem idea of physical immortality and both aged gracefully.

Chapter 6

Physical Immortality

February 1996:
It is interesting to note that aging and death can still be experienced by both pranic nourishers and liquidarians. Humanity has been locked into the consciousness and belief of limitation for eons of time. This mental expectation and belief in the necessity of death has been prevalent to the degree that glands such as the pituitary and pineal secrete 'death hormones' rather than fulfilling their natural life sustaining and regeneration patterns. The book *New Cells, New Body, New Life!: You're Becoming a Fountain of Youth!* by Virginia Essene, looks at this in the chapter written by Joanna Cherry.

Detailed research also reveals the body to be the most complex and self sustaining molecular structure imagined. New cells are created at the rate of billions, (e.g. a new stomach lining every five days), it is said that each two years a human being is completely new on a cellular level.

Then why do we age and die if we have the innate ability to renew and create all cellular structure? In his book *Quantum Healing: Exploring the Frontiers of Mind/Body Medicine*, Dr. Chopra says it is our programming and belief systems and that cells are just memories clothed in matter. Leonard Orr in his book *Physical Immortality: the Science of Everlasting Life* suggests that people die firstly because they expect to.

Having spent a decade or so in the business world, often working 50 to 60 hours per week, raising my daughters as a sole parent, plus attending to my meditation and esoteric interests lead me to be quite aware of time management so that a certain level of sanity could be maintained in the lifestyle I had chosen. Somewhere along the line I came to the conclusion that physical death was poor time management.

After twenty years of a vegetarian, then virtual vegan diet, plus gym work and relevant research to maintain peak health, I realised that the body was a self sustaining, wonderfully regenerating machine that only wore out due to high levels of toxicity. This toxicity came through diet choices, negative thinking and belief systems (remembering that our thoughts create our emotions and that emotional dis-ease creates disease).

My desire to maintain peak health was motivated simply because I could not afford the luxury to spend time being ill and as I had very little 'spare' time, I felt that I had better ways to spend it than ever being sick.

Apart from excellent time management, the attraction of the idea of physical immortality also grew as I did not like the idea of attaining a certain level of awareness, or awakening, and then have the physical vehicle fall apart due to my neglect. To then prepare a new vehicle and suitable conditions for the next life, be born, wear nappies, have parents, school and go through adolescence did not 'excite' me either.

(Please note I had a wonderful childhood, parents etc, a challenging but learning adolescence with the freedom to grow and develop and then 'flower' as I consciously chose. I was also aware at this time that I had consciously chosen, prior to incarnation, the garden bed that my seed of consciousness was to be planted in and the gardeners, so to speak).

To go through all that again and then finally remember what I'd already come to understand through years of research and experience in this and previous lives, seemed ludicrous to my logical mind.

At that stage I had been vaguely introduced to the idea of physical immortality and had definitely understood the opportunity of this to be my final incarnation on the Earth plane. I also knew I had "work" to do, a "role" to play and decided that I wanted to "check out" when I'd finished my work and when I was ready. I was no longer interested in dying through maltreatment, or ignorance, of the physical vehicle.

Embracing physical immortality is beyond fear of death. All immortalists I know see death as a more gentle, fearless and favourable process than birth – there is certainly less pain involved but that is another story.

Suffice to say that life on this plane of existence can be likened to school and the time spent away from physical embodiment is like wonderful holidays. Often people have equated an individual's desire for physical immortality as being afraid of death and the unknown and in some cases this may be so.

However there comes a point in the evolution of a Being where physical immortality is not only good time management but a natural consequence of their resonance. Physical Immortality is not possible without the corresponding resonance or the belief that it is a possibility for you.

In order to become Immortal (on a physical level which is a logical, conscious extension of soul immortality) one needs to address the following: -
1. Let go of the belief that we have to die
2. Release all negativity – of thoughts and emotions – from the energy fields of our bodies
3. Master the physical, emotional and mental bodies.

Letting go of the belief that we have to die is quite easy when one truly understands that we are simply systems of energy and that the level of cellular degeneration and/or regeneration is dependent on the level of Mind Mastery (mastery of the mental body) that a Being has achieved.

Releasing all negativity is covered in the visualization exercises in my book *In Resonance*. So, in essence, mastery of the mental body leads to mastery of the emotional body which in turn masters the physical body.

However there are also practical techniques that can be practiced that are reported to either reverse and/or stop the aging process.

Like being able to live purely on prana, physical immortality is simply about having real freedom of choice. It is not about being rigidly attached to life – for existence and consciousness truly are eternal. The more we expand our consciousness and remember all that we are, the more we recognise that our physical embodiment is just a small aspect of our BEingness.

However, information brings us the power to choose. It is simply time for all cultures to be made aware of ways of being and thinking and living that are now empowering others on this planet.

It is also interesting to know that there are physical immortalists in existence on this planet who have mastered their physical bodies. Like a person who parks their car, many yogis and meditators can 'park their body' and come and go at will. They can take their body up into light, move themselves into another energy band like discussed in *The Celestine Prophecy* so they are 'out of view' to someone tuned to a denser energy band. This finer energy band is one of higher consciousness and its gifts are immeasurable.

Also empowering can be the knowing that there are people now on the planet who have freed their body from the need to eat food and are now being nourished by prana, the God Force within. This is particularly empowering for those currently dying from malnutrition and starvation on this planet as living on light presents another option and path to look at and explore for those interested.

Continuing on with the idea of physical immortality, another wonderful source of information and techniques to stop, and even reverse, the ageing process comes in the book called *Ancient Secret of the Fountain of Youth* by Peter Kelder. We explore some of his ideas in this next chapter.

Regeneration & Rejuvenation

It is my understanding and conviction that the higher the quotient of Light within the body the stronger our natural ability for cellular regeneration on the purest level. Logically the freer our cellular structure is from all forms of toxicity plus the more Light and the higher the vibration or rate of oscillation of our energy fields, the less possibility of disease, decay and degeneration. Light attracts Light – light transmutes and dissolves that which is not of Light. Consequently, while we may reprogram our glands to produce only life sustaining hormones and/or use the Fountain of Youth rites as covered in this chapter, our main focus must be to increase the Light quotient within the cellular structure.

In the book *The Complete Ascension Manual*, Dr. Stone states that a light quotient of 80 – 83% allows for ascension, 96 – 98% for dematerialization, teleportation and rematerialization where one manipulates the cellular structure of the physical vehicle with a single command or intention. In these states physical immortality is a natural consequence as liquid light flows through the systems and the chakras become unified in one column of light. With the Lightbody complete and the monad (I AM) firmly anchored all becomes naturally self sustaining.

Excerpt from *Ancient Secret of the Fountain of Youth* by Peter Kelder – "the body has seven energy centres which in English would be called vortexes. The Hindus call them chakras. They are powerful electrical fields, invisible to the eye, but quiet real nonetheless. Each of these seven vortexes centres on one of the seven ductless glands in the body's endocrine system, and it functions in stimulating the gland's hormonal output. It is these hormones that regulate all of the body's functions, including the process of ageing.

"The lowest, or first vortex, centres on the reproductive glands. The second vortex centres on the pancreas in the abdominal region. The third centres on the adrenal gland in the solar plexus region. The fourth vortex centres on the thymus gland in the chest or heart region. The fifth centres on the thyroid gland in the neck. The sixth centres on the pineal gland at the rear base of the brain. And the seventh, highest vortex centres on the pituitary gland at the forward base of the brain.

"In a healthy body, each of these vortexes revolves at great speed, permitting vital life energy, also called 'prana' or 'etheric energy', to flow upward through the endocrine system. But if one or more of these vortexes begins to slow down, the flow of vital energy is inhibited or blocked, and – well, that's just another name for ageing and ill health.

"These spinning vortexes extend outward from the flesh in a healthy individual, but in the old, weak, and sickly they hardly reach the surface. The quickest way to regain youth, health and vitality is to start these energy centres spinning normally again."

The above book goes on to explain that there are six 'rites' or simple exercises one can do to stimulate these centres. These tools for longevity have been practiced for eons of time by Lamas at a Monastery high in remote reaches in the Himalayas.

The Lamas also eat lightly, once a day, are vegetarian and often usually only consume one type of food per meal and in small quantities. For example one meal may be of fruit, another of vegetables, and another of bread. They exercise via physical labour, which with their diet, and the rites they practice, apparently keeps them all looking around 25 years regardless of biological age.

The lamas also say that keeping the voice low keeps the base chakra vibrating healthily due to the vibrations of the lower octave of sound. They consequently do regular chanting as this helps greatly to align the seven vortexes. It is not recommended for women to adjust their voice too low as their resonance is different to that of a male. They also suggest one should think and act young as one attracts as per their thoughts so they obviously understand the power of mind over matter.

Due to copyright restrictions, we are unable to provide either the diagrams of these rites or full details. However for those interested we recommend that you purchase this book as it is well worth practicing. Many, including my now 80-year-old father, are experiencing the positive benefits of youthing and re-energizing through the practice of the rites covered in Peter's book.

Reprogramming the glands of the body for cellular Regeneration

Introduced to me by Joanna Cherry of Ascension Mastery International at Mt. Shasta, California USA, this is a simple technique designed to switch the production of all hormones to be life sustaining not life draining. As the mind is the master* and mind has mastery over matter, the glands of the human body have been unable to support the pure, regeneration of cellular structure due to the inherent belief in the need for death. As long as we believe that death is natural then our bodies must and will support that belief regardless of its ability to do otherwise.

A simple technique to reprogram the production of hormones within the body is as follows and can only be guaranteed to work when one has completely released 'deathist' mentality.

Sit in meditation/contemplation
- tune your energy fields with breath & Light,
- visualise a beam of Light coming in from the highest source, passing through the 12th chakra through which the I AM connects with your being, down through the other chakras and entering the top of your head through the crown,
- let this beam of golden, white Light fill every cell in your brain,
- instruct the Light to fully anchor in and activate your pituitary gland, then the pineal gland,
- instruct these glands to release old programming and beliefs and from this moment only produce life producing and life sustaining hormones that promote and support physical immortality,
- feel the Light beam go into the throat area filling every cell with Light,
- instruct the thyroid gland in the throat chakra to do the same,
- feel or visualise the Light moving down through the body filling every cell,
- next, instruct the thymus, the adrenals, the pancreas and the reproductive glands exactly as you have just done for the others above.

Thank all the glands for the wonderful service they have provided according to your previous instruction but state that you now embrace the state of physical immortality and demand them to support your new belief in perfect harmony according to your Divine and perfect blueprint.

Chapter 7

The Great Immortalists

February 1996:
I am guided to include with the story of Babaji and St. Germain, plus an extract of a channelling on the Arcturians for they are universally known as the Masters of Light technology. They are also the Masters of Immortality, of being able to rearrange molecular structure and take a body at will.

In Dr. Norma Milanovic's book *We, The Arcturians*, they say that within 100 years all of humanity on Earth will live on the Light of God alone. My personal dealings with Arcturius, began shortly after I underwent the 21-day process in 1993. He first began telepathic contact, then visual contact on the inner realms via meditation. He has been closely linked with me since that time and brought through the message "The Doorway of the Heart" while I was in New Zealand to share on Being sustained by Light. His focus was on the command over molecular structure that all who seek mastery must attain.

Arcturius has also shared that like Giri Bala and Teresa Neumann who have proved one can live by the Light of God alone, others such as Babaji prove, through their ability to dematerialize and rematerialize, that one can also have complete command over their molecular structure.

The Ascended Masters share that being sustained purely by Light, being able to dematerialize and rematerialize, physical immortality, healing by touch, manifesting purely by thought not action, are all natural abilities acquired or rediscovered when we embrace the God within.

Babaji

In his book on *Physical Immortality: the Science of Everlasting Life* Leonard Orr shares that while the majority of people think of immortalists only in terms of Jesus through His ascension, upon research one will find many examples of immortalists throughout history. St. Germain, Anna Lee Skarin, Elijah, various Hopi Indians and European Alchemists to name a few. Not all have chosen to remain on this Earth plane. One who has is Babaji.

There are many stories about the great immortalist Babaji. Based in Herakhan India, it is said that he was a Yogi Master in his first lifetime and conquered death, that he has retained his physical body and while thousands of years old, keeps the appearance of a youth in his mid twenties. Other stories say that he personally instructed Jesus, that he can turn his body into Light, dematerialise, rematerialise and age or youth at will.

It is said that Babaji dematerialized his previous body in 1922 and then rematerialized his present body in a cave in 1972 (although other sources say it was 1970). From 1924 to 1958 he lived as a simple yogi in Dhanyon village near Almora, India.

Leonard shares that one of Babaji's earliest forms was that of Shiva the yogi, then Ram, then Krishna. Then as Goraknath he gave physical immortality to two Kings in 57 B.C. Gopchand a King in Nepal and Bhartara in Rajisthan and it is said that both are alive and active today.

Leonard shares that as well as guiding Jesus, Babaji also worked with Moses and Elijah. There is also the Babaji of the Himalayas who has promised to stay upon this plane until all have gained their enlightenment.

While the Herakhan Babaji left his physical body in the 1980's the Himalayan Babaji is said to carry the energy of the immortal youth and represents the pure love stream of the Kumaras.

Comte de Saint Germain

When discussing any great teacher or Master, it is interesting to note that they always operate on two levels. One in the public eye and also in their role for the Divine One and the Spiritual Hierarchy that is currently overseeing the evolution of humanity upon planet Earth. Another well know immortalist and emissary of the Great White Brotherhood, working on the 7th Ray of Ceremonial Order and Magic, St. Germain is also known on the etheric realms as the Master Ragoczy.

Many would know of Saint Germain as the writer of William Shakespeare's plays. Previous embodiments are said to include Merlin and Christopher Columbus. It is also said that He was Joseph, father of Jesus and the Jewish prophet Samuel.

In modern times He is known for His books *The "I AM" Discourses* channelled through Godfre Ray King in the 1930's. One of His greatest claims to fame is that He founded "The Society of Rosicrusse Freemasons" under His identity of Francis Bacon. It is said that He also prophesied and then tried to avert the French Revolution.

St. Germain then spent some 85 years with the Trans-Himalayan Brotherhood and the Masters El Morya, Kuthumi and Djwhal Khul, they channelled the original Theosophical literature through Madame Blavatsky. It is also said that He was instrumental in the formulating of the American Constitution and the Declaration of Independence.

Believed to be born in 1561 and better known as the Comte de Saint Germain he is known as the Regent for Europe and is concerned primarily with the outgrowth of consciousness there. A master linguist he spoke all European languages, was an expert swordsman, a master violinist and possessed extraordinary mind power and a photographic memory.

Independently wealthy, legend marks Him as a master Alchemist able to turn base metal into high quality gold that never lost its lustre. It is reported that He also never ate nor drank and kept a youthful appearance of a man in his mid forties. Because He lived for such a long time as an immortalist, He was constantly staging His own death and assuming other personas.

Working with Archangel Zadkiel He is teaching humanity how to transmute the negative energy we have accumulated by using and upholding the Violet Transmuting Flame of forgiveness.

He is also helping humanity to embrace the 7th Ray of Spiritual Freedom as we attain our Ascension.

Freedom from the cycle of life and death.

Freedom to do the higher will of the Mother/Father Creator God.

Freedom to rise above earthly limitations.

Freedom to recognise and experience the Divine Life Force within us all.

Freedom to recognise that this Divine Life Force is God's expression in myriad's of individualized forms.

Freedom to recognise the wholeness of which everything is a part.

Freedom to release the veils of illusion, separation and ignorance.

Spiritual Freedom is the seventh step on the ladder of enlightenment and will be granted after one has learnt the aspects of: -
- Will and Power
- Wisdom
- Divine Love
- Purity
- Healing
- Peace

March 2006:
Many of the great light beings on Earth today keep a very low profile and hence there is no mass awareness of them. It is said that when a student is ready a master will appear, similarly with the immortals path. Once our hearts are open and we are in a state of sincere humility and surrender then our DOW can reveal all Its gifts – if this is our desire. It will also connect us quite synchronistically with all beings that we need to meet on the inner and outer planes.

Over the past decade, I have learnt so much regarding the gifts that our DOW has to give us and how they reveal themselves when we are ready to receive them. A year or so after I learnt that my DOW could physically nourish me with Its love and light, Leonard Orr literally appeared at my door. Fulfilling his own journey, to connect with the immortals on Earth, he arrived with a big smile to offer his support and to also leave me with some of his own research and findings. I share this next chapter that he has written as it covers areas that I personally have not explored.

The path of physical immortality was not something that really interested me until my DOW revealed more about it for me personally in 2005 and I cover this journey in the book *Harmonious Healing and the Immortal's Way*. Leonard's story adds another view.

The Yoga of Everlasting Life

Vrishvahan Samadhi (Soruba)
written by Leonard Orr

The pinnacle of yoga is the immortal yogi. The immortal yogi is a total master of spirit, mind, and body. The immortal yogis can survive and be in ultimate happiness without food and without the conveniences of civilisation which most people consider to be essential for human survival and well being. The immortal yogi is free – totally free.

To people the immortal yogi is the goal of human existence.

Immortal yogis are masters of earth, air, water, and fire. They are masters of death and time and space. They evolve bodies of light which they can dematerialize, travel at the speed of thought, and rematerialize. They are the great humanitarians. They teach by example rather than by lecture and writing. They are masters of their mind and emotions. Yoga practices which lead to the death of the body are only the shadow of the yoga of eternal life. And yet the yoga of everlasting life and total mastery is so simple. When you experience it you will wonder why you didn't think of it yourself.

Jesus is the closest example which Westerners know of the immortal yoga. Jesus spent half of his life in India studying with the immortals. However, the ministry of Jesus in the West was only three years and he didn't leave very much knowledge behind – unless you include the Essene Gospel of Peace which was evidently written after the resurrection.

After I learned all I could from studying the Bible for 22 years, the Angel of the Lord appeared to me and told me to go to India to study with the immortals. In 1977, I met my first immortal yogi. Since then, I've met eight. They have to be at least 300 years in the same body to interest me, because most of the writers and teachers of physical immortality have died already. Physical immortality is not meaningful until a person has kept the body in good condition for at least 200 years.

The yoga of everlasting life which follows are the main points – the common denominators of the practices of all the immortals I have met. Notice the main points are not intellectually stimulating. They are practices. They are not something you can learn. They are something which you do. They are like the water which runs forever, the fire which is always consuming. The wind which always moves. The Earth, always changing and nourishing. The immortal yogis who do these simple practices are always awake and alive. This is the foundation of personal aliveness. Physical immortality is quality of life, not quantity.

Human existence without the goal of total mastery to me is bland and meaningless. You could say that the study of the immortals is my major focus in life. It amazes me that people are content with superficial life and death.

Vrishvahan is a Sanskrit word which means having an immortal indestructible body of light which can transfigure or to dematerialize and rematerialize the human body at will. Soruba is a Tamil word which means the same, to have a perfect human body in which spirit, mind, and body are totally integrated. The basic practices described here naturally evolve the soul to this high state of body mastery. It may take some people a few decades of practice and others a few centuries. The yoga of everlasting life may be simple, but not superficial.

The secrets of the great immortal yogis of India are so simple and obvious that they are overlooked by philosophers.

The Eternal Sadhana of Shiva Yogi is built into Indian culture. Since I was born in the U.S.A. and became an evangelical Christian scholar, it may be easier for me than for people born in India to see the obvious. I've had the privilege of studying with Shiva Yogi Goraknath Baba Haidakhan. In the Bible, he is known as the Angel of the Lord, the eternal ABBA Father in human form, in the Lord's prayer of Jesus. ABBA is the word for Father in the Greek New Testament. It is an intimate form of Baba in Sanskrit. Jesus lived with Babaji, the Angel of the Lord, for 9 years in India.

Air, fire, water, and Earth are the secrets to the everlasting life, health and youthfulness of the body. Mantra yoga is the secret to mental health and the master of mind and emotions.

Everyone in the West has indoor plumbing and warm water. As a result, it is normal for most people to bathe twice per day which is the practice of the immortal yogis. I have found it necessary for me to soak for at least one hour in warm water each day to clean the negative emotional energy pollution which I receive as a result of normal participation in the world. Warm water opens the chakras and cleans them. Cold water automatically closes the chakras. I usually end my bath with a cold shower.

Many American millionaires received their mental inspiration and energy for their success by soaking in warm bath water.

Everyone in India who values the everlasting health and youthfulness of the immortal yogis can earn enough money to purchase a bathtub and water heater. When trekking in the Himalayas I use a simple sheet of plastic and heat water in a simple metal bucket. I put the plastic over rocks to form a bathtub. It is very inexpensive. Hot water bathing I value as the supreme gift of spiritual civilisation. Water can be heated by the sun – solar water heaters, or by your dhuni.

The supreme secret of eternal life is to clean the energy body. Daily bathing cleans the energy body. Water can clean the mind faster than the mind can clean the mind. Baptism is the Christian symbol of water purification. Daily bathing is the reality of this symbol.

From the example of Saddhus in India who live in a dhuni, I learned the value of fire purification. And, of course, by the grace and supreme example of Babaji (Shiva Yogi Goraknath of Herakhan), I have mastered the secret of fire. Elijah is the great fire yogi of the Bible.

I think I receive more value from sleeping with the fire every night as do saddhus, than from a yagna, but I am not sure. I received tremendous mystical value in the depths of my soul every time I participate in a yagna (yagna is a fire ceremony done by Sanskrit priests). Until 70 AD, the Bible religion was based on the fire ceremony.

When we sit or sleep near an open flame, the wheels of our energy body turn through the flames and are cleaned. The emotional pollution of participating in the world is burned away. The emotional pollution of participating in the world is burned away. Death urges are dissolved by fire and water working together as they clean and balance the energy body. Water and fire purification are great secrets of everlasting life and youthfulness. Fire and water nourish the body with life energy the same as food does.

Air means breathing. We must learn to breathe energy as well as air – pranayama. The simple pranayama which I practice is the pranayama of new born babies. Infants merge the inhale to exhale in a continuous rhythm. Connecting the inhale to exhale is the simplest and most natural pranayama. It is the pranayama of eternal life. Baba Goraknath also taught me the value of three alternate nostril breaths per day to keep the nadis clean.

I started a spiritual movement in the United States in 1974 that has spontaneously spread to over 10 million people all over the world called rebirthing. Rebirthing means to do pranayama while relaxing in a warm bathtub. Rebirthing also means to unravel the birth-death cycle, to liberate the soul and body of birth trauma and death urges. Rebirthing means to become a conscious expression of the Eternal Spirit and to include our physical body into the conscious expression of the Eternal Spirit and to include our physical body into the conscious life of the Eternal Self. Babaji once referred to rebirthing as the new yoga. Intuitive energy breathing in the bath is a very high and practical yoga.

Earth yoga means to master food, sleep and prosperity. The basic disciplines are to fast one day per week on liquids; milk or juice first, then drinking only clean water on our fast day when we are able to do this. To arise before the sun each day, and to have an effective exercise system.

The immortals of the Bible, Moses, Elijah and Jesus fasted without food or water for 40 days. The yoga immortals can go without food or water for years. We can master sleep by staying awake during the full moon as much as possible and by arising each day before sunrise. Sleep is death. Prosperity means to produce ideas, goods, or services of value for others as well as ourselves. Prosperity naturally comes when we serve others. We receive money from others when we give them ideas, goods and services which they are willing to pay for.

The great yoga for the kali yuga age is karma yoga. The saddhus of this age work in the world part-time and do austerities part-time. Karma yoga – all work – is also an austerity. True work in the world is dharma – sadhana. God says, 'work is worship'. But we cannot survive in the world without spiritual practices. People quickly lose their health and their bodies in this 'money mad' world without spiritual purification with earth, air, water, and fire. Fasting, breathing, bathing and fire cleans the emotional body and heals the physical body.

When we don't do enough spiritual purification we can develop a 'guru belly'. Excess emotional energy pollution accumulates in the solar plexus chakra and produces the guru belly – it may be called psychic fat or emotional energy pollution.

There are eight basic practices for the yoga of everlasting life. All these practices nourish and clean our life energy, our soul and body, the rainbow body aura.

Breathing, fire, bathing, food mastery and work are the four that yield mastery of the body. The body is earth, air, water, fire and mind. The Shiva Samhita says, 'energy and thought first created air, then fire, then water and finally earth.'

Mantra yoga yields supreme mastery of mind. Babaji taught me that 'om namaha shivaya' is the Maha mantra. In Hebrew the mantra is backwards – 'yava shim omen'. This is my steady diet. I also get value from working with a few mantras – 'bhole baba ki jai, on maha mrjitenjai, jai maha maya ki', and 'om Jesus Christ, jai Jesus Christ'.

The sixth principle is grace. Grace is when our love for God meets God's love for us. The grace of everlasting life may be expressed in the following thought – 'I am alive now, therefore my life urges are stronger than my death urges.' As long as I strengthen my life urges and weaken my death urges I will go on living in health and youthfulness.

We need to learn how to rest in the Lord – our Source.

Spiritual purification practices make us more alive but the grace of life keeps us alive while we are doing them.

The eighth principle of everlasting life yoga is respect for the saints. This means to learn from the great immortal yogis who have kept their bodies in health and youthfulness for over 300 years. Spending time with these people is life's greatest privilege. One thing they teach us is to find God in every person, especially those people who are close to us, our family and friends.

Thank you Leonard.

March 2006:
As I re-read this book with a desire to update what has been written, I remember one of the early weekend workshops that I did on the subject of living on prana in Switzerland in the mid nineties. At the back of the room was a very surly looking woman who seemed to get more agitated as the seminar unfolded. At one point she said: "I'm not interested in all of this sort of stuff, just tell me how to live on prana and not need physical food".

This 'sort of stuff' was the type of information the previous chapters here have contained, information that lays the groundwork for this field of possibility before I share my personal story with this reality.

One thing that I know for certain 10 years after writing this book is that there are many ways to magnetize enough cosmic particles (prana, chi) to healthily feed a physical body in an alternate way and yet our ability to do this is completely dependent on one consciousness, belief systems and personal frequency or keynote. This is not a journey about physical food it is a journey about the spiritual food that our Divinity has for us, a food that can nourish us on all levels, that can also flow into and through the physical system and free it from many limitations.

Prana & Interdimensional Life –
plus message from Arcturius
channelled through Jasmuheen 1995

March 2006:
Over the past decade some people have questioned the reality I have created around my own living on prana experience, and so before we continue with the following channelled message, that I received in 1995 from one of the Higher Light Being's who was overshadowing me at that time; I would like to add the following data to clarify this further.

PRANA AND INTER-DIMENSIONAL LIFE excerpt from *The Prana Program*

Q: What is inter-dimensional life?
A: It is the experience of our natural multi-dimensional nature that comes via a journey of expansion of our consciousness. By changing our brain wave patterns we can experience the different realities of more subtle and refined dimensions that exist within us and around us.

Q: Some people have criticized your first books on this due to your constant referencing to Holy Ones and Beings of Light. What relevance – if any – do they have to The Prana Program?
A: Nothing and also everything. Firstly the initial process that I underwent that gave me the gifts of being free from the need of physical food, came through the ascension networks. Downloaded from Serapis Bay, in the early 1990's, it was trialled by one group based in Australia, with various success. For some it was an easy conversion, for others not, yet all experienced an increase in their intuitive abilities. As those abilities expanded so did our contact with and understanding of inter-dimensional life.

Q: Is knowledge or experience of these Beings of Light an important reality in The Prana Program?
A: No, for example – to use television vernacular – some people only like the Christian, Buddhist or Muslim Cosmic TV channels and some of these may never channel surf, hence their experience of inter-dimensional realities remains vague or limited by choice. Others confine their dimensional experience to 3D Earth and its games of struggle for survival. Everything is possible and if we can think of something it can be brought into reality on some level or else we wouldn't have the thought. Hence we can access many of the benefits of The Prana Program using the science of the fields. Other benefits that are literally quite delightful – like liaising with inter-dimensional life – can only be enjoyed when we open to its channel. As creative beings we can choose to dwell in any reality we desire but choices are broadened with education, the expansion of our consciousness and experience.

Q: You often say that human evolution and The Prana Program particularly, is being overshadowed by inter-dimensional Being's of great light and love, can you share more of this?
A: In my experiential model of reality, there are many inter-dimensional groups tuning into Earth's evolutionary process, guiding and overshadowing and sometimes interfering e.g. A recent TV series director Steven Spielberg called "Taken" focused a lot on interference by the Zeta Reticuli and their experimentations. However there are also benevolent bodies who download to open minds – via the U.F.I. – lots of evolutionary enhancing technology to guide Earth; from The Prana Program to Tesla technology, free energy systems and so much more.

Q: But didn't The Prana Program's nutritional aspect originally come from ancient wisdom sources not inter-dimensional?
A: All wisdom – at some point – is downloaded interdimensionally through the act of consciousness expansion that allows an individual greater access to the U.F.I., the Universal Field of Infinite Love and Intelligence.

Q: For many years you promoted the Luscious Lifestyles Program as a way of increasing the pranic flow. How did you discover this?
A: An eight point action plan that includes daily meditation, prayer, mind mastery, a light diet, exercise, service, time in silence and the use of mantras and devotional songs, these points formed the lifestyle that I found to be practiced by everyone who was experiencing the most benefits of The Prana Program. It is also the lifestyle that I received telepathically from Mother Mary when I asked her for a recipe to eliminate suffering on Earth.

Q: In some very religious countries you are criticized more for your work with inter-dimensional life than for The Prana Program, why do you think this is?
A: Religion and power often go hand in hand with many promoting that inter-dimensional contact is only possible through intermediaries such as gurus or priests. However in my reality and experience it is our calibration that determines contact with the Holy Ones and/or Angelics. Many power mongers do not like to hear someone say that God is within and that we can go direct to Source for anything as it shifts the balance of power and eliminates the need for middlemen.

The Arcturians – Message

"Salutations dear ones of Light. This is Arcturius with your gathering. Tis such a simple understanding is it not – that one has within them the power to move beyond dimensions and through dimensions, beyond space, beyond time.

For we have shared with your gathering that your being knows expression upon all dimensions. For you are connected, are you not, to the Source of Creation, and you know also that all beings were birthed through the fire, the energy and the love of the Mother/Father Creator God. You have within your understanding the knowing that you are not separate, that this Mother/Father God resides within your being and is not external to you.

You have glimpsed the understanding, and some have a deeper knowing, that the dimensional shift, the access to the greater part of your expression lies through the doorways within.

You have understood that you are Masters, that you are co-creators and in the co-creation dear ones comes the creation, the knowledge that you can create the experience your heart desires through your focus. It is simple for every day that you focus on simply giving yourself, your physical being, a bath, a shower of the inner Light so you will become Light.

Understand the vastness of consciousness. The consciousness that is I, Arcturius, is individualized yes, it has a note of knowing but it is the same consciousness that resides within the vastness of the All That Is, that is you as well.

The consciousness within is so elastic and is governed by the higher mind, the Divine Intelligence that resides within, the ability that you have to move into that state of All Knowing. It is that aspect that the Light within will awaken, to allow you to simply shift your perception, your focus in this journey for reconnection to wherever you desire. For example, if you desire to be once more upon the Sirian system then you simply intend to be there.

It is like a fisherman that casts his line out into the vast oceans. It is the hook, the sinker, that lands so much further from the shore but it is the intention of the fisherman to cast his line, is it not, that creates that possibility.

And so it is where you move your consciousness across the galaxies and universes of this dimension to another. It is your intention, your focus of what you wish to achieve, of where you wish to go. There will be an aspect of your consciousness that will arrive thus, that aspect is like that hook, that sinker, it has the weight to emerge into that sea of energy that resides where you direct it, for it has the power of your thought, your focus, your intention and this is what sends it winging across time and space.

Your journeys, your inter-dimensional travel is simply that. The desire, the recognition that you are in essence, multi-dimensional beings. The thought, the knowing will propel your energy forward or backward simply by your thinking. It is your thinking that you are learning to bring into discipline is it not? For you can think that you are limited or you can think that you are unlimited.

Our star system dear ones is a system of Ascended Beings. All beings that move upon and within the energy fields that are known as the Arcturian system, understand the Divinity within, understand the power of the mind to create and we have all understood the harm that was created when the mind was filled with impurities. When, through discipline, the mind was focused on the purity of creative expression of the Mother/Father God then we moved into the Ascended state.

We understood that we could ignite the Light of the Divine Being within, allow it to grow within our cellular form, creating a new matrix of energy – you term your Lightbody – and dissolve the molecular structure of solid form into Light. This we did eons of time ago and this is the challenge for beings upon this plane in this point of your linear time.

This is a journey you have all undergone before and you hold within you the cellular memory of having done so, where you were beings fed from the ethers, from the higher planes, from the Universal Force. This was before your base changed from what you would term your silicone to your carbon, and now you reverse the process and when you reverse the process, you once again become the purity of the energy of the silicone substance.

Tis the same substance as your crystals, for those beings that are refracted in these energy beams known as crystals, hold unlimited power, they are conduits for energy. They light great cities, they balance the energy beams of great cities in complete harmony and alignment with the thought forms of the masses of individualized sparks of consciousness and energy that reside within the higher realms, in expression and acknowledgment of

Divine Power. And the key to the doorway, dear ones, of the higher realms is simply the desire within the heart.

It is interesting to watch your planetary system for many are exploring new ways of energy, from the fusion, the fission, the splitting of the atom, to the desire to explore your space, to create space vehicles of metal. Know that any civilisation that works with the vehicles of metal have not yet understood the Divine energy matrix within their being for it is the vehicles of Light – what you term your Merkabahs, it is also the power of thought beyond your Merkabahs – that allow for interdimensional travel. It is when you hook into the inner matrix of energy of Divinity, that will allow you freedom to access all the dimensions and travel so freely.

It is not until the scientists, your physicists, begin to open up to the Divinity within that will enable them to create the vehicles of Light to move beyond the limited technology they are currently exploring.

The gifts of your Divinity are so simple yet you have been trapped within the physical plane for so long you have forgotten the simplicity. Has it not been shared that it is the children that will create this heaven and inherit this heaven? It is symbolic dear ones. It is symbolic in the sharing of humankind to embrace the child-like innocence within.

It is time to understand simplicity as being the key, to understand that it is purity of heart, that it is the ability to love each other unconditionally; and that the Higher Light Science is simply the ability to move energy through your body, the energy of Light and Love - for it is this love alone that will propel you in to the next dimension. And you know within your heart what that promises for you have journeyed there before. It brings with it the ability of all beings to live in the honouring and acknowledgment of the Light within regardless of the expressions of physicality.

On the Arcturian system all of the beings look the same. We do not have the desire for recognition on that level for we tune, as we do with your gathering, to the emission of energy, the emission of signals of Light and Love that emanate from the heart within. We do not focus upon your physical form, we simply read the energy patterns of Light, the depth of Love that comes from the heart centre. For it is the heart that is the doorway to the higher dimensions is it not?

As with your system, the Arcturians are continuing to evolve back to the completeness of their being. Now that system is fifth dimensional and it is beginning to move into the higher octave of the fifth bordering on the sixth. We work freely with Ascended Masters and the other Light Beings that move within all other dimensions of expressions.

There is free communication, telepathically and using the languages of Light for the languages of Light are beyond your telepathic thought imprinting. The languages of light are the languages that allow you to recognise the vibration of the Light emanation of each individualized soul, of each individualized unit of consciousness.

From the fifth dimension, moving into the 6th and the 7th, the consciousness moves from an individualized state and becomes a mass consciousness working in unity and harmony beyond the individualization.

Your planetary system, and that of the 4th and the 3rd, has been individual units of consciousness trapped in limited form run by ego and your lower mind. You are beginning to awaken to the Supreme qualities within you, the unlimited nature of your being.

And as you are becoming aware you are not just one, but are masses, and you are learning to play the harmony of an orchestra, for you are individual instruments but there is great change upon your planet. You are learning to tune, to work, to harmonize your energy together, for there is a song to be sung, a tune to be played upon this Earth. The words of this song, the feeling of this song is simply that of harmony, of unity.

You have spent so long in judgment have you not? In the "this is the only way, this is my way, you must do it my way and if you do not you will be punished ..." It has not worked has it? To stand in judgment of one another has created only separation and pain.

The gathering here is a gathering of unity of hearts is it not? Of hearts that long for peace within and peace without, of hearts that long to know once more the greatness of your being, the unlimited nature of your being.

You have practice runs do you not? Often on the night realms you are freed from your physical body to go to the higher dimensions of Light, to other planetary systems for great learning and knowing. And you are remembering this more are you not? So you often find upon your return to your physical body that you still feel you are somewhere else – for you are.

You do exist in every dimension of expression and with every breath you can know more and more of the God within, until you are consciously that. And on every level of dimension of expression you have the power to move freely through the focus of your thinking; through the power of your intention of your thought.

Did you not know dear ones that in order to embrace your Ascension all you have to instruct your being is with the power of one focused thought. To simply chant to yourself with your heart and your soul with the power of your intention that: -

"I AM an Ascended Being of Infinite Light and Infinite Love" and thus you will become!

There is nothing else that you need to do in essence. And yet it is fun to play these games along the way is it not? Tis a process of rediscovery. Perhaps there is one or two who wish to share, to ask questions, we invite you to do so dear ones of Light.

Q: About bi-location and teleportation, what is your experience on that?
A: Beings such as myself do not take physical form so there is no requirement to bilocate or teleport for we do not need to manipulate molecular structure. We have had the pleasure of being in physical embodiment yet have not chosen to be in physical embodiment for eons of time. Our beings, our energy fields are manipulated through the universal expressions, through thought alone which happens instantaneously.

An aspect of my consciousness resides within all atomic structure, within all space and time for we have understood that we are the All That Is, we are the Creative Energy. But we can, through focused thought, gather together beams of Light energy that we may project into form and trigger knowing within beings.

On the Arcturian system one may take a 'body' that is quite small and fine but when we materialize to your realms we may take the form of angels if that is what is required to make connection with you. But back to the question for we digress ...

With your beings, the understanding of many is that your focus, rather than being on your multi-dimensional nature, is on your physical form is it not? Are you not now simply remembering that you have the ability to dematerialize, to teleport, and are not limited to the physical body at all?

As you change your energy matrix and thus your consciousness, and as you bring in more of the higher knowing of your unlimited being, you will be able to come and go freely from the physical body without concern of the physical form. If your focus is limited to the physical body it will restrict you.

The lessons and the knowing that you are understanding is that you can move from the physical at will and so you are learning tools and techniques of shifting consciousness which is what your bilocation is.

The beings of Light upon this plane that have embodied the Christ Self within, bringing it to the forefront, are in – for some – a role of teaching and igniting the hearts the of many.

Many when they understand the ability to move beyond physical form do not decide to play on these earth realms for there is not much upon this earth plane that you have not experienced in this or in other embodiments.

Many when they begin to understand their abilities, through the power of the mind to bilocate, simply do so to access the doorways to higher dimensions of expression. To explore what it is they have forgotten. That is all. Has that answered your question?
(Yes thank you more than answered it.)

Q: When bringing in the Light does the intention have to be kept focused?
A: The Light is unlimited, the Light is the force of God. I have found that many of you when you begin your manifestation, you still wish to hold on to the details of how it will be manifested do you not? Control is it not?

This is a process dear one of surrender, of trust. In your mastery, you simply need to have clarity of focus, clarity of intention. What is it as Masters you wish to create upon this plane? And then expect it to be so!

If your expectation, your desire is simply to reawaken to the God within, to bring the Light and Love of God within every cell of your being, command it! How it is done, it is done! And a 'by-product' dear one of that, is the realignment in whatever way is for the highest.

Q: Could you please elaborate to us on the meaning of Ascension, the changes we go through?
A: Ascension is the state of being, that state of perfection that allows one freedom to move through each energy band of each dimension. Ascension is the embracing of the complete nature of your Self. It is about being filled with Light once more for Light is the aspect of the God within.

Many beings are continually ascending. As you ascend from one dimension, you ascend to the next. It is like a graduation from your kindergarten, to your high school then your university.

And when you graduate you find yourself back in the arms of the Divine as a completely unified point of consciousness that is no longer a point of consciousness for it has become lost in the vastness of the All That Is. That is your graduation present. Does that make sense? (Yes). You ask for more?

Q: Perhaps some more on the changes involved?
A: Changes dear one. The fourth dimension is the last dimension that you need a body, that you carry your consciousness around in a physical form. When you move into the energy matrix of the 5th dimension you create a body at will. And having passed from the 3rd to the 4th the doorway is open to you freely.

Right now you are focusing on your form in this dimension with an awareness of doorways and access to other dimensions. When you are in the 5th it will be the opposite. The focus point of your consciousness will be in the 5th with the access back to the 4th and the 3rd as guided by your heart and your contracts and your service. For every dimension has these contractual arrangements with the Divine One.

And when you are in the 5th you will begin to access the doorways to the higher dimensions which you can also do now my dear ones. For of the Ascended Masters many reside upon the 7th dimension and access doorways back through the different realities, tuning into the mass reality that each dimension creates.

The mass reality of this dimension has been one of separateness, with limited beings of judgment, of disharmony. It is changing as the higher energies and the desire in the heart of all brings through a new formula of being.

On the 5th dimension all is created instantaneously through thought. As you think so shall it be. If you wish to visit temples, there is a temple right there. If you think it, it manifests. And there needs to be a discipline of thought, of a universal recognition of harmony, of the knowing of the God I AM in its expression within all beings so that none are harmed, so that all occurs for the highest. On that plane of expression one takes bodies as required, as you desire. There is no such thing as bilocation, as dematerialization for all just is thought and instantly occurs.

There is an energy of complete unconditional Love and yet excitement, of recognition, of the desire to see every being embrace the God I AM in every moment. For the being is the BEing here, we understand that level of expression.

And on the 6th it continues on becoming purer and purer points of expression of creative energies. Has that helped? (Yes thank you).

Q: Can you explain a little of the difference of physical death and ascension and ascension with this body?
A: Tis said to be nature is it not? The dying is really 'old hat' where we come from, on our plane of expression. For we know we created the body so we can de-create it or re-create it at will. You become so attached to the physical form upon this plane because you do not

recognise the unlimited nature of your Divine essence or the capability of your Divine essence.

If you did dear ones, you could take a body at will and drop it at will. If you wished to be a blonde Scandinavian you could create that. If you wished to be a tall Negroid you could create that, just for the fun of it like when you change your clothes.

It is from limitation that one clings so closely and fiercely to the physical form. The process of birthing on this plane is far more difficult than that of dying. The karmic repercussions, the understanding contractually of death is simply that …

One may be awake enough to understand the immortality of the soul, like your Buddhists. Many Buddhists feel that the physical body is irrelevant for the soul is eternal. But if one is truly embracing mastery then cannot one maintain the energy fields of the physical form, that houses this aspect of your consciousness, while you are in service and until you have completed your service?

You can still move to a higher dimensional frequency after death and continue your journey of ascension for it is a never ending journey not a destination. Because what is happening upon this plane is there is enough energy force building that will shoot the whole energy matrix into the next level including the disembodied ones attached to this plane and those embodied.

But Ascension in this body, is simply mastery of the now. Of understanding if your contract is to be here for some time, then to maintain the physical form in peak condition, and when the contract has expired, to take the physical body into Light. To keep its memory pattern, its energy matrix, stored on the etheric realms for you to take that 'garb', that molecular visionary concept and use it at will when required.

The Mother Mary that comes to many is a being of shimmering Light, golden Light energy fields. She works with the Angelic Ones, is the Mother of the Angelic Ones. And yet She has kept the imprinting, the imagery of her previous embodiment upon this plane because that is the One that when She clothes Herself in the garb of that molecular imagery, triggers within the heart.

If She came as little green monster, hairy with red eyes, people would not go "Oh that is Mother Mary" (much laughter) but when She comes in the garb of Her blue robes and Her angelic face they go "Oh Mother Mary, I recognise your image".

Thus it is with the One you know as Lord Sananda dear ones. The consciousness of that One is so vast. It is not Sananda that took embodiment of the being of Jesus – just an aspect of that – that sustained the vibration to the highest, finest frequency so that the individual known as Jesus could be used as a Holy Chalice by all of the Ascended realms to make the imprinting upon your plane at that time. To give the message.

But that being had its own individual consciousness, does that make sense? (Yes) That being continued its own evolution but was simply in service to the Greater Cause – to First Cause – sustained by that spark of Lord Sananda. And when that One brings forth an image it brings forth the image of the Christ, of Lord Jesus for it triggers the knowing in the heart. We have digressed but has that answered your question? (yes thank you!)

Q: I have one more question please. As we are going through the changes at the moment, most of us are putting more light into our bodies, we experience sometimes areas that come into conflict maybe, anxiety from the ego. Can you give us some practical advice on what to do at such times to stop the intellect from being in conflict, and pacifying perhaps that side of ourselves.

A: To simply allow dear one, sweet child of light. You have known great pain, have you not? (yes) This body has a memory of great suffering and pain. Many bodies are in a state of that of a frightened child. It is not the physical body dear one, it is the energy field that is overlaid by the emotional body.

But the emotional body has full understanding and feeling of every experience in every embodiment. It has been guided by the mind that has worked hand in hand with the ego. It is moving into an energy matrix where it needs to relinquish control – where the lower mind must go into the higher divine expression.

So the emotional body and the ego feel a little unsure as to what is going on, as if its power, its position is being usurped somehow. Simply love every aspect of yourself. And when these fears come up you may simply program with your higher knowing that "I walk in safety – that in joy, in harmony, in safety, I now step into the unknown" knowing that the unknown is also the known, just perhaps not in your conscious memory bank quite yet, not released.

It is a matter of empowering self with love. When these fears arise, acknowledge those fears momentarily. Know that you are now being given the opportunity to move beyond the fear, to counteract the fear through the knowing that you are vast, unlimited loving beings, that you may walk safely in your own divinity. Has that helped dear one? (Yes, thanks).

Q: I have a question about vibration. I've recently been practicing holistic pulsing. What I'm wondering is what are the higher depths of the vibration we create in the body – is that a beneficial thing to be doing?

A: Dear, dear one, whatever you are guided to do within the heart it is for you to do. For you are unique patterns of energy and when you follow that inner guidance it is giving you another flavour, so to speak.

So if that is your inner guidance to do such, it is because it something you are needing to embrace in your own energy field, and having embraced that, share of that knowing to others that magnetize to you.

Understand that there is a tandem process dear ones of light, there is your own unfoldment and there is your planetary unfoldment. You are working in conjunction with a mass matrix of energy. So as you change yourself you are changing others.

As you are guided to explore such things dear ones, any work that is refining your frequency, bringing in the higher frequencies is simply allowing energetically the opening of doorways for the light body to superimpose itself over your body.

Many of you have blockages in your electrical circuitry. These blockages have been caused from not allowing, from not understanding the need for the free flow of energy, and from previous embodiments of pain and suffering that have created thus.

So as you are guided dear ones of light by your inner calling to do something, know it is a gift, just something that will allow you to be refined a little more, realigned a little more. But be aware, all must come from the inner call, dear ones, of the Inner Teacher. It must be the heart –felt knowing that this is such, rather than the inspiration of others alone. So dear ones, perhaps one more question and then it's time for a break.

Q: Can you explain a little about the relationship of animals and our role with the other aspects of nature on this plane?
A: At which point of time? Perhaps that is a trick question, dear one. Dear ones, understand that when humanity, the humanoids took embodiment upon this plane of expression billions of years ago, that it was like you were being given from the Mother/Father Creator God the most incredible paradise.

For this earthly planet, the Mother Gaia, was abundant with everything the imagination could think of, the best of all creative expression that had been created on other planetary systems was brought into totality upon this plane – your life forms, your animals, your birds, the expressions of nature were all here.

Humans, when they took embodiment and energized upon this plane – the story of which is quite complicated and not relevant here – were given the guardianship of such beauty of expression, recognising that every creature held within it a spark of the divine energy that also pulsed through your very core. They were your brothers, your sisters, different form, but your brothers, your sisters. Perhaps they did not have the complexity of all the bodies that you have, but they have the life force nonetheless.

It was a wondrous time – you have forgotten such. The animals were working on intuitive levels of connected being, for they were so happy in the purity of their expression. The discord with the animal kingdom has come from that of the human kingdom as it has abused and tested and maligned and murdered and slaughtered in the name of survival. And yet if you understood the true essence of the energy that sustains you, you would not partake of such barbaric journeys.

We are not in judgment dear ones however. What has unfolded on this plane has also been in part of divine perfection, for as you have moved from your divinity in your conscious understanding, you can now embrace that divinity with heart-felt joy, having not felt it for so long. All is perfection.

The connectedness you have with these ones is just a deep knowing that they have an aspect of themselves – if you attune to closely, dear ones – that can blend into your being to allow you to be more complete in your expression.

There is a mutual exchange of energy. Your loving acceptance is healing the energy matrix of suffering from previous times and they are imparting an aspect of their resonance to your energy field as well.

Remember dear ones, that whatever you are guided to do, if you trust that, it simply because there is aspect of vibration of resonance that will allow you to be even more glorious, more beautiful than that you already are aware of.

So dear ones of light, perhaps our message has been simple, repeated, for this expression of your true essence is simple as it is all powerful, it's essence is love. It is the essence of love that glues the molecular structure of all expression harmoniously together and its aspect is great light. The darkness can be loved by the light and is all created by The One.

Love and honour all, dear children of light. See the spark of the divine in all. The next time you feel in judgment or anger of your fellow beings, move beyond that framework and look for the spark of divine expression in their eyes, and in their soul, and in their heart. And when each one sees that you look upon them with eyes of unconditional love, they will reflect that love back to you.

And do you not understand that it is the essence of love that will create the change upon this plane far more powerfully than that of your judgment? We love and honour the light of the God within you all. This is Arcturius dear ones."

- End of channelled message. -

Note from Jasmuheen:
I was guided to include this channelling in this book of my journey as there are many interdimensional civilisations who naturally live only from the Divine essence. Requiring no food, nor sleep, nor bodies, they open the door to us to embrace a more civilised world and inspire us to move Earth back into a state of Grace-filled harmony with all life.

Chapter 8

One Way

February 1996:
Having researched information as to how a being could live on light by explaining energy and prana, the following chapters will share of the practical application of this information. While our initial attraction to this journey has been deeply personal, in retrospect various individuals, including myself, have also been both 'guinea pig' and pioneer for this process in the West.

Learning to be sustained by prana is not a new practice. It is as ancient as the Vedas and beyond, with some research into the times of MU suggesting all beings were once fed from the etheric realms that it was only after 'the fall from grace' that we began to take nourishment from the atmospheric realms. We were given guardianship over the mineral, plant and animal kingdoms to love and honour and peacefully co-exist with all. Somehow along the way we became less refined, less civilised, less sensitive and less honouring.

To me personally, the process of allowing oneself to be sustained once more from the etheric realms is about returning to civility.

While I understand the Divine perfection of all, and recognise what has taken place in the evolution of mankind to be a natural, pre-ordained part of this journey, I also embrace the idea of living life in this NOW moment to our highest potential. I like the idea of also allowing all other life forms the freedom of full expression, to live without the fear or threat of 'being man's dinner', or senseless slaughter from ignorance. I also realise that this way of thinking is way ahead of its time for the mass consciousness upon the planet for I have witnessed first-hand that for Western culture the concept is very embryonic and threatening as it tends upset the deepest beliefs held by mass consciousness in the West today. In this work we are literally challenging the ideas of "If you don't eat you'll die"; "there are two things you can count on in life, we are all born and we will all die" etc.

I remember feeling – when quizzed by journalists earlier this year in Hong Kong – that if we were scientists in a laboratory, searching for and developing a cure for world hunger, we would no doubt have world press support, government and private funding and much more!

Then, having found this solution and experimented successfully on human guinea pigs we would possibly even be given some prestigious award like the Nobel Prize for our positive contribution and solution to this major world problem. Two thirds of the world's population suffer from lack of proper nutrition and hunger and live on less than $2 per day.

Nonetheless we are not scientists, just simple individuals listening to our inner guidance and exploring our human potential under the banner of 'spirituality'. Still our success is undeniable, the results can be proven and have huge ramifications globally which we cover in the chapter on "World Potential".

This information is revolutionary and will require individuals to consciously embark on the path of self-mastery for it to be fully implemented and integrated into society as a whole.

Chapter 9

Being Sustained by Prana
A Personal Journey

February 1996:
If it is possible to be objective, I would like to relay a process that I chose to undergo to be sustained by prana. I feel that this choice is a very personal one and must be under taken according to the dictates of one's own heart. Many will not make this choice at this point in time but some may readily embrace the idea. Regardless of individual choice, know that it is possible to be sustained by light alone and take no external food substance. Knowing and then experiencing that we can be nourished and sustained by light is a fascinating and uplifting experience and one that brings great freedom.

In early 1993 I was presented with an opportunity to undergo a specific process of realignment the details of which I will share throughout the following chapters. I must however share it from two points of view, my understanding at the time and my understanding in retrospect.

At that time apparently, maybe only a half a dozen people had participated worldwide in such a process. As such it was in its very embryonic and pioneering days. The information or "how to's" were being received telepathically and there were no manuals or guide posts, only an 'inner knowing' and confirmation of what felt 'right' in the heart of each individual who chose that path.

The history of this particular process began in late 1992 in Byron Bay, in northern NSW, Australia. At that time a number of audio tapes were sweeping the 'New Age' communities in Australia. These tapes were called the Ascension tapes and came through a channel in the US called Eric Kliene. I was later advised that the creation and release of these tapes was orchestrated by 'Spirit', or Higher powers; to create a mass awakening of the Lightworkers, which was what occurred.

Although I had been meditating for over 20 years, because it made life easier and more joyful, the information and energy from these tapes touched a chord deep within my heart and allowed me a glimpse of a much bigger picture.

Many others, like myself, had also felt a powerful acknowledgment in their hearts when they heard this Ascension message and call. Somehow we gravitated together and enthusiastically waited for further information. In early 1993 we received the news that a woman in Byron Bay had ascended!

Shortly afterwards her husband, came and spoke to a small gathering about how this had occurred. It seems she had long been clairvoyant and had begun to receive telepathic messages from the Ascended Masters about a specific process that would quickly and permanently raise a being's vibrational frequency. The energy fields of their bodies would be realigned to allow for the descent of the Higher Self and the individual's consequent Ascension.

When I was made aware of this 'process' I was open but detached. I thought it worthy of investigation and after research, and meeting those involved, decided to proceed. In retrospect I would expect that any choosing to undergo this journey have developed discernment and follow their own clear inner guidance each step of the way.

The process itself, was quiet simple and entailed a period of prior preparation where one was to have cleared at least 51% of their karmic debt and also healed their auric field.

Following that the process was a) to not eat or drink anything for 7 days; b) to sip water or very diluted juices and rest for another 7 days while the body healed and adjusts to the previous 7 days; c) to rest for another 7 days to allow for the integration of the energies of the Higher Self.

Now, what was the purpose of this 21-day process and what actually occurred? Firstly the 3 bands of 7 days is connected to the sacred geometries and a Being needs to dedicate this time freely and without interruption. It was to me, a sacred initiation, to be honoured and not rushed through lightly.

While for me it was definitely not just a process to stop eating food, this 'process' has allowed myself and many other beings around Australia to be sustained by prana alone for upon completion of the 21 days, we have not had to eat solid food. We are now completely sustained and nourished by the etheric realms. That is a fact. We are healthy, highly energized and inconsequentially, cheap to look after!

As the months rolled by, I felt great, my energy levels were high and I displayed all the signs of good health but my loved ones and relatives were not convinced. To allay their concerns, after 5 months of existing purely on light liquids and no vitamins, I underwent various tests and was not only given a clean bill of health but found that I had never been so healthy in my entire adult life! Good news for the loved ones and complete confirmation for me.

One thing I would like to mention is that as with all pioneers, there is no previous yardstick to measure things by. Anytime I have experienced aches or pains I have had to totally rely on my inner guidance as to what was occurring.

There was no way I could go to a doctor or alternative therapist and ask what was what. Generally speaking, the majority of Western doctors are still coming to terms with the idea that most disease is caused by emotional dis-ease and poor fuel choices that eventually disrupt the energy fields of the bodies before finally reflecting in the physical body. The alternative therapists treat a being more holistically and encourage fresh food, good nutrition, exercise etc. So in both counts the idea of being sustained purely by light energy can be very 'stretching' due to their previous training and ideas on what the body requires to maintain full health.

I even tracked down an Ayurvedic therapist who I assumed would be readily open to this idea due to their background and training. Upon discussion of the doshas and the revelation that upon testing since the process, my Pita was 13, the Vata 14 and the Kapha

15; I was greeted with scepticism and told that only rare individuals have such balanced doshas and further scepticism regarding the idea that an individual could be maintained purely by light.

The levels of disbelief that I have encountered in the non-traditional field of medicine, has been unexpected yet I understand it is simply due to their lack of previous exposure to this type of reality. How many liquidarians or pranic nourishers would either a Western doctor or alternative therapist encounter in their day-to-day world?

Eventually I developed my own system, using kinesiology, to keep track of bodily changes and use it in conjunction with my own inner guidance.

We are living in a society where the majority of people react to the idea of not eating with incredulous disbelief and/or total lack of interest in they themselves ever undertaking such a journey.

The motivation of individuals who have done this process is as unique and varied as they are. For me, it seemed a natural step. I had been a purist regarding fuel choices for the physical vehicle for over 20 years. At two, I rejected meat and by 15 had taken control over all my dietary needs, fasted for purification and learned to listen to the needs of my body. I found it spoke a specific language that was easy to interpret. I studied health, protein sources and experimented. For me, light and live food became essential and my body responded positively.

Creating, and then self-curing a cancer, also taught me about the effect that negative unresolved emotions that we store in our body, have on the physical body. It forced me to cleanse not only the physical body but also the energy blocks within the emotional body and to realign and release cellular memory. Due to my lifestyle choice, meditation, diet and exercise routine, the tumour had remained small and its growth had been slow. Still, through stress, unresolved emotional issues and the learning I required, it was there and very real and took four intense months to dissolve and clear.

Consequently, as I began the 21 days my system was very clean. I had eaten lightly of soups and fruit in the prior weeks as I wanted the experience to be pleasant. Previous fasting taught that the release of toxins (if any) can trigger headaches, nausea, muscle and joint aches, dizziness etc.

Foremost I was motivated by the desire for Ascension, to realise my full potential while in this body; to be a pure vessel or instrument for Divine Will to manifest through. Again this motivation was a natural progression for me after 20 or more years or regular daily meditation and metaphysical research. I had established via these practices, relatively clear inner guidance as to what was 'right' for me and this choice felt 'right'. To me the insights and the learning gained have been phenomenal.

So due to the preparation undergone I flew through the first 7 days with high levels of energy, I rested as was guided and was put on an etheric drip of Liquid Light so that when I felt hungry, I simply asked for an increase in the drip feed levels – this was always done as requested and the 'hunger' always dissipated. Like others, I have keep a detailed journal of this time and since, but my desire is simply that through the brief telling of my own story, others will understand the power of light or prana to sustain and the subsequent freedom gained.

In retrospect I saw that the 21 days was a process of great cleaning (1st 7 days), healing and realignment (2nd 7 days) and then filling with higher energies (3rd 7 days) that could be likened to the purification and sterilization of an old glass bottle to prepare it for re-use and refilling of another substance.

My research has shown me that this process that allowed for the descent of the Higher Self into the physical vehicle is comparable to the 3rd Initiation of the 7 level initiation process as discussed by Dr. Stone in *The Complete Ascension Manual* and by the Theosophists and Alice Bailey.

Inner guidance and research has suggested that due to the differing vibrational frequencies of the physical body (personality), the Higher Self (Soul) and the I AM Presence (Monad), that until the 4 body system (physical, emotional, mental and spiritual) is aligned perfectly neither the soul or monad can take full residence in the vehicle on this plane.

The 21-day process simply 'sped' up this realignment to allow the soul residence and upon completion the Higher Self, or soul, simply maintains its new home via Light energy – hence the cessation of the requirement for solid food substance.

However the 21-day process simply mastered the physical body and to a degree the emotional and mental bodies as it takes both emotional and mental fortitude to even undergo such a process. Nonetheless in retrospect, it is just a step on the "Ascension ladder" and while I did not attain the full powers of my concept of an Ascended Being, the benefits for me have been immeasurable.

I also soon discovered that for me, and many others, eating was emotionally based. After a year I experienced quite strong emotional stress with the sudden death of a parent, my energy levels dropped and my 'inner child' wished to seek solace in food. So I continued, with renewed intensity, the journey of cellular release and reprogramming and breaking of old patterns.

As the emotional body from each now point also serves the mental body (we are literally built to think before we feel), this led to the intensification of my apprenticeship in mind mastery to create a reality that moved beyond even the conscious awareness of food.

I learnt that I could program the body to maintain a desired weight and also to change its shape at will. I have learnt that my body reflects my emotional state and that my emotional body responds directly to my thought processes.

I have also learnt that the emotional body is like a wilful child and just because we have decided to keep the house clean from now on (through mind mastery) doesn't mean we don't have to clean out the emotional baggage from past thought processes that is held within cellular memory (or the cupboards of the attic!). Inner spring cleaning is imperative – only then can the house – our Being – be clean and function at full capacity.

This process also opened another door for me that has refined my vibrational frequency to the point that channelling, healing, clairvoyance, bi-location and creating by thought alone now seem natural and relatively easy. I have learnt to honour and love all aspects of my being, to love and honour the choices of others, to communicate freely with various Beings of Light and connect strongly to my own I AM. My life is joyous and abundant and purposeful. I not only know how, but do, create the reality I wish for in life and my life is exactly how I want it to be.

So since June 1993, I have existed on tea and water, then for pleasure tasted 'white' food (a potato phase due to boredom and lack of mind mastery) or the odd mouthful of chocolate and regardless of these indulgences I know that the only thing that nourishes and sustains me is Light.

I am not anorexic, I enjoy excellent health and am highly energized and often only require two thirds of the sleep I was previously used to. Having made this transition, I find my attitude towards being sustained by prana to be very matter of fact yet to many the idea is impossible and the reality ludicrous. It is neither.

May 1996:
In my inner communications I am advised that the 21-day process was channelled through to be used to integrate the Higher Self and that at this stage – 3 years later in 1996 – many have already passed this initiation either consciously or unconsciously on the etheric realms. As the higher self is Light, all can be sustained by Light having 'passed this 3rd initiation'. However as yet, many do not believe that they can simply stop eating and be sustained by the power of intention and expectation alone.

So this process continues to be offered and will simply allow for the physical body's transition to occur smoothly. It will also aid in the hastening of the integration of the energies of the I AM Presence (the 5th initiation).

It is believed that in Australia and New Zealand, over 200 have undergone this 21-day process, some with little understanding of the Ascended Ones, others with only the guidance of their 'guides'. Regardless of personal models of understanding and beliefs, the only 'belief' required is that as beings of light we can be sustained by light. This is simply the mastery of 'mind over matter'.

Footnote November 1996:
Many have labelled my approach and understanding of this journey to be of the 'Ascension paradigm' and it was the Ascended Master Serapis Bey, who originally channelled this 21-day 'inner ascension' process through to the Australian group. However as many are interested in the Pranic nourisher concept from more of a dietary point of view we will cover this in the chapter "Other Ways".

March 2006:
Since June 1993 I have existed on an average of 300 calories per day which covers the calorie content of sugar and milk in my tea. I am still amazed at what we have been able to achieve with this for I have travelled constantly, been bombarded with so much resistance and negativity regarding this reality and yet I have been able to maintain high energy levels throughout it all. My body magnetizes from the inner realms all the cosmic particles and prana that it needs to maintain health and apart from a brief period in 2005 when I was learning how to let go of old mortality patterns, the pranic beam of Divine Love has continued to feed me without further thought. To me it is a process of magnetic attraction that happens in response to the purity of our hearts.

Chapter 10

Questions and Answers

This chapter deals with what I have found to be the most commonly asked questions since I underwent the process. I have selected from the new Prana Program book Questions and Answers that I feel are most relevant, however, I recommend that you read both *The Prana Program* and *The Food of Gods* manuals to be well informed with all of our research. The book *The Law of Love* (released in 2004) covers more of the journey and also for being fluid free.

Preparation, Physical Changes & Pre-programming

Q: What do you mean by "learning to listen to the voice of the body, and the need to develop a strong mind/body connection", in preparation for The Prana Program?
A: This is one of the first requirements and it means accepting and experiencing that: -
the body is perfectly capable of telling us exactly what it needs. Even if it is suffering ill health or disease, it can tell us exactly what steps we need to heal it. We can access its voice intuitively on a day-to-day basis, and also by using a system similar to kinesiology, such as the tools we offer in the Comfortable Conversion chapter.

Secondly, a strong mind/body connection means experientially understanding that every cell of the physical system is constantly attuned to our thoughts and understanding the effect this has on the body via a process of thought experimentation e.g. thought monitoring where we see the benefits of positive thinking.

Both of these are important in experiencing all the benefits of The Prana Program.

Q: You also insist that people learn to hear and listen to and adopt the guidance of the Divine One Within them – their DOW – and that this is also crucial in the preparation process. Why?
A: As we are all unique, there is no one way to increase the pranic flow to experience all its benefits. Our personal field of resonance determines the cosmic particle magnetic process and this field is influenced by our environment, genetic line and also past experiences, plus the mindsets and perceptions formed by all of these. Hence the only one who has all the answers for us is our DOW as it is immortal and all knowing in nature and has no information or guidance restrictions. If we can formulate the question, the answers will come. How our body responds and what it needs to maintain perfect health and nutritional levels, in The Prana Program, can only come from this inner voice of intuition for only its intimate knowledge of our bio-system can provide all the insights and answers.

Q: You always say that a person needs to adopt certain mindsets with the prana program and engage in mind mastery, can you elaborate on this?
A: Our beliefs and self-talk constantly affect both brain and cellular operation and hence certain mental attitudes and mindsets need to be understood and adopted in order to begin to be nourished by prana. Once we understand what prana is, and how it can feed us, then we need to expect it to. For successful pranic nourishment an attitude that: "All my nourishment, all my vitamins, all my minerals, everything I need to maintain a healthy body, comes from prana" is step one.

Next an attitude that "I only eat for pleasure, not for need as prana provides all I require" is another new mindset. Both commands help to rewire the brain's neural pathways.

Q: Can you explain what you mean by the phrase "I only eat for pleasure, not for need"?
A: Firstly as mentioned this statement begins to reprogram the neural pathways in the brain. Secondly the statement accepts the possibility thus making it more real. An earlier survey found that 73% of people who do the 21-day process eventually go back to eating while the statistics for The Food of Gods prana program are a lot less. This happens because once you know you don't need food and have proven it by doing it then you have a choice. This is a great freedom – to not need food and to lose the attachment to it, and to randomly eat for pleasure only rather than regularly for need, which in turn has a huge impact on our consumption of global food resources.

Q: Many people say that increasing the pranic flow through their system also increases their sensitivity, often making them feel overwhelmed by denser energies in the world. Why does this occur and how can they combat this?
A: This occurs because we are in "unconscious absorption" mode, meaning we are too aware of, and sensitive to, what is around us and we allow it all to infiltrate our auric field and often drain and/or overwhelm us. Consequently we need to switch into a mindset where we only radiate rather than absorb. We do this by plugging into a limitless source of love, wisdom and power within us, and then we intentionally radiate this mix of energy through us, from the inner planes and out into the world. We can also cocoon ourselves in a field of violet light and utilise some of the bioshield devices we share of in detail in *The Food of Gods* manual.

Q: How does one become a pranic nourisher and increase the pranic flow? What prerequisites are there?
A: To do this successfully an individual needs to be a tuned instrument who practices mind mastery – that is conscious re-programming for the elimination of any limiting and non-honouring beliefs. By non-honouring, I mean maintaining beliefs that do not recognise the glory of the DOW and its gift of our life. We also need to recalibrate our personal field of resonance to specific frequencies in order to attract enough cosmic particles to nourish us in a healthy way. Other prerequisites for being a pranic nourisher would simply be the heartfelt desire to be limitless and to live life to the highest maximum potential in a way that is

harmonious to others. This is about honouring ourselves enough to open-mindedly explore exciting possibilities, to be passionate about being alive, to maintain a heart filled with joy and gratitude at the gift we have been given to simultaneously create, and also witness the majesty of creation. This mindset also increases the cosmic fire aspect of cosmic particle flow. Cosmic fire is Divine Love.

For some this also means to be able to absorb all that we desire, from all dimensions, through these five physical senses. As we shared earlier, increasing the pranic flow also requires us to utilise our two more refined senses of intuition and knowing by activating and stimulating the master glands in our body that govern these – the pituitary and pineal.

Q: What specific physical changes have you personally noticed?
A: My stomach has shrunk, my metabolic rate has slowed, and until I started 'nibbling' – to fulfill my interest in flavour – I never got hungry. I need a lot less sleep, my mental clarity has improved, I have become more detached emotionally, and I feel very 'light', vaster, more multi-dimensional somehow. Sometimes – when walking – I have felt that the only reason I know I'm physical is by my footsteps and shadow but this was only in the initial stages and as time goes by we become more grounded and integrated. Some of these things may be due to the current energy influxes on the planet also affecting many. In the first few months of the transition I also experienced a little extra hair loss when washing and brushing my hair which others have also reported. This is only temporary and settles down to 'normal' in a month or so.

Q: You often state, that it can take a bio-system 6-9 months to adjust to the prana only nourishment aspect of the program. Why?
A: Again this depends on an individual's calibration which we will look at in detail in the next chapter. However, my research has found that while energy levels are high, things like weight stabilisation can often take between 6-9 months so we need to have patience and give the program the time it needs for fine-tuning and adjustments.

Q: So how do you sustain body weight once you are on a prana only nourishment?
A: Through re-programming the body and a strong mind/body connection, plus having trust and faith that is also based on re-education into understanding how the body operates when we increase the pranic flow and act as masters of the vehicle.

The idea that one has to lose weight and/or die, if we do not eat food, is simply that – a belief. Society tells us we need a balanced diet, vitamins etc. to be healthy and, because of their belief systems, for the general population this is true. Being sustained by prana has more to do with our spiritual journey and awakening, a consequence of such is that we can be sustained by light and love of our DOW which has the ability to manifest all that we need on all levels.

The physical body is the servant to the mental body which when aligned serves the spiritual body. By changing our beliefs and mindset we can simply program ourselves to maintain a desired weight and we will. Every cell of our body constantly hears our self-talk and if our self-talk is limiting then the cell behaves in a limiting manner.

I also recommend that people do not weigh themselves as they transition through this change, as even thoughts such as "Oh no I weigh only ____!" can upset the new programming patterns we are laying into the system.

In India today there are yogis with such command over their molecular structure that they can be buried alive for weeks at a time, or drink poison with both having no negative physical affects. They achieve this due to their high levels of self-mastery over their physical, emotional and mental systems. Studies have also researched the benefits of intention regarding placebo medicine.

Q: Post conversion, why can some people stabilize their weight quickly and others can't?
A: Our research has shown that this depends on individual mind mastery and/or also the strength of past cellular memory influences and personal calibration levels.

Q: How come some people lose no weight when they convert to The Prana Program?
A: This is due to the fact that they are already calibrating at the level to attract the perfect flow of cosmic particles that they need to feed them and have usually been minimalistic in their physical diet before conversion, for example, one small meal a day of non-fattening type food e.g. fruit or raw vegetables combined with a mindset that all vitamins etcetera come from prana.

Q: What are your personal energy levels like, do you ever feel tired?
A: Rarely, of course this depends on how much I do. As my creativity levels have increased so much, I always have to be aware of balance and make sure that I spend time doing all the things that I love that keep my passion for life strong. Lack of passion for life can drain us as can choosing toxic ways of being.

Q: Do you need as much sleep?
A: As I find that my energy levels are consistently high with lack of energy being an absolute rarity, I find I can easily attend to my work/service commitments often for up to 20 hours per day before feeling any desire for sleep. One thing I have noticed is that my ability to be without sleep is dependent upon the 'type of energy' I am tuning to at the time. If I am 'working' and consciously plugged into what I call the cosmic service circuit board then I am so energized that I feel a vastly decreased need for sleep.

Q: What about physical body elimination, urination and defecation?
A: This depends on the personal program, some individuals who are nourished by prana have one small meal once a month for social reasons, others one small meal once a week, others live only on liquids which may include light soups, coffee, tea (which they transmute into a frequency beneficial for their body), others have mainly water with a fruit juice now and then for flavour. How much they ingest in addition to obtaining nourishment from prana then determines how much they will eliminate.

It also depends on if we are living in a highly polluted external environment like a busy city or if we are living in a purer atmosphere such as the beach or mountains where there is a high prana content in the air and surrounds.

It is said, via some research sources, that we can absorb up to two litres of water a day through the pores of our skin via literally drinking from the atmosphere, so even for the true breatharian who neither eats nor drinks, they still obtain external moisture in this way and will hence continue to urinate.

When I was taking a maximum of three small glasses of liquid each day I found myself eliminating fluid and approximately every three weeks what I call 'rabbit droppings' which for me was uncomfortable. I was intuitively advised that, as I lived in a city, pollutants and dead cells would allow this to continue. I later found that taking a small amount of prune juice once a week made this small elimination more comfortable. =

Q: What role does physical exercise play in The Prana Program? Why do you always encourage people to build muscle strength?
A: Basically a strong system can attract, hold and radiate more potent frequencies. Building muscle mass aids this so I always recommend a training program that improves both strength and flexibility. Ashtanga-Yoga/weight lifting, dance or whatever else a person is drawn to. Walking in highly pranic environments such as at the beach or mountains is also beneficial.

Q: What about menstruation?
A: It is said that woman are born with a certain number of eggs for fertilization so if a body is healthy and being nourished then menstruation will continue until all eggs are released. If a woman is receiving enough prana to keep her healthy then she will continue to menstruate until it is her natural time not to.

Q: Do you take vitamins?
A: No. One of the first things I realised was that I had to let go of the idea that anything other than prana would nourish me. If I was to change my mindset and totally trust that prana alone could sustain me then I could not take vitamins as there would be no need. This was a hard one for me as having been a vegetarian for over 20 years prior to my pure prana diet conversion, I had always taken vitamins, particularly spirulina and B12. If you trust prana to sustain and regenerate the body and align to its channel so that it can, then it will.

After discovering the body's need for good nutrition and vitamins, which is a must when we stay anchored in a brain wave pattern, it is wonderful to know that when we anchor ourselves in the Theta-Delta realm, that the body can access its nourishment differently and hence eliminate our need for vitamins and minerals through physical food or supplements. This alone is very freeing and financially beneficial as prana is free and available to all.

Q: What about if someone is on medication – is it safe for them to live on a prana only nourishment?

A: This is something that only their DOW can guide them with. Anyone doing this needs a strong mind/body connection and to trust and hear the guidance of their DOW.

Q: What has been your biggest challenge with this prana process and its aspect of no longer needing physical food?
A: For me I would have to say my challenge has been with a lingering desire for flavour and also having to deal with my blueprint of being public with this research. The physical body, due to my background, has been relatively easy to master. With my European upbringing and its social emphasis on food and sharing, dealing with the emotional attachment to food has been less easy. One only has to look at what and when people eat to see that 90% of eating is based on emotional issues, even social dining is both physically and emotionally driven.

Mastering the mental body has been the most difficult. And with any prolonged 'fast' the senses become enormously heightened – the sense of smell, touch, hearing, sight and taste, all of these are naturally satisfied in living, yet when one ceases to eat or taste, the sense of flavour is then ignored so this can take adjustment.

Others on this path have mixed up all sorts of flavoursome drinks to satisfy their desire for flavour. As I initially stayed mainly with water and tea and held the desire to move beyond the consciousness of food, then over time the desire for flavour variety became more of an issue for me and one I still indulge from time to time.

Q: If we choose to no longer eat and let prana nourish us, are there other ways to satisfy our desire for taste?
A: The Ayurvedic tradition offers a wonderful range of herbs and spices to totally satisfy all our taste desires, herbs which can be steeped in hot water and drunk like tea. This Vedic science of healing also links our taste buds and organs and some have begun to do further research on this connection. Also we have found that aromatherapy is a very powerful way of satisfying our sense of taste by using smell instead as many oils when smelt will alleviate an individual's desire for flavour.

Q: How beneficial are lifestyle tools, such as meditation and gradual dietary refinement, for the conversion to a pure prana nourishment stream?
A: The greatest source of physical, emotional, mental and spiritual nourishment comes via our day-to-day lifestyle and how we choose to spend our time as we keep repeating. Creating physical health, fitness and strength depends on a number of factors and much research has already been done in this field, for example, we know that drinking pure water, eating fresh healthy food – preferably vegetarian, exercising regularly and engaging in meditation to deal with mental and emotional stress, are all extremely good for us.

We also know as metaphysicians that time spent in silence in nature and that exercising self-mastery and mind control via re and de-programming our bio-system, is also beneficial in the creation of mental and emotional health, as is the use of devotional music or chanting and mantras. Add daily selfless service and prayer and we have a basic health and happiness lifestyle recipe that will help us tune to the perfect frequency field to eventually enjoy all of The Prana Program benefits. We share of this lifestyle in detail in my book, *Four Body Fitness – Biofields and Bliss*.

Q: You always say that success for a pure prana diet depends on personal resonance, what do you mean by this?
A: As mentioned already, personal resonance is a result of our lifestyles and how we choose to spend our time which influences the type of frequencies we transmit into the universal and global fields. Being in balance, being lovingly aware of self and others, living a life where we are listening to our intuitive voice, all of this affects our personal field of resonance and in turn how the universal field responds to us. The type of frequencies we transmit then determine the level of cosmic particles or chi that we can attract, hold, utilise and radiate. Thus we become a person who can feed ourselves internally by this flow and also feed the world by our Presence due to what we are radiating.

I would like to add that one of the main keys to access the Theta-Delta field of pure prana is our purity of heart. This means that our emotional field needs to pulse with the signals of sincerity, humility, surrender and compassion – things that cannot be taught except in the class called 'life' and via our interaction with living beings.

Q: How beneficial are colonic irrigations for detoxifying the system and readying it for a pure prana diet?
A: Keeping our bio-system clear of all toxicity – whether it is on physical, emotional, mental or spiritual levels is always beneficial, yet it is easier to do when we are well educated as to how to do this. If we have created high levels of toxicity due to dietary choices and attitudes then we can cleanse the system in many ways. A change in diet, using colonic irrigations to rebalance and stimulate a sluggish elimination system, as well as fasting, all of this has its place and needs to be undertaken if it feels right personally and is required by the body. Remember the body has its own voice that needs to be intuitively heard and listened to.

Q: Is it helpful to experience normal fasting before attempting a prana only regime?
A: Most definitely. Fasting and abstaining from food has many beneficial effects and with The Prana Program it not only helps in preparation, as far as detoxification goes, but also helps to decrease our emotional dependence on a variety of flavours and gives us insight into social reaction and new behaviour patterns that occur when one fasts and abstains from socialising around the sharing of physical food. Fasting intermittently can also acclimatize us to social reactions and can teach us new ways of interacting socially.

Q: Does the aging process automatically stop with pranic nourishment?
A: Not necessarily as this depends on mind talk and what type of hormones our master glands are releasing as they can either produce the death hormone or life sustaining hormones. What they produce is a mirror of our beliefs.

Q: Is stopping the aging process just a matter of increasing the pranic flow?

A: No we need to also work on mental attitudes. We also need to reprogram our master gland function to change the hormonal flow through the endocrine system which is the bio-system bridge between the physical and non-physical world.

Q: How do we stop the aging process of the body?
A: Similarly to the above in the preparation for physical immortality question – with particular focus regarding self-talk and also re-programming our master glands hormone production. Many people are unaware of how much damage limiting self-talk does to the human body, and how well it responds to limitless thinking, and how beneficial commands such as, "I am younger and younger everyday" are. Again the exact tools for this are provided in *The Food of Gods* and *The Law of Love* e-Books.

Q: Is the pranic nourishment that you practice based in Kriya-Yoga, as Yogananda describes in his book Autobiography of a Yogi?
A: In this work we are all tapping into the same blueprint, a matrix some call Universal Mind, which holds data like in a 'cosmic computer bank'. I assume that Yogananda also received 'downloads' of information from this field as in essence we are all talking about the same thing and although one doesn't need to do Kriya-Yoga to live on light, I personally feel that pranic breathing helps. Our work is based on the premise that even though we're all everyday people, we're also all divine instruments and we can consciously tune ourselves and have experiences which some people might term miraculous.

Q: How beneficial is yogic training for being a prana nourisher?
A: As Yoga has become so popular in our Western world, it is good to understand the different types of yogic practice and how they relate to pranic feeding. Firstly it is virtually impossible to provide a specific Divine Nutrition access procedure for as we keep stressing, it is all to do with our individual frequency which is determined by our past and present experiences and attitudes, and no two individuals are the same. However we can provide a selection of tools for tuning to the Divine Nutrition prana channel so that the individual can then experiment with this and yogic practice is one of these tools.

Chapter 11

Spirituality and Sexuality

February 1996:
One of the more 'delicate' yet common questions that I am asked in my travels is about sexuality and spirituality. Particularly with someone choosing to live by the light of the I Am. For example, how compatible are the energies of sexuality with the higher refined frequencies of the Divine One within? This is a huge issue for many and one that we feel has the requirement of a chapter in its own right.

Sharing of my own journey I personally found myself after the 21-day process operating on a completely 'different' wave band or frequency band of energy. Meditation over many years had allowed me a great degree of sensitivity to energies which was increased dramatically after the process. Suddenly I could see people's energy. Anger for example appeared like red shafts or swords emanating from their energy fields. It was at this time I began to further question the personal issue of celibacy. My motivation was once more regarding maximizing energy and empowering its direction.

The issue of celibacy is such a personal one. For me, after tuning in and researching further I came across the Taoist understanding as shared in the books *Taoists Secrets of Love – Cultivating Male Sexual Energy* and its counterpart *Healing Love through the Tao – Cultivating Female Sexual Energy* by Mantak Chia and Maneewan Chia. For those interested in continuing or developing their sensuous spirituality, both texts are recommended reading. While the exercises may appear arduous at first they are relatively easy to master and the following two articles with techniques are simple to apply and practice. My personal decision to explore these avenues was based on the fact that I wish to explore everything to its highest positive potential and this was something that my partner and I had touched on yet not fully explored together. As the Lamas from the *Tibetan Rites* share, celibacy should be a choice based on conscious desire to tune the energy fields further to a particular beat and not one borne from lack of opportunity for full expression and convenience.

While a human being is complete within themselves, romantic love is an aspect of Divine Love. Finding the never eternal well of love within by connecting with the Divine One is one of the most fulfilling journeys humanity can undertake and enjoy. Sharing this well of love unconditionally with others adds another level of expression to existence again. Two beings consciously uniting the energies of the sexual, with the spiritual and heart creates another beat again.

Sexuality & Spirituality – Male Potency

by Eltrayan

The following two articles are taken from *The ELRAANIS Voice*.

"You should be told at the beginning of this commentary that Eltrayan is of the male gender. I mention this to explain the particular targeting of males in this discussion, which is on the benefits that may be derived by the use of an evolved and refined version of celibacy. These are matters on which I have firsthand knowledge, and while not wishing to exclude women, the female model is outside my direct experience.

"The use of physical techniques to increase consciousness is both valid and sensible, since while we all have spiritual, mental, emotional and physical bodies and while the chain of command runs in that same order, the contribution possible by the physical body should not be underestimated, certain experiences and lessons being possible only at the physical rate of vibration. Enlightenment is the state of evolvement when these four bodies are revolving synchronistically and are perfect vehicles for the Self, the individual spark of the divine, to use to experience existing at the various frequencies provided by the bodies.

"Celibacy is traditionally defined as abstinence from sexual intercourse. While there may be males for whom this has appeal and to whom this seems the correct action, at least for a period of time, for most men it has little attraction. I suggest that from an esoteric view, the intimacy offered by the physical, tactile, sweet sharing involved in making love, particularly when at least a component of love is involved, is both positive and valuable. The negative aspect for males in making love is the waste of one of their most precious resources for spiritual advancement in ejaculation. It's time to lift the level of comment above whether an athlete's performance is affected by intercourse before a sporting event, to outline how this sexual essence can be redirected for spiritual enhancement, with the added advantage of converting an average male lover into a sensual and sexual treasure.

"It is said that the primary energy source we have at our disposal is sexual energy. Between 25% and 40% of the energy (prana or chi) we accumulate from breathing, drinking, eating, sunlight, moonlight etc. is used to manufacture sexual energy, which is stored physically in males in sperm. A single ejaculation has 200 million to 500 million sperm cells, each cell being a potential human being.

"Discharge of semen means that the body has to produce more, and the raw material is drawn from the blood, which in turn draws the precious elements from every organ of the body, including the brain. In an average male's lifetime, 5,000 ejaculations involve 15 litres of semen. With 200 million to 500 million sperm in each ejaculation, there are sufficient sperm cells for that man in his life to generate 200 times the current population of Earth. This is an enormous reservoir of energy and nature is not so extravagant or wasteful to apply such a large proportion of energy just to produce a few children over a lifetime.

"It is possible for a man to have an orgasm with little or no ejaculation as demonstrated by the Taoist masters, thus denying none of the pleasures of a physical relationship, but still retaining the sexual energy involved.

"Making love helps restore imbalances in body chemistry, the stimulation of sex hormones stimulating the hormones secreted by the other major glands – the adrenal, thymus, thyroid, pituitary and pineal.

"The practice of male sexual energy conservation and transformation assists in the internal equilibrium of the human energy system. The testes are connected to the pituitary gland in the male hormone system and they work together in transforming sexual energy. The pituitary gland regulates the activities of the other glands. The testes produce both sperm and male hormones, and when they are not ejaculated, these male hormones go into the blood stream and are carried to every part of the body.

"So the benefits of sexual energy conservation are substantial. The first requirement for its implementation is for men to understand the advantages offered, without involving any loss of intimacy or pleasure. In fact the reverse is true and an enhancement occurs, but for many men this requires a change in mind-set regarding what making love entails.

"To comprehend how to contribute to an enlightened state of consciousness by using sexual energy, an understanding of the subtle energy pathways of the body is necessary. While making love, and particularly at the point of male orgasm, a stream of etheric energy, normally only a small portion of the total expended since the majority is usually ejaculated, travels from the root chakra, at the base of the spine, up the central nervous system along the spine to the pituitary gland in the head. This is observed by seers as being effected by etheric pumps which are located in the lower back and at the back of the neck. These etheric pumps should be visualised during making love, which of course makes control of them considerably more effective.

"The Taoist technique for redirection of the sexual energy is traditionally called the 'big draw'. As the name infers, it involves drawing back the discharge of sexual energy and redirecting it up the spine to the head. This is the primary tantric procedure. Regarding the retention of semen, that is the control of its discharge at orgasm, the muscles involved in its containment are the same muscles used when a male stops urinating mid-stream. This exercise of stopping and starting the flow while urinating is a simple and effective method of identifying and acquiring the necessary physical muscular control, and it is highly recommended.

"Only practice will develop the man's retention ability. The increase in sexual potency that follows will be quite remarkable, and women should be warned that they will be dealing, in due course, with a sexual dynamo with great libido, remarkable capacity, and progressively increasing subtlety and sensitivity.

"A refinement of the energy redirection is for the man to pass the energy over his head and by completing the circuit with touching the tip of the tongue to the roof of his mouth, the energy passes down the front of the body back to his root chakra and then up his back again, in a circular manner. A similar redirection of sexual energy may be applied by women. Further, it can be redirected in a circle up the back and then down the front of your partner's body, then up your back and around your body, forming a figure eight pattern, and producing an extraordinary experience created by the shared energy pattern.

"Consequently, the new age male can reasonably aspire sexually to be a modern Taoist master and the quality of attention and focus you apply will determine your degree of success. Being lucky with money is another story, but if you accept the refined celibacy of sexual energy retention and redirection, then being lucky in love is for you."

Sexuality & Spirituality – Female Potency

"Following on from the male experience is the female. The difference in techniques is primarily anatomical and secondarily, a subtle fine tuning addition. Firstly is the gathering of sexual energy from the female reproductive organs where it is stored, and the base and second chakras. Then comes the moving of this energy up through the spinal pumps to complete the circuit – as described by Eltrayan – called the 'microcosmic orbit'. Secondly once the energy has been moved into the brain, the tongue and mouth roof circuits connected, we then recommend opening the heart chakra and overlaying the energy of unconditional love as you move it down the front of the body to complete the energy loop.

This technique takes the sexual energy, moves it into the higher spiritual centres of the crown and brow chakra then adds the vibration of unconditional love to complete the triad. This blending of sexual, spiritual and love energy creates enormous potency that can then be channelled into your partner, up their spine and so creates the symbol of infinity in its energy path.

As with anything, one requires practice plus intention and focus to feel the benefits which initially while subtle become quite powerful. The main difference between the Tantric and Taoist practices is that tantra uses more ritual while the Tao focus is more on energy flow. Both are powerful tools for bringing the sexual experience into the spiritual. Many practitioners of the Tantric or Taoist sexual practices report the following: -

- a deep sense of connectedness with your partner,
- feeling as if you are one (this is as a result of sharing energy flows and consciously directing one flow through each other's bodies with will and intention),
- improved health and vitality – according to Mantak Chia in his book *Taoists Secrets of Love – Cultivating Male Sexual Energy* the Tibetan Lamas feel that 'spilling seed' drains the life force from the body creating premature aging, balding of men and death the ability to have multiple, full body and brain orgasms,
- increase capacity and longevity of performance and joy in sharing,
- physical immortality and organ regeneration by redirecting and reabsorbing the 'life giving' properties of the semen and ova,
- telepathic connection with your partner,
- women can control their menstrual cycle for contraception and stop and start their blood loss at will and much more …

Also recommended with the above practice is the use of the mantra or program of "SEX, SPIRIT, LOVE BRINGS BALANCE". This is to be used repeatedly as one builds the energy in the perineum then moves it into the base of the spine (kundalini area) with the command SEX; then up the spine with the command SPIRIT when it enters the crown chakra; then use the command LOVE when it enters the heart; then command BALANCE when it hits the perineum area once more. Then as you shoot this balanced energy into your partner (or around your own body if solo) as in the microcosmic orbit and command the same – SEX, SPIRIT, LOVE BRINGS BALANCE. This mantra adds ease to the exercise for instead of visualising the energy pumping up the spine you can command its flow into designated areas with the intention to blend the sexual, spiritual and unconditional love energies to bring balance.

This technique can be used whether your partner wants to practice this consciously with you or not. Simply go through the visualization of energy flow and use the mantra as you feel the energies build and allow them to flow into your partner's body when you feel guided. It will still blend your energies together bringing a pure balance of the yin/yang energies within both beings.

Often as I travel I hear women (who tend to make up 60-80% of seminars participants) share of their desire to incorporate their sexuality with their spirituality when in relationship. The tantric or Taoist practices are now being widely used by many with great results and is ideal for achieving this blending, and directing and purifying the energy flow.

Due to space constraints we cannot delve too deeply into this ancient practice here but recommend the above book plus its counterpart *Healing Love through the Tao – Cultivating Female Sexual Energy* by Mantak Chia and Maneewan Chia; to all those interested. You do not need to be in partnership to practice these techniques or to gain the benefits of this mastery. Along with completing past connections and cutting psychic and cellular memory ties etc. these techniques are wonderful for regaining mastery over the four lower bodies and creating sacred sharing in relationships."

Chapter 12

The Journeys of Others

February 1996:
This chapter details the experiences of not great Saints and Masters but every day, suburban or country people living in this Western culture who are simply pioneering a new way of being. Or as some would say 'rediscovering how we used to be'.

Rose Witherow of Melbourne, Australia underwent the 21-day process in November 1994. "I was attracted by the possibility of detachment, death of ego, death of old outmoded beliefs systems. I wanted to connect to my Higher Self and move towards unity for one and all."

Affirming "I breathe, trust and believe (know) I am just as I need to be", Rose's weight stabilized in September 1995 (after losing 13kgs). Her energy levels remain consistently high and her need for sleep has decreased from 8-9 hours to 4-6 hours per night. Taking no vitamins Rose has 4 or 5 drinks each day of coffee, tea and sometimes light soup and ice cream for flavour.

On an emotional level Rose shares, "I am much less sensitive and can 'let go' of attachments more easily. I am happier, clearer and more relaxed. More heart". Also, "I have more mental stamina, in fact I have to discipline myself to listen when I should be taking time out." And spiritually, "I am much more at peace and happy. I am more trusting and open spiritually. I have a greater love for (and less judgment of) others."

Charmaine Harley of Adelaide, provided the questionnaire and details in some of the future chapters. She shares that doing the process in June 1994 "seemed to resonate with my heart, feeling like I was going home."

Her "Energy is great. I do not generally feel tired until late at night. With this new energy it is higher, more even, neutral. If ever I feel low I rest for a few moments, ask for help and all is okay again". Charmaine also takes no vitamins, drinks mainly tea and coffee and when out socialising may have a light soup.

On a physical level she has experienced "Weight change, new body shape, spinal alignment, new posture, different walk, pain free body, no more bruises." With more mental clarity, Charmaine shares that on an emotional level she "Feels more neutral, detached, when I feel emotion it is for such a short time, clears quickly". And on a spiritual level "Able to focus more, more connectedness, inner knowing is strong, feel peaceful, strong."

The biggest problem for Charmaine came after the process "feeling separate, feeling of alienation of not thinking like everyone else."

Footnote October 1997:

As I am invited to travel the globe we have now brought the idea of pranic nourishment (and the M.A.P.S. agenda) to over 11 countries worldwide. It is being particularly well received through Germany and Europe with many tuned individuals seeming to feel that it is the next step for them.

The Ascended Ones share that at this point thousands of individuals have now undergone this process worldwide. Constantly people ring and ask me where they can do the process and for contacts with people yet to date no 'club' or network has been formed. As it is such an individual initiation, usually those drawn to doing it are of the 'warrior breed' who trust their own inner guidance and are not the type to require support groups, they know that the most powerful support group is the God I AM within.

March 2006:

Q: Do you think that certain people are attracted to this reality for a reason?
A: Over the years, due to my close interaction with many thousands of people, I have come to believe that those attracted to The Prana Program, and particularly its freedom from limitation aspects, are pre-programmed prior to their embodiment to be part of this wave of evolutionary change. Hence they feel it is something natural for them to experience personally and exhibit.

Q: You often talk about fulfilling blueprints we set for this life before our embodiment, what do you mean by this?
A: Simply that prior to embodiment, souls look at their prospective life and agree to fulfill certain things on both a personal and planetary level. This is called a blueprint or loose set of plans – which are the goals that we set. How we achieve these goals and the detail involved in doing so is a free will game that we design to both test and expand ourselves.

Q: If people are pre-programmed to do this then how do they find out? Is everyone's blueprint held in the Akashic records?
A: It's held in our lightbody. The Akashic records record the etheric imprints from our lifestyle choices. Every thought and action we choose is 'rubber-stamped' etherically in the quantum field, plus those things that have impact are stored within Universal Mind, the matrix called the Akashic records. The data as to our pre-programming can be accessed from cellular memory during deep meditation and we discuss how to access our pre-programming for The Prana Program in *The Food of Gods* (Meditation technique no.12 – Chapter 11).

According to the U.F.I. there are now >64,000 who are capable of attracting enough cosmic particles to live purely on prana. Many of these may not choose to do so but their personal calibration will support them successfully if and when they are ready.

Addition April 2002
Prana
Mystery Building Stone of the Universe
with Gerd Lange

What Indian sages thousands of years ago called "prana", the ancient Chinese named "chi" or "ki" and the Druids refer to as "od" or "id". It is commonly agreed, that prana is the life force but too small or etheric to be perceived by any kind of instrument or measuring device to date.

Modern science has found that our seemingly so solid world vibrates in an eternal dance of swirling atoms. These in turn consist of even smaller and smaller particles, which finally turn out to be pure energy (prana) densified in various wavelets and aggregates to form matter.

In general, there are two things which we take in when we breathe. One is air and the other is prana, pure life-force energy itself, more vital than air for our existence. If you take away air, you have a couple of minutes before you die; if you take away water, you have even more time; and if you take away food you have much more time still, but if you break prana from spirit, death is instantaneous (1). So taking in prana with breath is absolutely crucial in sustaining our life.

Prana is not just in the air, it is everywhere. There is nowhere that it is not; it even exists in a vacuum or a void. Nothing exists without prana, neither animate nor inanimate. Prana is the smallest, most refined, miniature building block of life, subtlest of subtle energies which creates and sustains simply everything (physical matter, thoughts, feelings … etc.). Prana in my opinion is higher dimensional creative energy and inseparably connected to spirit, god or the creative energy.

I have always been interested in Prana and its spiritual capacity. Being a Rebirther for many years, I have discovered, that the amazing effects which I continuously witness in a breath simply can't be produced just by the oxygen content accumulated in the session or through my guidance alone. There always seems to be an inner intelligence at work which undeniably suggests to me a connection with the Divine.

So what actually happens during a breathing session? We humans are an intricately layered four body energy system, consisting of a physical, emotional, mental and spiritual body – made of prana in various states of densification (i.e. wavelengths or vibrational harmonies). Each of these bodies is an electromagnetic energy field in form of a grid system, which resonates, in a specific frequency, not unlike an electronic computer memory bank. Each of these bodies functions on a different level and performs vital life interactions, e.g. processes information, holds memory and performs a multitude of other functions. The four bodies are linked through the chakra system.

If unaligned (through shock, trauma, emotions) the mesh of these grids collects densified subtle energies (unreleased feelings, dysfunctional thought patterns … etc.) instead of letting them pass through. These unprocessed energies get trapped in the system. Moving through the layers, thoughts densify into emotions, emotions densify into physical sensations and finally solidify in physical symptoms – dis-ease and illness.

Breathing intentionally, in a conscious connected manner, increases the prana content in the four layers of the grid systems. Accumulating prana in the bodies helps to re-align the grids by energizing them, which raises their vibrational frequencies. This in turn entices all four grid systems simultaneously to resonate in a higher frequency and they automatically attempt to achieve a state of unity, a place of balance. Through the re-alignment the trapped densified energies loosen up, and get "washed out" by the free floating prana, to be transported to the electromagnetic surface (consciousness). There it is processed by re-experiencing and released as thought, emotion or sensation. This leaves your system more cleansed, realigned and connected.

As we have established a few paragraphs before, prana is in everything and everything consists of it. God (Source, the creative principle) per definition also is everything and everything consists of and through him/her/it. Therefore it seems clear to me that prana must be of divine nature and has to have a direct connection to Source.

As prana is pure spirit, the "breather" usually connects to Source in a breathing session via the spiritual body. Experiences include feeling warm and internally glowing, cared for and loved, mystical revelations and unity consciousness during the integration phase. Another fascinating by-product of this breathing technique is that it facilitates permanent Higher Self-connection. Initially you just get in touch with your Higher Self but over time you can establish a permanent conscious connection to your inner knowing, the Divine One Within (DOW) and your true nature as soul having a human experience.

Newest information suggests that once upon a time we actually were consciously and continuously connected to the infinite supply of prana and existed purely of it. Not too long ago –about 13000 years – before the last pole shift erased our conscious memory of it (as Drunvalo and Bob Frissell state), we used to breathe in such a way, that while air came in through our mouth and nose, we would take prana in through the top of our heads – what once was the soft spot on the top of our heads. Simultaneously, we took the prana in from below, through the perineum. If you carefully observe how new-born babies breathe you can actually observe this – a gentle pulsation at the fontanel and the perineum. The prana channel goes through the body like a vertical axle and is about two inches in diameter. It extends one hand length above the head and one hand length below the feet and connects with the crystalline energy field (Mer-Ka-Ba) around the body. The prana then flows in from above and below the body and meets in one of the chakras. The chakra in which the prana meets depends on where you are mentally, emotionally, and dimensionally "tuned".

After the poles shifted, we stopped breathing in this manner and started taking in the prana through our mouth and nose directly with the air. The prana then bypassed the pineal gland in the centre of the head. The pineal gland is an eye – the third eye – not the pituitary gland as often thought of. It is shaped like an eyeball, round, hollow, with a lens for focusing light and colour receptors. It is designed to receive light from above to go to every cell in the body instantaneously. Normally this gland should be about the size of a quarter but in us it has become the size of a pea because we haven't used it for about 13,000 years.

The direct result of turning off the pineal gland is polarity consciousness – good and bad, right and wrong. Because of the way we breathe we see things in terms of good and evil, but in fact Unity is all there is; there is just one God and one Spirit that moves through everything.

When I met Jasmuheen, 2 and a half years ago, at an international conference for Breathworkers (GIC) things got really interesting for me. She gave a lecture there, about the possibility of being able to live without eating, living on light, purely being sustained by prana (which was the way we existed in the times when we utilised the prana tube). All you had to do is to connect to the Divine One Within (DOW) and to allow yourself to be fed by it through an alternative source of nourishment, the most refined, most pure form of energy, by God him/herself, by prana.

This genuinely blew my mind, especially as my immediate, internal reaction was a huge YES!!! Actually being quite fond of eating and cooking, with a rather strong tendency to overeating, I was surprised at having had such a reaction. But over time and through my growing involvement with her example (and that of thousands of other people having done this 21-day re-programming process successfully in the meanwhile) it became very clear to me that living on prana is a true and mind-expanding possibility. Being able to be sustained on energy alone would mean to me the definite proof that I am a light being, that I am not the body, but something much more refined and expanded. I had always intuitively known and felt this, but there hadn't been any definite proof so far. Her theory, however outrageous it was, made total sense to me. Based on the information of the prana tube, my firm belief that prana was everything and of divine nature and my strong connection to my DOW simply urged me to give this possibility a try.

The good news was that, if properly prepared and trusting, anyone could do the 21-day process. You didn't have to be a saint, which would have definitely counted me out. The biggest challenge for me now was to actually find a month of free time in my absolutely busy schedule. I had to wait for nearly 2 years before my chance had come. In hindsight of course this waiting period was very valuable, as it gave me the opportunity to research in more depth and to speak with lots of people who had done the process already. Through their reports and experiences I reached a place of knowing in me, beyond any trace of doubt, that it is truly possible to live on light, to live on prana.

My partner Yamini, who had also met Jasmuheen at this conference and had the same reaction as me, found time to do her process 2 months before me. Seeing her going through the process with all its challenges, but coming out of it renewed and changed in a more empowered, grounded way, inspired me even further. Then finally my time had come too. I won't go into details of the process here as there is not enough time and space for it right now, but it was an amazing, yet ordinary time. I feel totally changed, yet curiously the same. A definite transition has happened to me, including a complete re-alignment of my body and physical structure, and yet I feel "it's still me", just with a difference. The most obvious difference of course is, that I don't have to eat anymore.

For me it is now over 160 days (5 months+) since I stopped having to eat and Yamini is over the 200 days mark by now. Our weight has stabilized, our energy levels are high and we fully participate in life. Yamini is working out regularly at the gym, whereas I, of course, still have no time for that as usual (working some days up to 16 hours). By now our initial thoughts of "did it really work?" have been totally removed. We both know for certain, we are fully sustained by pranic energy alone – which is amazing. Somehow a miracle and yet it seems quite normal and ordinary to us.

I am comparing the process (and the fact that we don't need to eat anymore) to an enormous fire walk. You can only do it safely when you absolutely know that you can. If you have any doubt about it, you will burn your feet and it's the same with the process. As long as you have doubt and disbelief it will be impossible for you to do it. This seems total proof to me that thought is creative, that we are consciously creating our reality at any given time, and that there are amazing possibilities out there which we haven't explored yet.

As we have established beforehand, prana is of electromagnetic nature. This suggests that it is possible to charge and program prana with your intentional thought energy and that you can use it for conscious creation and healing, for yourself and for the highest good of this planet and its people. So if you are interested in global issues and want to make a definite contribution start breathing in love and light and breathe out love, peace, compassion and positive intentions for the highest in humanity. Create your own reality, your own vision version of paradise on Earth, and radiate out your personal (and hopefully) positive charge of that. Have fun!

With love and light Gerd Lange
(Co director London College of Holistic Breath Therapy, Member of BRS)
Tel: 0044-208-455 2420, e-mail: gerdlange@cerbernet.co.uk

March 2006 Update:

Q: There are various models or processes for accessing the "living purely by prana state", can you share about these?
A: Yes below are the ones that I have personally experienced and also a few others that I am aware of.

The paths of Giri Bala and Therese Neumann as discussed in *An Autobiography of a Yogi*. For Giri her method was Kriya-Yoga and for Therese great faith, trust and love for, and in, the Divine.

The ancient yogi path as spoken of in Vedic literature – using again Kriya-Yoga and Pranayama processes of breath and light work.

Morris Krok using various lifestyle refinement methods as detailed in *Diet, Health, & Living On Air*.

Wiley Brooks in the early 1970's – I am unsure as to his exact model.

The 21-day process – as outlined in the book *Living on Light* – a spiritual initiation to increase the pranic flow, a small by-product of which can be the freedom from the need for physical food. **This model can be dangerous for the unprepared.**

Prahlad Jani's model of being fed and hydrated through a hole in his soft palette. As researched by Dr. Sudhir Shah in Ahmedabad in India.

The model offered in the book *The Food of Gods* which combines lifestyle tools and Taoist and Vedic methods.

Hira Ratan Manek's Solar Nourishment method which we discuss in more detail later. As researched by Dr. Sudhir Shah in Ahmedabad in India.

Zinaida Baranova's method of supreme trust, faith and love.

The model offered in *The Law of Love* that shares of a fluid and food free existence using ancient Taoist tools and futuristic science.

According to an ABC news story, there is also the case of the 15 year old Buddhist boy in Nepal called Ram Bahadur Banjan who has sat under a tree, in the jungle of Bara, since May 17th 2005 and as at the time of the story in November he had not eaten or drunk anything, nor spoken, for six months.

* Note: points 5, 7 & 10 are covered in Jasmuheen's manuals of the same names.

Q: You say that the qigong community have done a lot of research into Bigu, can you provide more data on this?
A: Yes, on page 286 in the book *Scientific Qigong Exploration* by nuclear physicist Lu Zuyin, he shares further about the state of *Bigu* and also about the experiments conducted on people who have not eaten for up to 6 years. Dr. Yan Xin is one of the most respected and widely recognized Qi masters in China and it is with his co-operation that in-depth studies have been conducted and shared with the world. Many people have spontaneously entered into the Bigu state as a result of being in his presence, and much research has been documented in the Chinese language. In fact over sixty books have been written covering his research into the power and benefits of Qi emissions.

Q: Is there a common calorie intake level between the pranic nourishers that you know and the Bigu practitioners?
A: According to the scientists measuring qigong emissions and studies on the Bigu state, many people in Bigu live on less than 300 calories per day for years without any damage to their physical bodies. In October 1987 Ding Jing, aged 10, went into the Bigu state and stayed there for over 6 years with a calorie intake of between 260 and 300 per day. We have found the same and many continue to live very healthily on calorie intakes that are continuing to defy and challenge modern medical and scientific belief. Personally I have become healthier through the Bigu states and have long ago proved to myself beyond doubt that some other power is nourishing my body.

Q: What is a true breatharian?
A: A true breatharian is someone who survives purely from cosmic particles and magnetizing enough of the pranic flow to feed them and maintain health and perfect hydration levels. They neither eat nor drink as they have moved their consciousness beyond the need or desire for food, fluid or flavour.

Q: How many true breatharians have you met?
A: One. Zinaida Baranova in Russia who as at 2005 has been 5 years without food or fluid. She says her biological age is now 30, although she is nearly 70, and tests that we did together in Russia in 2005 proved us both to be extremely healthy. I have met others who

have gone without food and fluid for specific periods of time yet when I met them they were choosing to drink for social reasons. I am sure that there are others but many prefer to remain private with this choice and work behind the scenes and I only meet the ones that I need to connect with.

Q: You often talk of the power of prayer and programming in The Prana Program. How can this aid starving children for example?
A: While we will address the 'starving children' issue shortly, people often underestimate the power of the human heart and mind and the benefits of mental programming and the power of set intention and prayer. In 1997 I heard the story of an orphanage in Germany who after the war had very little food. While one group of children were starving, another group remained really happy and healthy. The young children in the healthy group had a carer, and they asked her what she was doing different. She said they just started the day by forming a circle and praying to Mary and Jesus to love them and care for them, and make sure they got through the experience without harm. Because these kids believed in these prayers, they stayed healthy and were fine. If guided by an aware adult, our children can exist in very supportive paradigms of which The Prana Program is a part.

(Alternate feeding programs for starving children are covered in detail in *The Prana Program* e-Book.)

Chapter 13

A Sacred Initiation

February 1996:
Converting the body to live on prana using the Ascension Paradigm …

As previously mentioned, I have never been guided to physically help others undergo the 21-day process That we are about to focus on yet due to continual interest being expressed in being able to be sustained purely from the etheric realms and no longer eat, I am guided to offer as much information as possible.

However I personally feel that if you need to ask anyone if this journey is for you, you are not ready. Seek only the confirmation from the Inner Teacher. If you do not have clear inner guidance, then you are definitely not ready.

The following 21-day process is for individuals who have a deep 'knowing' it is for them. It is for people already connected with the voice of intuition and the process will strengthen this connection. I recommend that it be approached as a Sacred Initiation, that you dedicate this journey to the merging of the God within so that it may be fully expressed through your four body system and then sustain you by the light of that which it is.

This is the path of the goddess and the warrior. A time of solitude. A time of knowing that while you physically take this journey alone you are not alone. For under the ascension paradigm you will call to your presence the energies of the Ascended Ones to work with the Inner Teacher and many gifts will be given and much learning gained if you allow it.

As I travel and share of this journey some ask if they can continue to work or socialise over the 21-day process. Those who are ready are aware that it is a time of honouring and in understanding the power of this initiation such an idea would not even occur to them. I have watched many undergo this process and return to eating and the reasons are wide and varied. We cover the social pressures at the end of this book. Some are drawn to undergo this journey to lose weight, to gain inner guidance, the reasons are so varied. We ask that you be aware of your agendas, do the questionnaire.

Please note: In essence this is a high level esoteric initiation.
This is not about eating or not eating.
It is about the aligning of the energies of the I AM Presence and a by-product of this initiation is simply that one no longer requires to eat from the atmospheric realms.

The information, in the next chapter is quoted verbatim from booklets issued by Charmaine Harley in Adelaide, South Australia. Charmaine and others were instrumental in acting as both caregivers and clear-givers to many since they themselves underwent the process in 1994.

In a recent conversation with Charmaine she shared that, as with everything, it is important to use individual discernment. It is not imperative to have a care-giver or clear-giver but she feels it can be helpful. Charmaine is no longer personally involved in overseeing the 21-day process.

Again I personally feel that if you feel the need for a clear giver you are not ready for you are the master and only you can advise you. If a being is a tuned instrument then they will not suffer confusion during this process. If they have enough mind mastery and have prepared the vehicle they will not get weak or drained. It is important to recognise and eliminate limiting beliefs. If you expect to lose weight you will. You need to reprogram the body to stabilize weight at the perfect level to demonstrate and express the essence of the I AM fully merged into physical reality. Reprogramming before you start is much easier than losing lots of weight and trying to regain the weight through the power of intention or eating again.

It is my recommendation that one prepares the vehicle in an honouring way to guarantee ease and pleasure in this transition process. Some individuals go out to restaurants for breakfast, lunch and dinner for weeks before enjoying their fill of all that they love to eat, feeling it will be their last meal. Then when they do the 21-day process they suffer great discomfort through release of toxicity etc.

We recommend a gradual elimination of red meat, then white meat, then to go to raw foods, then soups and liquids and then begin the 21 days with a clean and tuned system. How long it may take to go from being a meat eater to raw foods then liquids will be up to each individual. Do it in a way that gives joy and comfort. The body will guide you if you listen.

Having been involved as a 'pioneer' to this process then witnessing many others, I have found that the more tuned a being is to their inner spirit and body consciousness the easier the journey has been and the greater the likelihood of that being adapting it as a way of life and not a short term adventure.

March 2006:
Q: What do you feel is the main requirement to live purely on prana, what is the secret to living only on Divine Light?
A: After over a decade of personal experiential research and interviewing hundreds who live successfully via Divine Nutrition, my one conclusion is that it is our vibration that determines our success with this, nothing more, nothing less. Our vibration allows us to draw this nutrition from the inner planes and back through our cellular structure, if this is our intention. It also allows us to attract increased doses of both internal and external chi, or prana – in the form of a greater influx of Cosmic Fire, Akasha and Astral Light – which are the main elements sustaining all life particles. Things like a pure heart, the ability to serve with compassion and kindness, the openness to the Higher Laws and to using our higher

mind, all these tune us powerfully to the channels that can reveal our paranormal powers, of which the ability of Bigu is just a small by-product.

I would also like to add that after watching the 21-day process spread throughout the world over the last decade, I have understood that as a higher level spiritual initiation it often has many gifts. There is a village in Brazil where this process is attracting many young people who have estranged from their families and rather than give these ones the gift of being able to live purely on prana, it has instead given them the gift of healing their family relationships. The caregivers at the village work closely with the Madonna whose focus is on family and the emotional nourishment that our DOW can provide. The 21-day process can provide physical, emotional, mental and/or spiritual gifts and it will come exactly as we need it but it will necessarily free us from the need to take physical food.

Chapter 14

Guidelines for the 21-day process by Charmaine Harley

February 1996:
The following guidelines were prepared by Charmaine Harley as a result of her answering the same questions over and over, as during the period of a year or so in the early to mid nineties, Charmaine was instrumental in aiding many people through their conversion process for pranic nourishment. Please remember that they are only guidelines and the only voice you need to listen to is the Divine One Within. If you do not trust your inner voice of intuition and knowing – your 6th and 7th senses – completely, then **DO NOT** attempt to undergo the following initiation until you do. – Jasmuheen.

Charmaine begins ...

"If you are contemplating doing the 21-day process you will need to read these guidelines carefully and thoroughly:

Guidelines for the "21-day process" – Part 1.

The three week process is just one of the steps you will take on your journey home. However, it may well be the most important time in your life and by this I mean in all your lifetimes on this planet.

What you are considering is a courageous step and is honoured by us, by your spirit and by God. One can make a major difference on this planet by following their own heart and acknowledging God as their only true Source of love, light and nourishment. You can achieve Self-Mastery in this life and go beyond the birth/death, cause & effect cycle. This is one of the steps to assist you.

At the completion of the 21-days you will no longer require food to nourish you or provide your energy needs. Your nourishment and energy (or food) will be provided by Light or God. You will be taking a Leap of Faith and for this I acknowledge you in stepping beyond the Illusion.

While you read these guidelines, you will notice I make a reference to God or a higher power. For the purpose of going beyond and Self-Mastery, you will need to believe in something. There is no attachment to us seeing it the same way – I use the word God because I am comfortable with that. Whatever you are comfortable with is right for you. We are all one consciousness anyway so there is no separation in the true sense. There is a clumsiness with words for sure – they can be limiting and appear to put labels on things and put our beliefs in boxes. For the purpose of my explanation I will use the word God.

Some people have found that some possible explanations for parts of the process have been beneficial – particularly in bridging belief systems and developing trust.

In these guidelines we have put some of the possible stories or truths in italics, this does not mean that other explanations may not be more appropriate for you.

The experience of this 21-day process is really a paradigm shift of our old reality to a totally new belief system. We are really going beyond – and into the unknown.

The original messages for this process were channelled from The Ascended Masters … as a process leading up to the Ascension. To name a few, there is Sananda, St. Germain, Archangel Michael, Serapis Bey, Kuthumi, Lady Mary, Ashtar Command and Hilarion. These Masters are believed to be here at this time to offer their love, support and light and to assist in the mighty transformation now taking place on Earth. They readily offer assistance and information to those open to their energies. Planet Earth is ascending to the fifth dimension and any being on Earth wishing to ascend at this time is offered the love and guidance to do so. It is said that while one is in the 21-day process these Masters and your spirit/higher self/I am presence are with you any time and you only need to ask for their assistance. Some feel their energies, some see them and some are not aware of anything. No matter – the process safely goes on.

Sunshine for Lunch:

There is a book that I read recently and it talks about 'Pranic nourishment' and as I see it – the 21-day process is a step towards becoming a pranic nourisher and immortal if that is your choice. I have quoted part of the book for you to read just to give you an idea of the true potential of your being.

"Pranic nourishment was the most perfect state of the human being. He and she lived on solar radiation. The food and drug addicted masses, through habitual gluttony, have closed the entry of the spirit. When the stomach works, the vital force is centred in the digestive organs instead of the five sinus chambers in the head. Few search out the cosmic truths of life and put them into practice. O how narrow is the door and how difficult is the road which carries to life, and few are those who are found in it." (Mat. 7:14)

Every life process is reversible. It might take from a few weeks to many years to make the transition back to the most fitting diet for the human being – paradisiacal fruit. Those who have the soul of Methuselah and a body fit to climb the peaks may well transcend even this height to attain pranic nourishment. Professor Hilton Hotema discussed the subject in Man's Higher Consciousness. The lungs, not the stomach are the life organs. The life line is the spinal cord, not the alimentary canal. The most vital function is breathing. "If human beings consumed only radiation through his and her respiratory organs as they did in an early Golden Age when they lived a thousand years according to tradition … sickness would be unknown.

"When people lived on solar radiation and air, they received the exact energy needs of the body. Lungs and skin collected the needed energy and also eliminated waste. When you try to balance food intake you are apt to get too much of one nutrient and not enough of others. Depending upon the climate in which people live, in order to compensate for the intensity of sunlight, the skin pigment gets darker or lighter to insure that the right amount and quality of rays will enter the cells of the body. Pigment acts as a filter which reduces both the intensity and the quality of the light spectrum that penetrated the skin."

From *Survival into the 21st Century* by Viktoras Kulvinskas.

And … there is other interesting reading on the power of God.

"Never believe that you live by the power of food and not by the power of God! He who has created every form of nourishment, He who has bestowed appetite, will inevitably see that His devotee is maintained. Do not imagine that rice sustains you nor that money or men support you. Could they aid if the Lord withdraws your life breath? They are His instruments merely. Is it by any skill of yours that food digests in your stomach?"

From *An Autobiography of a Yogi* by Paramahansa Yogananda

And …

"On September 18th 1962, Teresa Neumann died at Konnersreuth, the little village in northern Bavaria where she was born and had lived all her life. Resl, as she was known to her family and close friends, was sixty-four and had borne the stigmata for thirty-six years. Before receiving them, she had been miraculously healed of blindness and paralysis of the legs. From the moment at which Teresa received in her hands, feet and heart wounds of Christ crucified, she no longer needed to eat and drink: strict investigations ordered by the Church and confirmed by doctors established the reality of this absolutely unique state of affairs. When people asked her what she lived on, Teresa would reply in all simplicity, "On the Lord!", that is, on the consecrated host which she received each day."

From the book *Teresa Neumann* by Paola Giovetti

And then …

Illustrating that there is a higher power beyond our thinking as we know it, Deepak Chopra says …

"Our human body is a field of infinite organizing power. There are six trillion reactions occurring in the human body every second and every one of them is correlated with every single other reaction; every single other biochemical event knows what other biochemical event is occurring in the body. A human body can think thoughts, play a piano, sing a song, digest food, eliminate toxins, kill germs, monitor the movement of stars and make a new baby all at the same time and correlate each of these activities with every other activity."

From the book *Creating Affluence* by Deepak Chopra

It seems to me rather arrogant if we think that we can do it alone without the assistance of a rather infinite Source. There is a loving design, a loving Creator that will support each and every one of us if we allow it too.

And this ... from the book *God I Am* by Peter O Erbe

"Our bodies, for example, have the ability to transform, that is to articulate, the photons of starlight, or sunlight, into the sustenance required by the body. It is a process similar to photo-synthesis. This ability will surface of a collective level when Man enters super-consciousness. It may already be developed in the state of True Perception. This "developing" is not a conscious process. It occurs on a soul-essence level, meaning this ability to feed the internal combustion of the physical body from the electrums of the ether directly – without the detour via carbon-based matter – shall surface naturally. It comes in the measure of our awakening. The process goes further: in a state of super consciousness we shall cease drawing energy (e.g. fossil fuels, minerals, etc.) from the Earth but transform light directly into the forms required by our day to day needs."

Where do you start?

- You need to consider setting a date to commence the process.
- Speak to one who has done the 21-day process, ask lots of questions and be certain you know all there is to know regarding your fears, hopes and joys.
- Read the attached self-screening questionnaire and be truthful and honest with your responses. This process is not an escape from the world or from things in your life that do not work – if you think it is, you may be very frustrated afterward when you discover that all of your baggage is still there awaiting you. In fact, it is right in your face. With the insights and detachment one gains from the process, however, it does seem to be a lot easier and clearer to observe and release.
- Attempting this process for improved health or perfect weight is not recommended.
    - These may well be side benefits of going for mastery, however, attachment to them – like all attachments – needs to be surrendered.
- We make no medical claims of any nature and take no responsibility for or provide advice on any health condition or treatment.
- After this, please be certain that you seek inner guidance with regard to your readiness and your commitment to this 21-day process.

Note from Jasmuheen: This process is only for those who when they read this book find that their heart responds with great joy! For joy is the voice of the Divine One Within and when we are in alignment with our true blueprint it communicates this to us the emotion of its joy.

Questionnaire
by Charmaine Harley

When one first hears about this process, the responses are numerous! For the ones who resonate with it and know in their hearts it is for them, that's great. However – no matter how much excitement there is – at the end of the day, the mind has to be won over as well. The challenge with this can be disheartening and confusing, so the first thing to say here is that even though this process will take you home to God, beyond all that you know – there are a few hurdles to jump or bridges to cross and obstacles which have been created by the mind which are denying your greatness and authenticity.

See! If you really knew the wonder of what you are, your true potential, this process would be unnecessary, we could all just pack up and go home right now! However our nature to date is one of struggle and pain rather than peaceful and flowing so we have needed to create a process that enables us to STOP and go within. A process from the mind to release us from the mind. And that is what you are probably looking at doing, so the purpose of this self-screening questionnaire is to enable you to get an idea if the 21-day process is really for you at this time.

Because the process is about surrender of the ego and all your beliefs, it is important in your decision making to really look these questions straight in the face. If you are unable to say yes to the questions, then you may want to ask yourself "why would I want to do the 21-day process?" You need to honestly be able to say yes to all of the questions.

Self-Screening Questionnaire
with Charmaine:

I. Are you prepared for anything to happen?

II. Are you willing to surrender to God's way?

III. Are you prepared to explicitly follow a set of "rules" for 21-days?

IV. Are you willing to put your entire life on "hold" for 21-days?

V. Are you able to give up the attachment to "things" in "your world" if it were asked of you? That may mean your family? Your relationships? Your children? Your home? Your car? Your career? Your money? Your lifestyle? Your possessions? This could be for 21-days and/or beyond!

VI. Do you know that the attachments you have to people, beliefs or things may hold you back from realising your true potential, your greatness and achieving Self-Mastery?

VII. Are you aware of the difference between giving people and things up to giving up your attachment to people and things?

Do you fully appreciate how powerful the mind can be and that it creates your so called reality 100% of the time and that would include the time you are in the 21- day process?

IX. So do you also know that this means that whatever happens in the process has been created by your mind? And is part of the process you created to surrender to – for release and healing?

X. As an example, say that after 11 days into the process you haven't used your bowels. Shall we say you create a pain in that area and you become fearful that you have a bowel obstruction. Are you aware that even though your mind created it – it may also tell you that this could be real. You could get more frightened and your mind and body might tell you to get to a doctor quickly. If you succumbed to this fear based drama, you would be saying no to the wonder and greatness of your being and the ability to heal yourself with the God energy. Because you created it with the mind, you can heal it, simply by your belief, going within and asking for assistance. This process was created by the mind and it can release you from the mind. Do you understand this? There is of course no need for you to have this happen during the process.

XI. Are you understanding that the 21-day process will change your life from the very moment you hear about it and that you may never be the same again?

XII. Do you know that you do not have to do this process? and the challenges it can bring are yours and yours alone so it is really important that you understand what it is you are committing to – so have you spoken to someone who has done the 21 days? and do you feel absolutely positive that you know what it is about and what you are choosing?

XIII. Are you 100% certain you are choosing to do this process for you and no other. Not for your family or friends, your leader, your teacher, under group pressure, etc.?

XIV. There are many benefits that can come with this process like improved health and ideal weight. However your desire for these alone are not enough for you to commence this process. Are you aware that your faith in God or a higher power is needed to get you through to achieving Self-Mastery or expansion in consciousness?

XV. Are you aware of the possibility of your beauty, the clarity, the lightness, the state of being, the connectiveness and bliss, the gentleness, the love and peace, joy and freedom this process can bring to you? and are you ready for that?

XVI. Do you truly desire for God and to be in a state of Oneness?

If you are able to say yes to these questions, then you may be pretty well tuned into the purity and able to honour the sacredness of this process.

**Guidelines for the
"21-day process" – Part 1 with Charmaine**

Care-giver:
- In these guidelines I have suggested that you have a care-giver and a clear-giver.
- A care-giver is a person who understands and is willing to support your process.
- A clarity-giver is a person who has clarity and one who has completed the 21-day process.
- Clarity is a term used for good, clear communication with Spirit and has the knowing of how your process is going for you.
- What is important during your process is that you have a person of clarity informing you of various parts of the process that you need clarity on and a care-giver to physically attend your needs. So the care-giver can be the clarity-giver as well, can be the contact between you and the clarity-giver or you can elect your own clarity-giver. Phew!! That was long-winded and I hope I have made my point.
- The person of clarity will be very aware of what their role is. The clarity-giver may visit you or can be contacted by telephone.
- Let it also be suggested here that you only have one of each, as otherwise there can be a lot of confusion created with too many opinions!
- A care-giver is a warm, loving being who may have done the process or may not have. They are accepting and understanding of your commitment and have committed themselves to support you through the process 100%. If you are not living in the same space as them, they visit you each day to physically take care of your needs. This would be: change the linen on your bed, wash your clothes, help you to the bathroom if necessary, shop for your juice, arrange the flowers, water your garden, feed your chooks – whatever it is you require.
- Their role is mainly on a physical level and then to remind you of your process and keep you on track. I say on a physical level mainly because even processing on an emotional or mental level is a distraction. They also filter out the so called "real world". They do not discuss worldly things with you and distract you from your time with you. They basically keep you quiet and free from any distractions.
- During the process, many people experience irritability and being a touch unreasonable (this is fine and to be expected), however, please do not blame your discomfort on the care-giver. They are human and doing their best for you, be grateful to them for offering to be there for you.
- All arrangements with the care-giver and what you require of them is discussed and cleared before the process. This is important because the three weeks is a time for you and spirit.
- This is a time of surrender, detachment and letting go of control, and you (your ego) will think of ways to sabotage your peace, and distract you from the moment.
- If you elect a care-giver and go into their home, be aware that there are costs to be covered.

Most care-givers ask for a donation and/or the expenses to be paid. Clear this before you start your journey. A care-giver is happy to give their time and love as part of their service, however, they may not necessarily be able to support you financially.

The Role of the Care-giver:
One who chooses the role of a care-giver is to be acknowledged. Not only is it a large responsibility, it is a huge honour to share this journey with another. The role is one of love, understanding and strength. Your love and courage can make a huge difference to their surrendering process and feeling safe. As many individuals that there are is as many types of processes there are and each one and their experience is unique.

At times the role can be challenging for the carer and as a carer we guide the person in process to trust in God, surrender and ask for guidance – so we do the same – when we need the love and support, we ask God for the guidance.

Be very aware of the individual you are attending and their personality/ego. Treat the personality with love and at the same time be firm. Be sensitive to their needs without necessarily giving in or controlling.

Remember you are the only contact with the outside world for three weeks. Give them a stroke and they will be grateful forever. Be insensitive and they will remember that forever. Liken each individual to a "vulnerable new baby" – they are dependent and impressionable and almost at your mercy. Your love and trust is important to the relationship that has been set up for this process.

It is advised for you not to be caring for two people in process in the same space because of the difficulties involved.

When preparing someone for the process, make sure they are organized beforehand, have been well informed, and have all that they need. Once they are in process – that's it – not a lot of things are up for discussion – so as far as getting things for them or doing errands ... if it hasn't been organized prior (as this is a distraction to them), then it is not on.

Enjoy your part in their process and see the beauty that begins to shine in them more and more with the lightness that comes from their experience.

Note:
The care-giver will need to read these guidelines for understanding and perhaps talk to one of us to assist in a smooth journey for all concerned.

Preparation:
- Be ready for three weeks of nothing worldly, no phone, no computers, no work or employment, no social life – this is a point that cannot be said enough for the level of surrender required for you to benefit 100% from this process.
- Give up all tasks and thoughts of doing anything for this time.
- You cannot be concerned about anybody else during this period – your only concern is yourself.

- You withdraw as much as possible from the outside world and by this we mean from your work, family, friends, social activities and even from the attachment to the company of your pets. It is preferable to be away from your own home where there would be easy distractions.
- Once you commence this process you are not able to leave your immediate environment or concern yourself with anything of a worldly nature. So have all your errands complete or organized for someone else to do, e.g. appointments, meetings, bill paying, garden watering, pets, etc.
- You are being asked to give up everything for the period of three weeks.
- If you are doing the process in your own home, make sure all your needs are respected and any necessary shopping is done beforehand.
- Although it is not encouraged to be in a space with family and friends or pets, if you still choose to do that – ensure that you are not required to be with them or visitors or answer the phone (get an answering machine or unplug for the times no one is at home to answer it)
- Hand over to spirit – this is a journey and for most a challenge where you are asked to surrender.
- A detoxification program a week before your process is recommended – this basically means lighter foods and no red meat for the last week. At the same time still enjoy the foods that you feel you may miss or would like to have e.g. lobster! Spoil yourself.
- Every individual has a different understanding of 'lighter'; however, start to clean up your diet in preparation.
- Alcohol – preferably give it up a week before, but definitely three days before as it often takes this long to clear out of your system.
- You are asked to give up any drugs and/or cigarettes.
- No sexual activity of any kind during the 21 days – after the process you will need to seek guidance from your Higher Self on this matter.

If you feel tempted in getting help from outside influences or other parties, e.g. body treatment, medical advice, nutritional supplements … it is important to be aware that this is a response from your old conditioning and programming. Our suggestion is for you to consider being your own physician. Ask what this is maybe teaching you or showing you – then to go within and ask spirit to assist you with this situation and trust that spirit is more than capable to heal the problem. This is a time to remind yourself of the surrender and trust that is required of you for this huge leap you are taking. For your future progress in Self-Mastery, this is the requirement.

During the 21-day process, the body shows signs that it is cleansing and there is absolutely nothing to fear. Mother nature knows best and she will see you through any crisis because she is God's true physician. (Please note that if you have detoxified your system before hand then none of this is relevant.)

Some of the signs that the body has begun to cleanse may be:

- Inability to sleep; Headache; Nausea
- Irritability; Aching muscles
- Coated tongue; Bad breath
- Sense of weakness; Restlessness

The first few days are generally the most difficult and if there are signs of discomfort, they usually do not last very long. If there is pain, it passes in a few hours so at this point, simply rest until it has gone. The discomfort is the result of the toxins releasing which can irritate the tissues and nerves. In any area of your body that is congested with toxins, this will determine the type of eliminative crisis that may occur. There is no need to ever be concerned, as these are all common signs with the cleansing of the body and Nature will only eliminate what it can handle without overloading your organs. You are perfectly safe, Nature is performing its inner 'spring clean' and you are more likely to feel the joy of your cleaner body, a feeling of lightness, love, beauty, clear-headedness and connectedness to spirit or God.

(Note from Jasmuheen: I strongly recommend to everyone that you prepare yourself sensibly BEFORE the process. 1) get strong and fit and 2) gradually eliminate heavier foods especially meats and alcohol 3) fast, and if guided have colonic irrigation's to cleanse the bowels and release toxicity. The more you prepare the easier the 21 days are!)

During the 21-days there is no particular schedule to follow. This is free time and one of surrender. However, you may want to discuss with your care-giver – if you have chosen to have one as this is not a requirement but a personal choice – about the time they visit if you feel it is important to you.

The 21-day process is broken up into four parts:
    First three days before spirit leaves* on the third night
    Fourth to Seventh days
    Eighth to Fourteenth days
    Fifteenth to Twenty-first days before completion

(*This simply means that the energy field of the spiritual body merges with the higher frequency energy field of the Higher self or I Am presence – depending on the initiation level being undertaken. This does not mean that you vacate your body and leave it unattended. It means that the spirit body is pure in itself and does not need an energy adjustment like the physical, emotional and mental bodies. – Jasmuheen)

Your Requirements for the Three Weeks will be:
- A warm, nurturing, quiet space with a bed and, preferably, with a comfortable chair, plenty of light and fresh air. A small outside area for fresh air and sunlight could be most beneficial.

- Heaps of comfortable clothing and warm clothing depending, on the weather. Be prepared, because you may find your body thermostat is different than usual.
- Sarsaparilla and water in the ratio of your individual taste. *(or substitute)*
- Ice to crunch in the mouth then spit out. Some like the cold.
- Spit bucket with fresh slices of lemon for freshness.
- Face cloths.
- Phone for limited calls in contacting your care-giver and clarity-giver on the 4th, 7th and 21st and any other needed days concerning your process.
- Essential oils and burner – frankincense, sandalwood and lavender recommended for aromatizing the air if you desire.
- Candles for atmosphere.
- A bath could be enjoyed.
- Stool for shower in case you are feeling weak.
- Menstruation during the process most often remains unchanged, however be prepared for variation as some have experienced irregularity, heavier flow, lighter flow etc.
- Some creative work like art, knitting, guitar playing or a gentle hobby, as long as you enjoy it and do not have to do it.
- Reading that is light and makes you feel good. The material to read at this time is not to be judged as good or bad – it simply occupies the mind for a short time. The novel *The Mists of Avalon* is recommended or any other good stories, magazines, romance novels etc.
- Music that is meditational and inspirational.
- For the second week 'orange fruit juice drink' (or apple or what you are guided) that is only 25% concentrate. Note that junk juice is recommended rather than fresh juice – one of the reasons is because fresh is too acidic and can cause discomfort to your system at this time.
- For the third week, any fruit juice and no more that 40% concentrate.

(**Note from Jasmuheen:** Remember that the whole idea of this process is about listening to the Inner One so regarding juice flavour just use your own discernment but keep the juice taken weak so it's easier for the body to assimilate. If you feel to stay on water, do so.)

- A sketch pad and coloured pens for creative writing or drawing.
- A journal for the purpose of writing about your personal experience and your journey along the way.

What you do not need is:
Television; mind work; reading; material that conditions the mind; visitors; phone calls; music with lyrics if you feel it can distract you; vigorous exercise routines; going outside of the boundaries of your residence OR anything that will distract you from being in the present moment.

Additional note from Charmaine:
The completion of the process can be prolonged for very individual reasons. However, if the guidelines are followed, it generally assures a flowing, easy time for you. The reason there are guidelines is to provide you with as much support as possible to go beyond the ego mind, to give up the making of decisions based on habit or conditioning. You surrender totally without reference to the mind. If you could envision yourself as a discerning disciple to the guidelines, I feel that you would begin to discover the master within and no longer a slave to the mind. The more you are able to surrender to be with what is … just to allow … the sooner your essence is able to shine through. Any fight you have or are holding onto is simply against yourself.

The caterpillar does not question or fight for its old form – it simply does and becomes a beautiful butterfly. There is no pain, there is no resistance, it is a natural transmutation.

March 2006 with Jasmuheen:
I feel guided to add additional points regarding caregivers …

At the end of the nineties an Australian women, Lani Morris, died in Brisbane Australia. Her caregiver said that she was experiencing many difficulties but refused to stop and that on day 7 she drank 1.5 litres of pure orange juice, consequently she collapsed into a coma and was later taken off life support. Her caregiver Jim Pesnak and his wife – a couple who were in their 70's who I had never met – were arrested and charged with manslaughter and jailed. The court said that it was their duty to stop this woman from proceeding as soon as they noticed she had difficulty. At the time they felt that as a responsible adult it was her choice whether to go on or stop.

Personally I feel that the only caregiver we need is the Divine One Within and as I keep stressing, if its guidance and voice is not 100% clear and trusted by you then the 21-day process is not for you.

August 2012:
The 21- day process is a sacred spiritual initiation and it needs to be treated as such, with the recommended guidelines being followed as suggested. Over the past twenty years since the process was initially downloaded by Beverly from the Universal Field; I have found that seven out of ten people who do this initiation ignore the guidelines that we offer here.

As I travel I continually hear of all the different ways people have elected to do this and some of them just aren't physically safe. **Physical safety and health with this needs to be our number one priority as no initiation is worth losing our life for!**

Also it is now well known that I do not recommend that people do this initiation any more as the energies on our planet are now very different to what they were when this initiation was downloaded in late 1992. Still while it cannot guarantee the gift of being nourished purely by prana as only our personal resonance can do this, many people are being called to do this process. For those of you who are, then we stress again, please follow the guidelines as offered.

Also use the following breath test to check to see:
   a) if it is in your divine blueprint to live purely on prana physically this life and

b) to determine exactly what your current prana percentage is. If your current prana percentage is say 60%, then if you stop taking physical food then your body will go into fasting mode for the additional 40%. You will also not be able to stabilize your body weight post process unless you are at the 100% nourishment level.

The following Breath Test is an excerpt from my new book *Being Essence*.

Apart from trusting our initial intuitive reactions, there is a simple method we can use to do this, for this Baseline Essence breathes us and when we make a statement that is not in alignment with Its' will, then It will change the way that It breathes through us.

We call this method of testing the Breath Test.

Remember we live in a time now of great chaos and change, it is a time of self-reliance, self-responsibility and learning to trust and listen to that divine voice of infinite wisdom and love within.

So let's practice this breath test now …

Baseline Essence Guidance System - Breath Test
Just think for a moment about something simple that you know is a complete lie for you, something simple like, "My body really loves meat" for example, which for a vegetarian is not true.
As you chant this over and over as if it is a truth, just watch what your breath does …
breathe normally as you watch what is happening in your body as you keep chanting this lie over and over as if it is a truth.

Now take a moment to think of something that you know to be absolutely 100% true for you, something simple, like perhaps the statement, *"I really love my family"* or find something else to chant that is absolutely true for you
then begin to chant this simple truth over and over as a statement of fact while again you watch what your normal breath does
be very aware that there is an energy force breathing you and how it is reacting to this chant …
Take a moment to practise this before you read on.

Results or signs:- Many people find that when they make a statement that is true for them, that is 100% in alignment with the will of the Essence that is breathing them, that physically it feels as if the breath drops right down to the stomach, or to the intestinal area, and that the organs, especially the lungs, seem to expand or open up.

They also find that when they make a statement that is not a truth for their Essence, then the Essence that is breathing them lets them know by allowing the breath to rise up towards the nose or else it seems to get stuck in the throat, often with the feeling as if everything, including the lungs, is closing down or contracting inside. Others can also notice a change in the beat of their heart or sense other signs in the physical body that are a clear physical response as directed by their Essence, to a statement they are making.

Just play with this rhythm for a while, thinking of something that you may not be sure about in your life that you would like confirmation for, always make it as a statement as if it's true for you, whether you know that it is or not, and then watch what your breath does.

I like to always start this breath test with ...
"It is beneficial for me to … (insert the statement)."
Or
"It is for my highest good to … (insert the statement.)"
Or
"It is for my highest good, and the highest good of my work in this world, to … (insert the statement.)"

While many long term meditators are great at receiving clear inner guidance, sometimes tuning ourselves into true stillness, to be able to hear our inner voice, can take time.

This breath test technique is a quick and simple way for us to receive inner guidance from our Essence wherever we are and whenever we need quick confirmation without having to go into deep meditation. It also means we never have to give our power away to anyone again, as through this simple technique we can always know what is true for us.

If there is no response when you are well practiced at receiving results from this technique, it may simply be that regarding this information you are seeking confirmation on, that it is not your time to know the answer yet, or that what you are seeking to know is none of your business.

However this technique tends to work very well when we check information for others and when we seek data that is for their highest good as well, for our Essence is their Essence and it is all knowing, all loving, all wise, existing everywhere and breathing through us all in every moment.

So practice this technique until it becomes a quick response mechanism for you, where you find that you can simply make a statement once or twice in your head telepathically to Essence within and see how the breath responds … breathing always naturally … always making a statement as if it is true.

This technique can be used before making any important, potentially life changing decision.

So make the following statement and watch how your breath responds.

"It is in my divine blueprint to demonstrate being physically nourished purely by prana this life."

Keep chanting this over and over until your breath responds. If you get a yes then trust that as is this a pre-agreement prior to your taking embodiment then you will be given all the support you need to bring this into truth.

If you get a 'no' then why do an initiation like the 21 day process, which for some is very challenging?

Also then check the following:

"It is beneficial for me and for my highest good to undergo this 21-day initiation."

Again if you get a no then do not do it.

Also now using this same method, make the statement ...

"Prana now provides more than 50% of my physical body nourishment!"

If the breath confirms this, then check using the same statement for more than 60% and so on until you ascertain your exact prana percentage.

Anytime you get a *no* response with the breath test, then drop the percentage amount you are checking, down as maybe your prana % is 40%, or even 49% for example.

If you get a yes to 50% then you can safely reduce your physical food intake by that % amount.

However if you do this, you must also hold the intention that:

"All my vitamins, all my minerals and everything I need to be a healthy, self regenerating, self sustaining system comes directly to me from prana as my Essence."

Full conversion to living purely on prana and our Baseline Essence cannot be attempted until this level reads 100% and your complete bio-system is hooked in.

Now read on ...

The 21-day Day Procedure - Converting the Physical Body
by Charmaine Harley

First Three Days:
- For ease of remembrance, you may wish to begin your process at midnight and from this time on there will be no more food and nothing to drink for the next seven days.
- This is a quiet time to settle in, meditate (whatever that means to you) and stay with yourself.

- Go within to further open a pipeline of communication with your spirit, your inner teacher.
- Affirm you want the process to continue.
- This is your time to be still and communicate with God.
- In the stillness, you may like to ask for your I Am presence name.
- On the 2nd day you may find there is pain in the kidney area, lower spine and/or thighs. This can be usual, as being without liquids to flush your kidneys may cause some discomfort or headache. Toxins that have been released inside the body will not yet have been flushed out – and this takes time. *(This will probably not occur if you are toxin free before you begin – Jasmuheen.)*
- You may find you are urinating a lot and there may be a burning sensation for a short time.
- Do not be concerned with your bowels as they may not empty as quickly as you think they should. *(You may decide to have colonic irrigation's before beginning the process – Jasmuheen.)*
- Your body may feel weak and shaky so have a stool in the shower for support. If this is the case, have your care-giver around to help you. You may use the bath if you prefer.
- When you need to use the sarsaparilla – swill in your mouth and spit into the bucket.
- Crushing ice in your mouth and spitting out is another option – no other form of thirst relief is suggested.
- No fluid is to be swallowed at all.
  The mouth could become thick with toxic build up or feel mucousy, so continue to rinse out. Clean your teeth as required. *(If your body is toxin free this will not be required – Jasmuheen)*

Third Day:
- Keeping quiet is the order of the day!
- During this evening the spirit* is going to depart for a period of time waiting until your body is ready for it to re-enter in its greatness.
- Affirm your desire for spirit to leave* on this night and the process to continue.
- You could ask to be aware of when your spirit has left.*

* [The idea of 'spirit leaving' is about the merging of the energy field of the spiritual body with that of the finer vibration of the Divine Self. All energy bodies are held within the field of the I AM Presence that is always with us, is our essence and guides this whole process divinely – Jasmuheen]

On the Fourth Morning:
- Spirit is most likely to have left during your sleep.
- You may feel different. When the spirit left your body, all the feeling and love left also – therefore, you may feel empty.

- If you have chosen to have one you may contact your clarity-giver if you wish, to see if spirit has left.
- Your Divine Self together with the Ascended Ones will begin work immediately after spirit leaves to prevent "the death process" commencing. They will have begun their work days, perhaps weeks before, but they will not do anything that cannot be reversed in case you change your mind before this time. During these four days, they are working with the energy fields of all your bodies, altering your system to use light energy to raise the vibration of your body.

Fourth to Seventh Days:
- From day four to seven, still no liquids can be taken.
- If fluid is taken it is assumed that the retuning work will stop and not resume for another 24 hrs after the liquid is taken (delaying your process). Many have felt that an etheric 'drip' is inserted into the back section near the area of the kidneys so there is no need to fear regarding this period without liquids
- Keeping quiet is still the order of the day!
- You will need to be aware of the needs of your body during these four days.
- It is suggested that you remain still and quiet at three intervals during the day.
- Choose your times and stick to them. Suggestion is 10 am, 1pm & 4pm.
- This realignment process often can last for approx. 2 hrs at a time.
- You may feel something of this realignment process
- You will instinctively know when to roll over, be still or go to the toilet etc.
- You may feel groggy or heavy which again is less likely if you are well tuned beforehand.
- The most important thing is to be quiet at this time – you may not think you know that anything is happening however if you are still you will be aware and it can be very subtle.
- Your Divine Self is guiding you. You are safe and protected.
- All you need to do is surrender to the process.
- You may wish to speak to the angels as they will assist you.
- You may bathe and shower as you like.
- You may experience what is called an "etheric temperature" where you feel very hot. This is a sign that all is going well. You could be tempted to have a cold shower or jump in the swimming pool, however, resist – this is too drastic for the body at this time. To bring the heat down, get a cold ice pack or wrap ice cubes in tea towel and place it at the nap of your neck – this is a centre that will be sensitive and cool you down.
- During these days you may feel really thirsty. So, be aware, but do not give in as you will only prolong the process and postpone your first drink on the seventh day.
- Because you are more in mindspace, your thinking may be very erratic and all over the place, like so many thoughts with no feeling. Try to quiet the mind and meditate for your peace of mind.

- You may be very irritable, idiosyncrasies you have may come up and you need to be aware and quiet the mind.

On the seventh day ...
- Contact your clarity-giver – if you have chosen to have one – to ask what time you can have your first drink – generally on this day, it is later in the afternoon or evening and juice is allowed.
- This will be juice at 25% concentrate, it will be of a cool room temperature, and it will be small. One hour after, you may partake in another small drink of juice.
- Remember your body has not had anything for 7 days ... so take it slowly – be gentle with yourself.
- You will be given specific instruction at the time with your drinking.

Eighth to Fourteenth Day:
- Keeping quiet is still part of your day.
- Talk with the angels, so that they will assist in your healing. Be happy. You will soon be feeling wonderful.
- From now on you may drink juice 25% concentrate.
- Please understand that you may have undergone major realigning, albeit etherically – so please rest accordingly.
 (Again the more tuned you are before the 21 days, the less energy realignment work will have to occur during the first seven days – Jasmuheen.)
- Now comes the healing process. This will last for the next seven days and the above instruction must be strictly adhered to at all times.
- Food is something that is no longer a part of your reality because your reality is no longer that of what it was.
- Should you be bombarded by thought projections from an external source (that being negative), then you must find a way to occupy the mind with something more peaceful. Your logical mind and ego/personality may be out-of-control at this time. You are very safe – of this, there is no doubt. So, please, do not give negativity any credence whatsoever.
- This is the healing week a very beautiful time, so enjoy it and rest.
- You could be likened to an invalid, so please accept this and behave accordingly.
- You may sleep a lot.
- You may feel spaced out.
- You may continue to have discomfort in your body.
- Everyone's experience is unique *(and depends on how well they have prepared themselves – Jasmuheen).*
- You may feel quite energetic, however, do not use this energy – reserve it for the healing.
- Some people have found that when they are not resting enough they start to feel sick or experience discomfort of some type – a sign that spirit wants you quiet.
- You may enjoy a bath at this time.

- Rest, read and spend these days becoming close to the Divine One within.

Fifteenth to Twenty-first Day:
- Integration week and the healing is nearing to an end. The higher energies of the next finer energy band of consciousness – the Divine One within – will begin to be released within your body, a little more each day.
- You will start to feel stronger.

Ask :
- What is my role, my purpose?
- What have I come here to do?
- You may be able to watch a video sometimes ask your clarity-giver and they need to be 'feel good' videos.
- 40% fruit juice concentrate is all that is allowed – no soups or milks are recommended.

Take each day as it comes and still continue to be in the moment.

21st Day:
If you are using one, contact your clarity-giver for clarification that you will be complete at midnight of that day. *(Please note that the use of midnight is not to do with the 'witching hour' as interpreted by a dear French lady – but are simply to signify the end of a day. – Jasmuheen.)*

Having completed the 21-day process:

Changes – Charmaine continues

You may already notice your detachment. You may feel ordinary or extra-ordinary. You may experience a heightened sensitivity of smell, taste and touch. Your teeth may be sensitive. You may experience some painful feelings in your body ... just know that healing is still taking place.

At this time, it is not unusual to be wondering if there are any changes at all or, perhaps, you are not noticing them. The changes will be subtle to start with, however, your feeling of lightness and well-being will be evident. I, myself, noticed small changes and, as time went on, I noticed more that was changing. My walk was different (my feet were more aligned instead of facing out) and I was standing taller and straighter. My real feeling of connectedness and a strong sense of being one with God took a couple of months to embody. Be patient with yourself, love your journey and above all – enjoy!

Authentic Freedom is Permanent.

Now that you have completed the 21-day process the door is open for you to go beyond the old beliefs. Living with the old beliefs, while also trying to trust in God, may be difficult. You will not be able to live with conflicting belief systems. It is helpful to remember that the process is really the beginning of the rest of your life – so embrace the new you. To be born again is to let go of the past and place your future in God's hands.

As of now you have no physical or nutritional need for food or drink. Whatever you decide to drink it is important to not give the ego/surface mind additional power. For example, some people for example have been tempted, out of old conditioning, to add a blended banana to a milk drink. The ego will justify that you need the banana for fibre or potassium. Some see natural, pure and healthy a consideration when choosing drinks. You no longer need to choose a drink based on its nutritional value.

Your desire for drink or food is not physically originated but comes from a mental or emotional source. Be aware that if this desire occurs, you may well want to suppress it with a drink. This is okay, and we suggest that you be witness to what you are doing. By being a spectator to these feelings or thoughts, you usually obtain insights and grow. Change will occur over time. However, it is possible your taste buds may desire certain flavours. This will also change over time.

Be gentle with yourself. You do not have to be a proud "no food or drink" person. Some will only drink water or herbal teas because it is considered healthy. As part of the ego's self sabotage in creating the illusion it could make you believe that there are set rules, a regimented drinking system or a particular way it has to be. Whatever drink you desire is okay.

Decide what to drink without losing the joy of living. If you want coffee, that's okay … if you want water, that's okay … and if you want juice, that's okay. You can determine what drink is right for you by the way you feel when you have it. If it is too heavy, you will definitely know. Going for the Light and love and enjoying ourselves is our first consideration. There is a fine line between denying yourself and the application of self-discipline. You need to discover the balance, so you do not feel deprived.

Do not judge yourself too harshly about what is right and what is wrong about drinking. After the process, some people are very good with self-discipline and do not look for a distraction with having to drink something. Others find they need to drink more and need that nurturing pleasure to feel good. Everyone is different – that is for sure – and everyone is at a different stage of the journey. We are here to enjoy our evolvement, so have a good time and be kind to yourself and others.

Socially, there is no reason not to be present during lunch and dinners with others. For instance, one can have a bowl of clear soup and a drink without drawing any attention to yourself or seeming to be different. Once you are comfortable and accept your new way of being, others will not even notice or be concerned that you are not eating. We have found that our social and business activities around meals in restaurants, cafes, etc, is actually easier. Because we used to be health conscious and concerned about things like white or raw sugar, quality or freshness, level of preservatives, etc. we find now that we can be more relaxed and able to have a good time.

You are now at a point where you are able to go within and ask for all of your needs to be provided for. During the last 21 days, we have suggested that you trust for all healing and wellness. It may take some time – even months – before your body is in full alignment, allow this process to continue without external interference. You are more than capable of healing yourself. We have decided that for our optimum and increasing health, we partake in no physical treatment by another e.g. chiropractic, doctors or bodywork. Your perfect weight and health will manifest automatically.

A final note …

You are encouraged to ask for any support you may require. While you are discovering your own wisdom and clarity, it may be helpful to speak to another, perhaps the one who assisted you through the process or another who knows the path you have chosen. No one else knows any more or has any more insights than you do, however, in talking to another, your own clarity becomes apparent. Often as you ask the question, you then realise you also have your own answer! You are welcome to contact us, as we are willing to share your experiences.

With much love – Charmaine Harley
and please enjoy the miracles …

When one commits to God Over The Illusion – the effect on humanity and the planet is immeasurable and the healing power tremendous. Every time a being raises their vibration, the effect ripples to the farthest edge of the Universe …

Note from Jasmuheen: Charmaine's comments on junk juice has caused some 'purists' to react, however I would like to share here that prior to the 21-day process I was a pure food, spirulina and vitamin junkie. I realised that a huge part of this journey is about trust, that to complete the process and then still take vitamins or only 'healthy' drinks etc was not trusting the forces of light to do their job and sustain me. This realisation was a big leap of faith!

Logically I reasoned that if I trusted – and then experienced the benefits of that trust by maintaining a healthy body – that all my nourishment, vitamins, sustenance really did come from light then I could have any junk flavour I wanted for I would be indulging in it purely for its flavour value and not for its nutritional value. I began to exchange my pure fruit juice preference for the odd cappuccino or the odd mouthful of chocolate just because I felt like the flavour of something sweet but I also learnt to transmute these things.

For me, as an absolute food purist for some 20 years, the process was extremely liberating! To be nourished from pranic energy and then be free to have a stage of tasting chocolate, or to have a potato scallop now and then through winter just for fun was fun!

The true gift of this process is freedom. Freedom of choice, freedom from limiting beliefs, freedom to allow the Divine One within to sustain us on all levels not just nutritionally. Personally I would like to recommend that anyone undergoing this process stay with it, without taking any food, for at least 6 months or until you have proved to yourself beyond a shadow of a doubt that prana really does sustain you. Yet as always, this choice must always be only yours. Know that your weight will stabilize if you have reprogrammed your beliefs around this, and know that your energy levels will become very high and you will find that you need to sleep far less than before. These are three definite signs that you are being nourished from prana.

As this process is about merging consciously with the Divine One Within then always use your discernment, always trust your own inner guidance for you will be tested on this again and again in many ways. The process is not a path of guaranteed 'enlightenment' or a quick fix it for any problems we may have, it is just another step in our continuing journey of self-mastery.

If you have doubts about doing the process then do not do it yet – ask for the Divine One within to make it very obvious to you that it is part of your blueprint! It is not a 'fad' or the latest 'new age' trend, and again personally I only recommend that you do the process if it feels absolutely like the next step for you, without doubt, without question, without fear.

Doing the 21-day process can be considered a very 'radical' thing to do, yet for the one tuned to the Divine One within, for the warrior or the yogi, it is often perfectly natural as they understand the true gifts of this journey instinctively.

If you are strongly guided from within then ask the Divine One Within to prepare you perfectly on all levels so that you may flow through the 21 days in joy and ease and grace!

And be sensible, the more you prepare yourself beforehand the easier this transition will be! Do not do anything to endanger the health of your body for it is a Divine Temple and needs to be acknowledged as such. Careful preparation and responsible action regarding this is recommended at all times.

Chapter 15

Other Ways

February 1996:
For those not tuned to or perhaps interested in the Ascension paradigm and the creation of a sacred space and initiation understanding, we offer the following.

The idea of living by the light of cosmic forces has been in existence for eons of time. Personally I cannot separate this from its spiritual base into a simple dietary matter yet the work of Wiley Brooks and others does attempt to do so. The program that they recommend is quite simple.

Firstly prepare as you would if undergoing the 21-day process. Be kind and gentle to the body. As mentioned previously: - "It is my recommendation that one prepares the vehicle in an honouring way to guarantee ease and pleasure in this transition process … We recommend a gradual elimination of red meat, then white meat, then to go to raw foods, then soups and liquids and then …" continue as you are guided intuitively. "How long it may take to go from being a meat eater to raw foods then liquids will be up to each individual. Do it in a way that gives joy and comfort. The body will guide you if you listen."

Regardless of how one converts the body to take nourishment from the etheric forces, there will still be commonalities regarding emotional and mental body reactions that are both cellular and cultural. Working with greater cosmic forces and the reality that we are spiritual beings having a human experience seems to empower people further. Especially as at this point in our linear time, the choice to be pranically sustained is neither a common nor a popularly supported one. For those of us 'pioneering' this to the Western world, all documented information of the journey is beneficial and we share it freely.

While my personal reality was firmly anchored in the Ascension paradigm, my background regarding dietary choices was intuitive until I understood about tuning for maximum potential on all levels, consequently I admit that it is hard for me to comprehend anyone undergoing this journey who is not consciously spiritually aware.

If you are working with your guides or intuition the 21-day process will still provide a 'fast track' conversion process. From liaisons with those who have had the Ascended Master connection, the gifts of the journey seem to be quite miraculous in itself. Others without this connection have shared "What gifts? The whole 21 days was a challenge and a bit of a struggle".

Not taking food or fluids for a seven-day period can be an extreme process and a challenging experience for an unprepared or untuned vehicle. However when one has a strong inner connection this initiation has the potential to BE sacredly joyous.

For those wishing to eventually live purely from prana we recommend that you begin the following instruction immediately as it will set the conversion process, to be pranically fed, in place. Then listen to your body. It will guide you to begin to intuitively and effortlessly eliminate various substances from your diet quite naturally.

Call forth the body elemental and command ...
"I command that from this now moment you absorb all the vitamins, nutrients and nourishment – required to maintain peak physical health – from the pranic forces."
Act as if you are the master of your system as you say this and that it will automatically be done.

You will know when the conversion process is working as your weight will stabilize and your energy levels will be high and you will naturally find yourself eating less and less.

March 2006:
As I have discovered that 7 out of 10 people ignore the guidelines offered in this book and follow their own inner guidance or preconceived ideas as to how this should be done, since 1997 with the first death around this process, I began to develop another system that we outline in detail in *The Food of Gods* book. Slower and safer, it shares another paradigm that I prefer, re dealing with pranic nourishment.

August 2012:
Please note that our research has now shown that the long term success rate with conversion to pranic nourishment is as follows:-
   The 21-day process as offered in this book – 10%.
   The slower method offered in the book *The Food of Gods* - 70%.

One reason for this is that for most people the 21-day process is just too fast for both their emotional body and their social adjustment capability; with most returning to taking smaller amounts of food so they can feel less socially isolated. Using the slower process seems to help enormously with these adjustments, hence the better long-term success rates.

Chapter 16

Future Potential – World Hunger

February 1996:
As I shared in the Foreword "They (the Ascended Masters) show me visions of a world without hunger, no food outlets or farming except to grow for the sake of beauty not need. Imagine how many billions of dollars could be diverted to other things if everyone trusted they could be fed by Universal substance, by God's Light alone?"

More and more are becoming aware and entering into a deep knowing that what we focus on simply grows and becomes. To recognise the power of the mind to create is the true potential of humanity, this means also being able to recognise the power of thought to create and then to be disciplined enough to focus only on what is for the highest for both individuals and the masses alike. This requires the marriage of the human heart and mind, where "True intelligence is the capacity of the mind to honour the wisdom of the heart". Emmanuel Book 11 *The Choice of Love*.

This also means understanding that if we, as the masses, keep focusing our thought-forms, media, attention, on world starvation affirming outmoded beliefs that "if you don't eat, you must die" then the starving masses will die.

It also means understanding that if we, as the masses, keep focusing our thought-forms, media, attention, on affirming outmoded beliefs that "if you don't eat, you must die" then the anorexics will die. (The problem of anorexia must be dealt with in a twofold manner. Firstly to address the 'lack of self worth' emotional issues that are the root cause and secondly the belief systems within mass culture that keep insisting that "if you don't eat you'll die".)

It also means understanding that if we as the masses keep focusing our thought-forms, media, attention on affirming outmoded beliefs that "everyone is born and everyone dies" then everyone who is born will naturally die.

Just take a few moments, or hours, in contemplation and think -
How much time do you spend in the preparation of food?
How much time and money do you spend shopping in crowded supermarkets?
How much of your income is spent on food and socialising around food?
How much of each nations energy and resources are focused on the cultivation and production of food?

Imagine …
A world without abattoirs. (the vegetarians and animal liberationists would love it!)
A world without animals bred, and grazing on valuable land, for eventual slaughter.
Imagine no farms or pastures utilised for food production.
Imagine no McDonald's or take-aways (a horrific thought for some no doubt!)

Imagine ... No starving children – every second, somewhere in the world a child dies of hunger and malnutrition.

Imagine no anorexic teenagers.

Imagine no world poverty as the billions of dollars we spend on food could be diverted for social change and equality of living resulting in ...
- no ghettos
- no crime
- no need for social welfare.

Imagine ... A planet united for the good of all as living on pure prana is either motivated by, or brings, a spiritual awakening to a better state of being.

Know that: -
Change comes from being open to new ideas, daring to be different, rising above mediocrity.
There is a better way of being, a more complete way of being. A way of being that embraces our full potential where telepathy is normal, being sustained by only Light is normal, physical immortality is normal.
This is the future of our planet. Someone must pave the way by embracing these ideas as reality and then living them.

Footnote October 1997:
It is time for us to move beyond words and platitudes and demonstrate our mastery as we pragmatically begin to re-tune the various systems on our planet. This is what M.A.P.S. – Movement of an Awakened Positive Society is about, re-education and refinement of existing systems in a manner that operates for the good of the whole.
Through introducing the idea and method of fine-tuning it is our intention to aid in the elimination of world hunger through pranic nourishment which will also then benefit the environment and create a more sustainable future for the planet.
Many comment that this is a huge project for us to undertake yet we live in a society with amazing technological ability. One of the most powerful forces for change is the media. Used positively with integrity and a desire to honour the intelligence of their audience, great changes can occur globally in a very short time with media co-operation.
For me personally one of the biggest challenges is to get past the mainstream media's initial disbelief and the sensationalism aspect so we can do some in depth reporting on this 'new possibility' as a practical solution to world hunger. The journey of re-education continues ...

Footnote 2001:

In August 1999 I completed a two year research project interviewing over 100 people who did the 21-day process and converted to living on light and included it all in the book *Ambassadors of Light*. With an average age of 47, the oldest was a woman of 93 who lived in Vienna Austria, the youngest was 13. In this next book I also look deeper at weight loss issues and dealing with family and friends post 21-day process. We also address the various media misconceptions that have occurred around our research and also add research by Dr. Karl Graninger, Dr. Barbara Ann Moore, Choa Kok Sui from the Pranic Healing network, Dr. Juergen Buche, the Qigong Masters with their natural state of Bigu, and more.

In this second book we also look at the redistribution of the world's resources, including the benefits of global vegetarianism, disarmament, and other issues that if addressed will substantially free up much needed funds that can be applied to feed, clothe, house and holistically educate all in need.

We also address issues such as Third World debt, raising money for social welfare, genetic engineering and our global position re the cultivation of livestock and its environmental impact plus health and longevity.

March 2006:
At the beginning of this year I completed *The Prana Program* which offers a safe simplified version of obtaining pranic nourishment for Third World countries.

Q: You have said that the idea of just being free from the need to take physical food, is not enough motivation for people on this journey and that people wishing to be involved with it need to be aware of the 'bigger picture'. Could you explain what you mean by this?
A: Humanity has been gifted with an amazing ability which is to re-discover, recognise, experience and demonstrate the God Force within. We have been programmed to demonstrate this Divine Force and be one with it, any time we choose – for on one level we operate like mini computers that are run by the same software as the Cosmic Computer called God. This Divine Force, or God, radiates Its nurturing love and light through our inner sun centre to feed our chakras, and through our physical world sun, and It has the power to feed our cells by both internal and external means. However the remarkable thing is not to see a human being become free from the need to eat physical food, but to see a human being radiate such light and love that all are fed by their presence.

Q: Why have you decided to offer The Prana Program for Third World challenges, surely this is something just for aid agencies?
A: I believe that the wider we spread our research and share its relevance to such challenges, the sooner it may be accepted. The benefits of this are not just for the chosen few and by educating widely at a grass roots level we can address the challenge on many levels. It may also inspire others – apart from those in aid agencies and the U.N. – to share the data here with appropriate channels that they know. I also believe that as more adopt this mental paradigm, it can be more powerfully holographically projected and imprinted into areas of need to change the field dynamics and soften the suffering.

Chapter 17

Paradigms – Kuthumi

Received through Jasmuheen 2nd September 1996
And so dear ones of light, you gather together this evening as pebbles upon a beach ... you come in many forms, with many different understandings do you not? You have been washed by a wave of energy together in this gathering, like a tide that creates the waves upon a beach. This tide, this stream of energy, is simply the enactment of one of the laws that govern your space time continuum, one of the laws that govern the formation of life and matter and energy in this quadrant of the universe you call Planet Earth.

When we read the light that shines from your heart centres it comes in various gradients, it shines forth in various degrees of brightness. For you are all unfolding and gathering information that is aiding your personal evolvement, your personal understanding. Your heart centres can be likened to a doorway where there has been perhaps a darkened room. And yet when this doorway has been opened, it shines the light from another room where all the lights are on. Some of you are searching for the doorway. Some of you have found it and the door is a little ajar. For some of you the doorway is open and the light from within is blazing like a fire.

As we have shared often, humanity is evolving according to a Divine Blueprint. You all have different roles to play in the unfoldment of this blueprint. It is like the information gravitates to your being in direct relationship to the energy signals you emit, for you are forever emitting signals, whether you are aware of this or not, and everything that is within your life, within your gravitational field is there in response to a signal that you have emitted.

The energy and the consciousness of the Ascended One called Kuthumi is a vast point of consciousness. One of the roles that this consciousness has taken, to enact within your physical plane, is that of World Teacher. The reason we (we meaning the Ascended Ones) and the consciousness of Kuthumi have been brought to your grouping this evening, is to talk about a game that is being played upon your planet, to talk about the creation of a trinity of paradigms.

There are three paradigms that are being played out within the microcosm of your grouping, and your grouping dear ones is purely a microcosm of a macrocosm that is being played on the world stage. For the essence of that which you are, in your various unfolding levels, can be mirrored in the world today can it not?

The first paradigm is the creation of a personal reality that allows you, as was shared earlier, as individuals to live your life to your highest maximum potential. To no longer run on one cylinder, or two cylinders or three, where all you feel you are is perhaps a physical, emotional, mental being, but to understand that you have another aspect to yourself – your Divine Self, to command that self to be fully present in your waking reality in a manner that lets your heart sing.

When you have created a personal paradigm that allows you to express your divine nature fully upon this plane in a way that keeps you joyous, impassioned, living life to your highest according to your standards, you then find yourself gravitating into what we term a global paradigm.

A global paradigm is a pattern of energy where human beings are gravitating together and form an orchestra instead of being individual players, to be part of a collective group consciousness that forms a divine orchestra. This paradigm globally will be manifested in the physical plane according to your vision as a collective whole. This paradigm will be manifested in your political, educational, social, and economic systems. There are beings present amongst you who are consciously working in the implementation of a global paradigm that will allow the new millennium, the prophesied Golden Age, to become a physical reality upon your plane, and no longer just a dream sought by few for a better way of being. You feel the changes among you in the speeding up of time do you not? It is because the vibration is changing so rapidly as you unleash the Divine forces from within your being.

As more and more of you seek the inner doorway and allow the light of your Divine Self to be fully made manifest upon your plane of physical reality, that is what is speeding up the changes. The Divine Self lives within a paradigm of simultaneous time, where there is no separation between past, present and future, where the rate of vibration of electromagnetic energy moves with such force and creative power that there is no separation of linear time.

So it is your heart that is allowing these energies to flow through from the inner doorways, to create great changes personally and then flow into the global paradigm.

How many of you here present are working on the third paradigm creation? This is the final leg in the trinity now being revealed, and it is a paradigm of universal belonging. It is the preparation of humanity to understand that there are other life forms present in other energy bands, in other galactic expressions, other planetary expressions. That is why there is the release of information of other life forms, of extraterrestrial intelligence now coming in to your plane of understanding.

So simultaneously there are three paradigms always constantly interconnected and being played out. The state of awakening within each individual depends on which paradigm is being accessed at any given moment. Many of you have put in place the personal paradigm. Many have moved on to be active in the implementation of a global paradigm. And now you are beginning to work to prepare the rest of your brothers and sisters for the incoming information that you are part of a universal whole as well.

It is interesting to read the energies of humanity, for in the process of awakening, there are some who feel that all there is in life is your third dimensional reality. They are operating out of the energy beam of lower mind and lower emotional body. Lower mind – that is being caught with the issues of survival, of your jobs, of procreation, of continuation of the species upon this plane.

There are those who have now hooked into higher mind – that aspect of yourself that is truly divine, that is seeking answers as to why you are in embodiment, that is looking to work cohesively as group consciousness to bring a level of experience physically across the globe, where you work with awareness for the good of the whole. That is the driving force of higher mind – to work collectively so that when humanity upon this plane has reached a point of awakening and consciousness, you may take your rightful place within the universal paradigm.

This universal paradigm dear ones (and we speak to the ones of you present where this understanding is perhaps still a little far-fetched and there are some present where that is real also) – this universal paradigm sees your Planet Earth and humanity upon her as one piece of a gigantic puzzle, one piece of a myriad of expressions of life forms, through all the dimensions of time and space, created by the one force in its experience of expansion and contraction.

It is known to many as the 'in breath' and the 'out breath' of God. It is known in the quantum physicist's field as a unified field of energy continually expanding and contracting. It is a fluid motion of consciousness, of which you are interconnected and a part. One per cent if that, of your being resides in physical embodiment. And yet for many, 100% of your perception feels that all you are is the one per cent. And yet when you open the doorways to the higher realms through your heart centre and allow the greater aspect of yourself to express through into this physical plane, that is when the magic begins, that is when you feel fulfilled as human beings – for that is when you begin to tap into your full potential as divine sparks of consciousness.

So we ask that as you research and understand the laws of creation – the universal laws – that as you understand that all is simply responding as fluid streams of consciousness, that when you understand that you truly create your reality by what you choose to focus upon – then you start to consciously create personal, global and universal paradigms that work harmoniously in alignment for the good of the whole upon this plane.

It is a simple game and it is a game that many are being asked to play if it feels right within your heart. For it is the heart that is the doorway. And it is the heart that has the true intelligence and the connecting link between higher and lower mind. It is the door that allows you to access the four-fifths of your brain that you are being asked to begin to activate and utilise, so you may be a complete being operating on all cylinders.

You may play the game of suffering and lack if that brings you satisfaction. But all present, and those who have been working consciously with the reality of the Ascended Ones, have decided now that enough suffering has been experienced in both this and in previous embodiments. And that when one awakens to the glory of the Divine One within there ceases to be a requirement for suffering. For the true nature of divinity, the God within, is a being that knows boundless, limitless love and joy – and that is the quality, the essence, that it brings as it manifests in your life upon this plane.

We feel in reading the energies of those present that there is information needed for each and every one of you to create the perfect bridge – the bridge that forms the inner doorway. All here are seeking further information are you not? (yes)

Understand dear ones that your physical being is simply a mass of cellular memory as has been shared, and as such you hold within you data bases that can be likened to computer files that hold all the knowledge of your past embodiments – your present and your future embodiments as well – so that if there is something you are seeking, know that the information is held within. And if you command this information to be revealed to you, then it must.

We have been bringing through a series of programming *(see next chapter – Jas)* that allows those utilising such to be in alignment with Divine Will to honour their agreed contractual arrangements with the Divine One. For every being present has signed a contract with the Creative Force prior to taking embodiment upon this plane. That contract was like a role that you agreed to play at a certain point in Earth's unfoldment – to really be part of a greater whole, to really play a piece in an orchestra, divinely and perfectly, once you have learned which instrument was yours and which song was to be played.

When you are seeking the next piece of your blueprint knowing that you have programmed to be in alignment with Divine Will; you may wish to simply ask that the next perfect piece of the Divine Blueprint reveal itself clearly to you now and that it bring with it, the perfect individuals that will allow you to manifest, into physical reality this piece of the blueprint, now. That program and instruction dear ones that you give to universal forces will allow such to be revealed to you clearly, for you have instructed thus and it will bring through the other beings that will aid in the manifestation.

You are all aware that you are working triadically in nature, that you are working as a group consciousness for the anchoring of the blueprint for the Golden Age. For it is a huge paradigm to be anchored and created, is it not? It is a bigger paradigm to implement it into physical reality, to cross the borders and unify your social, political, economic and educational structures.

This anchoring of the global paradigm is the creation of the twelfth level of your light body. Those present are activating various levels of light body creation within them, becoming aware, should we say, of that which is already within. It is, like you may say, going into a mansion that is in darkness and when you turn the key, which is the inner doorway, and open that doorway, you switch on the whole light. But you systematically must go through every room of the mansion and switch on each light. That is the activating of your light bodies, for all is already present, you just have not seen it before. And when you switch on the inner light, it will reveal itself to you.

So some present have opened the door and activated the light that is to reveal what is in the foyer, the corridors. Others have activated the lights to your lounge, or your kitchen, your bedrooms and so forth. The twelfth level being anchored is being anchored by those who have gone through, activated, switched on every light within the inner mansion. This makes sense does it not? So they have become a beacon for the new global paradigm.

For when the personal paradigm is anchored and all the lights are on, when you have become an awakened being, when you have awakened to the glory of the Divine One and recognized that you are ascended, then you also recognise that you are a descended master now anchoring a global paradigm as part of your pre-agreed contract with the Divine One.

When the lights are on, it will act as a lighthouse, as a beacon to other beings who are still searching to create a powerful personal paradigm.

So the global paradigm dear one, must be made manifest physically. So many of you are now feeling the call are you not? To group together, to network, to create physically upon this plane for the good of the whole. And also to bring through the information to have the pride, the courage, in the face of ridicule. For the collective masses dear ones have not yet found the doorway to the inner mansion, let alone switched on the lights to all the rooms that abide there and discovered the magic, the true divinity and awareness that such brings.

So to stand tall and to speak of a universal paradigm, of space brothers, of space sisters, of extraterrestrial intelligence, of beings of love and light, of being given the invitation to humanity to become part of the Intergalactic Federation of Worlds (the body of consciousness that governs other paradigms of all the planets in other energy fields). This, dear ones, takes courage.

And many here are not yet consciously wishing to speak of a universal paradigm, yet there will come a time in your near future, where all such things will be discussed freely, collectively – this information is coming through your media, is it not? Planted, so to speak by higher consciousness. And yet in response to the call within the hearts of the awakened ones, it is time to get the ball rolling dear ones.

As we have shared there is all the time in the world, yet there is no more time to waste. It is time to dive into your heart centre, to find the inner doorways. To understand that you are these vast, multidimensional beings. To discover the 99% of yourself that may not have revealed itself to you fully upon this physical plane. For your mission is to be here, but to be unlimited. It is not a time as we have shared, of personal enlightenment and leaving this plane. It is a time to be personally enlightened and then enlighten the globe, to switch on all the lights, within all the hearts, within all the rooms, within the inner mansions of all humanity who continue to remain in physical embodiment in this time of now, upon your planet, in your planet's history.

So dear ones, you may stay in an understanding that perhaps this is all nonsense, and some present have wondered if perhaps it is. And yet you may decide to listen to your heart, to be open to explore these other paradigms, to understand that there are other realities that many are now choosing to explore. And in the exploration it is bringing great fruits within their physical world.

It is bringing gifts of telepathy. It is bringing gifts of clairvoyance, of being able to see energies, and into other realms. It is bringing gifts of the ability to self-heal and to heal others. It is bringing gifts of being able to tune to the heartbeat of the Mother/Father Creator.

God as it emanates from the heart centres of all of life forms and expressions on this plane. It brings a gift of great magic as well.

So choosing dear ones – and the choice is whether to live in the light of the God I AM and know great magic and limitless being or to continue perhaps in the realm of fear and doubt and uncertainty – the choice is always there dear ones, for all paradigms exist within the physical reality of duality upon this plane."

Chapter 18

Programming – Mind Power

February 1996:
I have been guided to include this chapter as one of the most powerful gifts that undergoing the process gave to me, was the understanding of the need to de-program cellular memory and re-program ourselves into the self-mastery of limitlessness.

As I have come to understand …

"Your body is a bio-computer, your thoughts are the software, your life is the printout of the two. Change the software, rewrite or modify the program, and change your life. It is that simple."

The following is an article I wrote for the Silver Cord magazine October issue in Australia then rewrote for *The ELRAANIS Voice* to include some additional programming tools. Due to the high level of reported success from many utilising this information we include it here for your enjoyment and the positive power of transformation it will bring into your life if utilised.

"After the completion of my second book *The Art of Resonance*, my inner guidance was to stop reading. Perhaps it was because the project had been intensely focused for over 6 months as I wove together the researched material gathered from well over 40 texts previously read. My intention was to present a manual of easy to utilise, self-help tools that honoured the heart and the intellect by providing well-researched data from many sources.

More than just the idea of 'taking a break' from research was the understanding of the importance of allowing what had been absorbed intellectually to settle into a cellular knowing which can only be achieved through living it. I also intuitively knew that I held within all the knowledge needed to be the limitless being I was seeking to demonstrate.

As I witness others make this journey, a pattern appears that seems to utilise all our inner 'knowing'. The soul stirs, we begin to awaken. We thirst for knowledge. We honour the intellect by researching and we find the commonalities – the threads of truth that emerge through all the teachings of the indigenous ones, the ancient schools and Earth's religions. We combine the knowledge of quantum physics. We discover Universal Laws and we recognise that they govern all energy and matter and are the foundation of all science and religion. We understand that these laws are unto themselves, for they are the Laws of Creation and when we work with them magic happens. We practice, we play, we create consciously.

Knowing we create reality via our vision we diligently monitor our thought processes deleting all but limitless thinking. We refine, we re-program, we witness the laws of energy respond and deliver this new paradigm in our day-to-day reality.

Meditation brings the gift of detachment and we become the witness, the creator, experiencing and living within our own creation. We have realised that the impact of BEing and living what we intellectually understand, empowers the reality further. For a beam of energy of thought is less powerful than deep cellular knowing that emanates out of every cell, every fibre of our being altering the energy patterns electromagnetically around us. The whole body sends out a frequency, a resonance that makes a statement to a responding fluid universe. It is said that the universe literally rearranges itself to accommodate our model of reality for that is the Law of Resonance at play.

Through conscious creation, via tuning and programming, we find Universal Mind speaks to us as we plug into the Divine cosmic circuit board. We are free from the need of food or sleep, free from suffering for our divinity as we consciously program in joy, grace, ease and more. Awakened and empowered via intention, programming and playing by the rules of the Divine game we create a bridge between the worlds, between paradigms, and experience the Oneness in all.

We witness the beat of the Lightworkers and of 'mainstream' society. Many are seeking to have fun, make money, and also now 'do good'. Many simply wish to create a model that allows them to live their life to their highest maximum potential physically, emotionally, mentally and spiritually in a way that honours all – positive paradigms for a new age.

Positive paradigms can be created by specific, intentional programming. Programming is repetitive instruction. As the physical and emotional bodies are governed by the mental bodies – higher and lower mind – in each 'now' moment, effective programming frees us and also directs us through life. It allows the journey of survival to be simplified so we can then thrive harmoniously. The following are a few programs that many have found most powerful:

"Dear Mother/Father Creator God, I ask that each and every moment of each day unfolds in complete and perfect alignment with Divine Will, in Divine timing."

[This program guarantees the successful fulfilment of all aligned dreams and visions and stops us constantly wondering if we are 'meant' to be doing something. It also allows us to know that if something doesn't manifest it is not in alignment, or ready under Divine Timing, so we can let it go.]

"I ask that all my sharing in each moment be for the highest good of others and the highest good of myself."

[Why would we want our sharing to be anything other than the highest? This also gives our relationships permission to be all that they can be, free of our expectations.]

> "I ask that the energy fields of my physical, emotional, mental and spiritual bodies be brought into perfect alignment for my Divine Self to consciously be made fully manifest on the physical plane, and all planes of existence, in a manner that brings me great joy, ease, grace, pleasure and abundance."

[The most powerful transmuting and creative force in the universe is that of our Divine Self (our I AM or monad). Commanding it to align us means it is done powerfully in a manner that is also joyous for we really don't need to suffer for our Divinity any more or stay in the cycle of constant processing.]

I term the above a 'baseline' program and it is designed to achieve what we wish to create. Programs can be long term – baseline – or short term to achieve a specific result. However, after re-programming, we also need to be vigilant with our thoughts choosing only to accept thinking that is aligned with limitlessness.

The reason that many experience life to be less than perfection is due to cellular memory and what we choose to focus on in each 'now' moment. Dr. Deepak Chopra shares that cells are just memories clothed in matter. The Ascended Ones suggest that if a being has had 1,000 embodiments at an average of 30 years each (to use a round figure) then we hold 30,000 years of cellular information based on memory and that's just from our Earth cycle!

So to delve into cellular memory without specific programming can keep us amused for eons and can also be time-ineffective. If we seek to know our true selves, to experience limitlessness then the most logical approach would be to focus on our limitless Divine Self, remembering also that whatever we focus on grows and becomes our reality!

A specific maintenance program for those already tuned is the one printed in our last newsletter which is designed to keep us primed during busy times where we cannot always implement our 'normal' or desired routine.

Programming for Limitlessness

> "All my bodies are tuned, toned, fit and healthy. They vibrate, and also express themselves, in perfected and synchronistic harmony to the beat of the Mother/Father Creator God. This is truth whether I eat, sleep, exercise or meditate."

This program overrides the 'self talk tape' that we continually run about the above habits and any guilt or limiting thoughts we may have about e.g. our eating, sleeping, exercising, meditation or other habits. If you are already programming, insert your own agendas. The above program simply overrides.

One of the challenges in manifestation – after aligning our will with the 'bigger picture' (Divine Will) – is timing. No doubt many have also found that just because you are in alignment doesn't mean things will manifest when you expect as there are often other pieces (and people) of the puzzle yet to be revealed, created, manoeuvre into position etc. I have been using the following program with great success as it allows for a guaranteed, perfect step by step, aligned unfoldment.

It also allows all to unfold fluidly, in Divine Time: -

"I ask that my next perfect piece/step in the Divine Plan Blueprint clearly reveal itself to me and brings to me now also the perfect players that share the creation and implementation of this blueprint so that it can be physically made manifest NOW".

As many are now aware we are now undergoing a "group initiation" where we are learning to work harmoniously together on this physical plane. This program also calls forth the right people (those who share in the manifestation of our piece of the blueprint) for us to be working with to make our visions manifest now.

For those working with or understanding simultaneous time patterns the following program allows us to re-access our past and future gifts to empower ourselves in our fulfilment of our pre-agreed piece of the 'bigger plan': -

"I instruct my I AM Presence to bring to my conscious awareness all talents, gifts, information from all past, present and future lives that will empower me further in the fulfilment of my piece of the Divine Blueprint upon this physical plane NOW."

The main benefit of mind mastery and conscious creation via programming, focus and intention, is the ability to attract, harness and direct raw creative power!

When in alignment with the 'Divine Game' this power is limitless in its capacity to magically benefit the whole!

NEW MILLENIUM GUIDELINES

- Focus on the quality of the information being shared, not external structures;
- Do not 'reinvent the wheel' – utilise the gifts and talents of each other to join together to create a powerful whole;
- Open to co-operation not competition as competition promotes separation;
- Check all guidance with the voice of joy within the heart's response;
- Take up the invitation by the Inner Teacher to attend classes – on the inner realms via meditation and quiet contemplation – and get to know who you really are;
- Be limitless in your thinking – quality thinking brings a quality life;
- Let your imagination flow – remembering that the imagination is a gift given by God to connect us to the realms of spirit;
- Be clear in your vision and share freely of this vision to those who ask;
- This is a group initiation so all must volunteer themselves motivated solely by the joy in their heart and their recognition that you share a common vision;
- Pay attention to all who may volunteer to aid the physical manifestation of your vision, for all have a part to play, a gift to bring;

- Be aware of the power of language and use trigger words. Use positive language in the oneness paradigm if you seek unity;
- Walk your talk – be a living demonstration;
- Share information, time, abundance freely;
- Remember you cannot copyright Universal Mind;
- Be fluid and flexible – expand into newness and BE in each moment.
- Tune in, chill out, let it sprout!

the Ascended Ones
A Sweet Revolution

Chapter 19

Self Healing

February 1996:
One of the greatest gifts that you can give yourself is complete mastery over the molecular structure and all of your energy fields. Mastery is about being empowered to exist in a state of pure health, constant regeneration, and freedom from dis-ease on all levels of our being. One of the first things that we may learn is to tune ourselves, realign dysfunctional energy patterns and then create perfect health within the physical body. Apart from conscious programming and indulging in quality thinking, quality feeling, and quality feeding (either from pranic nourishment or live food), there are also various practical exercises one can do daily to strengthen our energy fields and create radiant health especially prior to attempting to undergo the 21-day process.

This article elaborates on an exercise given to me by the Ascended Ones that allows us to do just that. Due to our busy lifestyles you may wish to incorporate this exercise in the shower, or as part of your meditation routine and also just as a stretching/exercise routine as an act of kindness to the body. We will be using our muscles, our minds, our intention and will, and working through the mental body to 'download' programs into the physical body.

When one is in synchronistic alignment with the divine blueprint and has no internal sabotage programs running, the following is guaranteed to work. For those interested in becoming aligned to both the timing and the unfoldment of the greater plan and realigning the internal saboteur, please refer to the "Mind Power – Beyond Psychology" chapter in the book *In Resonance*.

Firstly, understand that all is energy and that there are electromagnetic grid lines – also called meridians – that surround the Earth and that move through all matter, space and time; and that our energy meridians in our physical bodies mirror these – as above, so below.

The healing power comes from our intentionally hooking into these energy grid lines by visualising and imagining that the energy lines in our bodies can connect to the grid lines and energy matrixes in higher dimensions. For example:- when you are in the shower, rather than thinking you are being washed by water; you can imagine that what is coming out of the shower nozzle is pure liquid light, grid lines of energy that are like spaghetti, and are flowing in through the top of your head (your crown chakra), to be eagerly absorbed by your inner meridian lines.

Simplistically on one level, how physical form is created with each new embodiment is from an etheric blueprint or pattern which magnetizes to, and forms around grid lines or these energy matrixes. Through repeated embodiments, the cells, which are memories clothed in matter, densify and become heavy – basically through toxic thinking and toxic feeling – before we were practicing limitless being. As the molecular and atomic structure magnetizes into the etheric blueprint, through life experiences, the meridians that have become the inner energy lines, often atrophy or dim under the weight of what we collect in life. Therefore, by increasing the lightness in our cells and our light quotient, we are not only taking command over our molecular structure once more but we are activating fully the energy matrix of our light bodies.

Meditation

- So the visual imagery may be that you are stepping into a special chamber where golden/white emanations from the Great Central Sun (this is the source of power esoterically for this universe), begin to stream in through your crown chakra when the connection has been made. The connection is made by your visualization and intention – it is that simple. So the meditation/exercise begins as follows:

Close your eyes and take a few deep breaths.
- Ask your God Self/I AM Presence that you absorb into yourself the perfect voltage of electromagnetic/life-force energy from the highest and purest source that is perfect for your attunement NOW.
- Next visualise matching your inner meridians with the etheric grid lines – they may appear to be fine or heavier lines.
- Command, intend and visualise that once the connection is made, pure life-force healing energy begins to flow into your body, right down to the finger tips and the tips of your toes.
- Visualize and command that you are pumping up the volume – like turning a switch on a dial – until you have pure streams of golden white light energy running throughout the energy matrix in your body.
- You might like to visualise that these streams of light move out through your fingertips, through the hand chakras, through the soles of your feet and toes, hooking you into planet Earth, and allowing this pure energy force to use you as a facilitator so that it not only cleans and tunes your meridians, but the energy empoweringly moves through you and then aids in the healing of the Earth.
- You may visualise that as this energy pours into your body, it is beginning to spin like a vortex, widening the meridians and then spinning off streams of light into all the supporting cells, organs, blood stream, and bones in your body.

- Once you are hooked in and you have consciously widened the energy flow and have commanded pure life force energy to begin the healing/realignment process, you may begin further conscious programming.

- The mantra for the first aspect of healing is for forgiveness. It is not as if we are less than perfection, it is just that we carry cellular memory from other timeframes where we may have believed we were.
- So the first mantra while you are watching these energies flow through you is to open your heart and to say to the universe, "I forgive and I am forgiven".
- Keep visualising the energy moving through you, breathe in deeply, and on the out-breath, repeat the mantra, "I forgive and I am forgiven" until the Inner One guides you to stop. Trust your intuition on this.
- The next healing mantra is, "I now release all discordant energies from all my energy fields". This may be shortened to the word "release".
- Visualize that as the light floods in through your crown chakra pumping up the meridians, that it is coming through with such force that it is expelling from all your cells through the pores of your skin, all discordant energies.
- You may wish to imagine that as the light flows into your body and fills every cell, that it floods out through the top of your head, like champagne being poured into a glass overflowing, and begins to create an electromagnetic bubble of light around you.
- Visualize that it extends as far as your outstretched hands and at least six inches out again. This electromagnetic bubble and force-field that you create, you can intend to be completely impenetrable to all energies but those that are for your highest good.

- If you keep this bubble permanently placed around you and filled with pure God force energy, then all energies around the planet from sources known and unknown will either be rejected or absorbed and transmuted without actually touching your core.
- So as you do your release, and visualise these discordant energies moving through the pores of your skin, when they connect with the light around you, know that they too are automatically transmuted and realigned and therefore have no detrimental effect energetically to your environment.
- The next step after you have been intuitively guided to stop using the "release" command is the "heal" command. Again, the power of this is in your intention and the belief that you have the power to heal all discordant energies and disease in your fields.
- Visualize that as the energy floods in through your crown chakra and is pumping up the volume and power of life-force within, that this energy as it floods into every cell begins to transform your cells from shrivelled up sultanas to round, luscious, light-filled grapes (or whatever imagery that will create the effect of your cells healing, regenerating then renewing into perfect health).
- The next command is "renew". The visual imagery is similar to the above.
- You may then begin to use the mantra:
- "Release, forgive, forgive, release, heal, renew, renew, heal, heal to perfection as divinely intended NOW".

- Once you have done this you may visualise that your hand chakras have been fully activated into their healing power, are plugged directly into the purest healing power of the universal life force.
- As you sit in meditation, you may wish to place them on any particular part of your body that may need healing and command and visualise that this is done.

- A good way to test this and measure your abilities as they grow in self-healing, is to pick one aspect of your body that you would like healed, concentrate on it daily until physical change is witnessed.
- For example, a vein on your leg, or a mole on your hand, or a small scar. As you sit in meditation having plugged into the grid lines and tuned yourself as previously recommended, while your hands are laid on your own body you may command on the out-breath:
  - "Heal body NOW" or "heal veins NOW".
- The visual imagery is that you are attracting to your hand chakra pure and powerful forces of healing energy that are moving through your hand chakra and being absorbed into the part of the body that needs healing, and you visualise the cells like sponges absorbing the light, transmuting toxic energies, and healing itself into perfection.
- Next, (for those who wish to do physical exercises with this) visualise yourself plugged in to the energy matrixes of the pure healing forces, that you have pumped up the volume, and the energy is flowing through you now like a wide fast-flowing river. You may begin to intuitively move, either like you are doing a sacred dance or more isometric exercises. You may use this to go through a whole series of stretching exercises as well as yogic postures and exercises. The benefits will not only be increased suppleness and grace, but also the healing and realignment of your energy fields. When you do your dancing or stretching extend your muscles to their maximum capacity by contracting them and then releasing them in a pulsating rhythm, stretching further and further as you progress.
- All the time you are visualising that flooding in through your hands and feet and crown chakra and also through all your other chakras, is pure healing force energy that you are magnetizing into your body, by your command and intention. The visual imagery then becomes that you are interconnected with the energy streams of all creation and hooked into a river of oneness. You may then also focus your mind on a particular organ or area of your body that you intuit may need healing or extra attention, as you move.
- Daily practice of the above techniques will ensure a strong vehicle, especially when coupled with pure feeding, pure thinking, and pure feeling, and whatever other exercise program you are intuitively guided to do.
- The Ascended Ones say that the stronger the physical vehicle, the more intense light energy we can carry and can emanate through us, changing the pulse of, and transmission from, our electromagnetic fields. As we consciously realign

our energy fields we will attract to us levels of reality that reflect our own expanding consciousness. The above techniques will also ensure the full activation of our etheric energy matrixes termed our light bodies and will prepare for conscious future teleportation.

March 2006:

Other Self Healing tools and methodologies are covered in my e-Book *Harmonious Healing and the Immortals Way* released in 2005.

Regarding exercise and the prana program over the last decade, I have noticed so many people who post-conversion look undernourished and underweight. I cannot stress enough the need to treat the body as a temple and to exercise it lovingly. Find or develop a cross training program that suits you, that you enjoy so you do it and that will build muscle mass.

Chapter 20

Postscript end May 1996 – Press Reaction

May 1996:
I am guided to add the following notes after my recent tour to Hong Kong and the USA, where I had the opportunity to interact with radio, television and newspaper journalists, and many others, regarding the issue of Living on Light.

It is important to understand, for those who choose to undergo the aforementioned process, that in doing so you will literally push many Western people beyond their 'acceptable framework of reality'. One thing I found in doing press interviews is that it was a challenge to explain in a five or ten minute timeframe a reality that has personally taken over twenty years to create.

In order to understand the so-called phenomena of living on light one must have some understanding of the higher light science and laws of energy. The experiential and intellectual research my colleagues and myself are undertaking in these fields is literally creating a new language and a new paradigm of reality. This new reality is also quite easy to understand for those interested enough to study and work with their own intuitive knowing and discernment.

I was asked by a journalist about the fact that young children die each minute from starvation and malnutrition and that surely changing our beliefs and mindset about nutritional requirements of food would not save them. When one understands the dynamics of energy one understands that children are interconnected to their parents energy fields, particularly the mother until 18 months to two years. They then begin the process the separation which some schools of thought say is completed between 14 and 21 depending on the individual soul. As each adult group is exposed to the reality of many individuals worldwide practically being able to live on light they will lose their fear, change their mindset and consequently the energy transmissions they emit will change to which the children will respond. All is interconnected and the secret is in the understanding of the power of the mind over our molecular structure.

So, it is also important to keep the focus clear. This is a process of freedom. It is not about whether one eats or doesn't eat. Statistically approximately 98%, of over 200 or more individuals who choose this 21-day process journey return to eating food and 60% of those do it via slower methods. Yet they hold within them, on a cellular level, both an intellectual and experiential understanding and knowing that they can, if they choose, be purely sustained by Liquid Light. Thus they have removed another fear.

Globally we are pioneering a new way of being that has huge social and economic ramifications. If either of the scientific or medical fraternities were busily pioneering a practical solution that may save two thirds of the world population from dying of hunger they would gain tremendous positive media exposure. However because this path challenges deeply held belief systems in Western culture many find themselves confronted by old paradigms of fear, especially fear through ignorance.

We, as Lightworkers, are creating the new paradigm of love and light and living on light is a simply a by-product of this. We are learning to utilise the 4/5ths of the brain that science and medicine say we do not use. That is because living in this third/fourth dimensional reality only takes 1/5th of our brain power. The rest is to be used for accessing higher consciousness. This paradigm is about consciousness, defining energy by the consciousness attached to it – highest consciousness, highest energy bands, highest possibilities.

Also having available an extra 90-95% amount of energy, that we currently use in the digestion of food, (some sources say we use 40% of our energy to digest food) means we are free to use this energy for truly exploring our unlimited potential. Sometimes this creates a challenge especially when you are with people who believe they need fuel (food) and rest stops and as with everything we need to honour all.

Recently while travelling I had the opportunity to explore the reality of living without sleep. As my energy was so synchronized to the energy of the Mt. Shasta vortex I found that I was not tired and couldn't sleep for nearly a week during my stay there. Normally I would find in the morning that I would be tired, listless and have telltale 'bags under my eyes'. Aware of this 'old' reaction to sleep deprivation I simply surrendered to my state of awakeness, used the time to reflect and meditate and deprogrammed then reprogrammed the body to be energized and fresh in the morning and so I was. This was simply an experiment that worked and has given me the gift of a new level of freedom. I know when I am supercharged with prana that I do not need sleep, I do not need food and so I am freer, empowered, independent from beliefs that confine so many upon this plane simply through their lack of understanding.

As more and more individuals explore the unlimited nature of their being the path becomes easier, the inspiration of living examples more obvious and commonplace. As a "cosmic telepath" – a being who receives and transmits telepathically to beings on many dimensions – I am advised that due to the transformation occurring on the planet and the influx of finer vibrations it is not necessary for anyone to undergo this 21-day process. One can simply decide to let this unified energy field (as named by quantum physicists, God by the religious; and Universal Life Force by the new agers) sustain them and so it will be for the potency of the field has increased. The success of this is dependent on the individuals command over their molecular structure and the levels of trust and faith they have in their own Divinity.

To some this is like saying, "don't catch that plane to Paris just dematerialize then rematerialize", which to many is easier said than done. Having a set process, that allows for the conversion of the energy fields of the lower bodies to be sustained by light, is like the plane. The end outcome is the same but it is quicker and simpler than the years of training and de & re-programming a novice may take to learn the art of dematerialization.

We all have these abilities but we have simply forgotten them and the process of remembering tends to also bring up doubts and fears. We, humanity as a whole, are being asked to take a quantum leap from fear to love, from darkness to light. The new paradigm of this 7th Golden Age is the creation of the Diamond Age where love and light are here to break the cyclic pattern of the rise and fall of humanity.

My personal paradigm of reality is to live my life in a manner that utilizes my highest maximum potential physically, emotionally, mentally and spiritually. I see my body as a bio-computer, my thoughts are the software, my life the printout. Myself, and many others, are now consciously rewriting our individual and collective software programs so we can exist harmoniously, as unified fields of energy on this plane, in a way that honours all lifeforms. Living on light is a by-product of this that also acknowledges and honours our own innate ability to allow the 'God within' to sustain us on all levels.

Universal Laws of Energy decree simply that what we focus on will grow, so as we choose to focus on our perfection, on our Divinity, so will we recognise and experience the Divinity and perfection in all. It is a time of having the courage to shine this light, 'walk our talk' and enjoy each step along the way.

2nd Postscript – Social Reaction

November 1996:
One of the early decisions that I made when offering to share the information of this journey in book form, was whether to do a further chapter on the "after the process" reality. As time goes on I have witnessed many individuals go through this 21-day process, or similar 'versions', remain on liquids for a week, a month, six months or a year or more. Somewhere along the way they make the decision to return to social eating once more. Again the reasons are as varied as each individual yet as a detached observer and researcher I have again been interested in the commonalties.

In New Zealand this Spring I had the opportunity to reconnect with numerous individuals who had undergone the 21-day process since my visit there the previous year. Discussions revealed that the common desire to return to eating was due to social pressure, lack of support, feeling alienated or isolated in their choice. Readers are aware from earlier sharing in this text that the general Western society reaction to individuals being sustained by light at this time varies from outright disbelief to a reaction of "why on Earth would you! I'd never give up my food – I get too much pleasure from eating and socialising over food!" plus other reactions along that line.

There is very little support or understanding regarding this type of choice at this time. After the excitement wears off from being able to live by the pranic forces, a day to day reality check sets in. You may find yourself no longer invited to dinner parties as people may not feel comfortable with you being there and not eating or 'breaking bread' with them. Others somehow seem to feel guilty that they still wish to eat when they may intuitively know they really don't need to and your presence serves as a living testimonial which may trigger feelings where they may feel they are weak willed (so some say). Again there is so much that is triggered by your choice and example.

This is a very complex and confrontational issue. At this time this is not a path walked by many. Some feel lonely, get tired of being different, miss feeling 'part of the gang', stop talking about it, stop feeling joyous about it, play games of 'pretending' to eat in some situations that require their presence and where they feel it is inappropriate to draw attention to themselves. The list goes on.

It is important to realise that all pioneering work stands alone initially, that's what pioneering is about. Daring to be different, having the courage to forge a new path. Accepting the ridicule and judgment in your stride. Knowing that ignorance breeds fear and that in the West this is a journey, an understanding that many are uneducated in, unexposed to.

Personally I rarely arrange social occasions over dinner as I have found that for whatever reason it can cause people discomfort to see me there and not sharing on that level. Socialising over afternoon tea or in coffee shops avoids the eating or not eating issue. To many people when they hear you don't eat the issue becomes very black and white. If they see you having soup – due to the social game – or honey in your tea, they immediately say "I thought you didn't eat. You can live on that!" in a manner that can be so cynical and judgmental it is outstanding. Once or twice may be fine but this is a typical reaction by many to many on this path. After awhile you may feel as though you are walking into the eye of a hurricane, swimming against the tide of conventionality and one can get quite weary. I hear the feedback. I've experienced so much of this myself and yet … the gifts the journey brings re self discovery and magic truly are limitless.

So if you undergo this journey be aware. it may be natural for you but it's not natural to 99.9% of the Western population. Structure life so that you create the least reaction if you wish for ease or non confrontation. Apply some common sense. Tune to the energies of those around. Program so the highest may be shared. Be aware that what excites you often hold no excitement for others. Just because you may feel that your new ability of not eating and maintaining full health and energy is miraculous, most people still dismiss it as ludicrous.

Even in the 'new age' arena and among alternative therapists there is a high level of scepticism. Alternative therapists are just getting mainstream consciousness to take responsibility for their own health through improving diet, exercise, nutrition and educating people to understand the role that unresolved negative emotions have in the creation of disease. This idea of no food, no vitamins, no nutritional supplements rocks that industry as deeply as the alternative therapy "heal thyself or prevent dis-ease in the first place" idea is currently rocking the billion dollar pharmaceutical industry!

Often when we have been involved with TV work the program concerned will also interview a medical practitioner who always says that it is impossible to live without nourishment and the fuel one gains from food. This is true as we do require adequate nourishment to maintain a healthy system. What they fail to realise however is that we are being nourished just from a different fuel source. As many Western practitioners have not heard of prana then the idea that we can survive without food sets up an immediate reaction of "well she is either deluded or it's an absolute miracle" to quote a doctor from Huntington Memorial Hospital in California when questioned about our work on the show "Strange Universe"!

Chapter 21

"To Eat or not to Eat"

November 1996:
Now what? You've been through the process, you've gained great insights, you KNOW you can live on light. You've realised that the needs of the physical body are minimal, that it really is the emotional body missing the dinner/social agenda or the mental body's boredom with lack of flavour or whatever your particular challenge is.

For those who have no challenge – hats off – you truly are unique! Enjoy the journey and take it to the next level! Ask your DOW to teach you how to access cosmic particles in a way that you can safely stop taking fluids. Just breathe and enjoy and write to me of your insights and learning so it can be shared with others as we continue to research and report on this 'experiment' down under!

To me again this journey is not about whether one eats or not. Its importance is in the freedom it provides. The freedom to be at choice, to dictate to the body as the master in a house; to free oneself from limitation, from beliefs that we need to eat or sleep or age or die; to have the courage to explore our full potential.

It is about laying a new pattern into cellular memory based on first hand proven experience! Whether one lives for months or years from the pranic forces is irrelevant. The body knows it can once you have allowed it to be for it retains the memory. The more who are aware of this, the more common place it becomes, the more every day and the less miraculous.

Being all we can be is our God given right not a state reserved for holy men or ancient sages. It is about being the Christed One, it is a time of the second coming where the coming is each individual coming into full conscious awareness of the Divine One within. It is then allowing the Divine One within to take care of all our needs on all levels as we traverse this path through life!

Once we have given the Divine One permission to be fully evident in our lives we may consciously begin the process we call RE-IMAGING.

Re-Imaging

RE "IMAGING" is channelling change by recreating positively from cellular memory. Its conscious application allows us to bridge the veils of linear time into simultaneous time.

In the Mind Mastery article (TEV August/Sept. 96 issue) we instructed that "All the gifts and talents, plus power and learning from initiations in past, present and future lifetimes be brought into our full conscious awareness, in a manner to empower us fully in the creation and manifestation of our piece of the Divine Blueprint into physical reality NOW".

In the Mastery game of "conscious reality creation" we can literally re-invent our physical imagery by tuning all the energy fields to their perfect beat. This is also enhanced by focusing on our cellular memory of perfection and Divinity, when we expressed fully our Divine nature.

This understanding was enhanced for me when recently working in the field of those addicted to the vibration of the drug, heroin. Dr. Deepak Chopra's research shares that cells are memories clothed in matter, cells are 'homes' or data storage units for memories.

Consequently we have within us 'reels' of memory – emotional experience – footage. When one consciously tunes oneself through meditation and programming our vibration changes as does the electromagnetic signal we emit and life can become limitless depending on our intent and programming into cellular memory.

We instructed the individual that while in meditation he could ask "that the memory and consequent vibrational experience of the drug heroin – be released from cellular memory into his conscious awareness through the endorphins of the brain". This way he could enjoy the 'flavour' of the drug based on the stored memory of the previous experience rather than physically injecting regular 'fresh doses'.

Combined with the energy state change – beta waves to alpha to theta – that meditation provides, the body's cells, via memory, would then overlay the feeling that the drug heroin released.

Similarly we can 'state change' via connected conscious breathing and while in the meditative states begin to access deep memories and literally reconstruct ourselves.

We may begin the exercise by calling forth the memory of our time
- as Priest/Priestess in Lemuria;
- as Priest/Priestess in Atlantis;
- as Priest/Priestess in Egypt;
- as Priest/Priestess in Avalon or Glastonbury with the time of the Druids;
- as Priest/Priestess in the Ancient of Days;
- memories of our training in healing temples; music and art temples, crystal caverns, memories of our Earth Goddess self; the monk, the Gypsy.
- Imagine yourself once more in these times, in your power, tuned and masterful.
- Feel the energy flow into your emotional body as these memories are released from the database of your cells into your conscious awareness.
- Imagine your physical form as you stand tall in your power. Perhaps tall and muscular or small and refined. Whatever – just allow the image to flow into your mind's eye. Again keeping any image that makes your heart sing.

Re-imaging is about re-formulating from a cellular level, without the cost and pain of a surgeon's knife or a psychologists couch.

I recently had the pleasure of connecting with Rhys Hart, a Brisbane naturopath (and an Elvis Pavarotti impersonator for fun) involved in the research of limb regrowth. When a person loses a limb their body still retains the physical imprint in the etheric body energy field so regrowth is again, mind over matter.

Similarly with cellular memories. We hold the memory, the experience of so many lifetimes of being tuned, talented, excellent at some thing or another.

Re-imaging is about selectively choosing the brilliance from the memory pool within to re-create ourselves into the physical, emotional and mental image we wish to be now. Mind over matter. A Master living within a physical vehicle commanding and guiding the emergence of Mastery.

Imagine all the things you'd like to be. Whatever flows into your mind comes to be acknowledged and is a mirror of what has been. This process is like a smorgasbord where the creator (you) selects the best from each lifetime knowing that what we focus on – by Universal Law – must be. As we envision so shall we BE.

ALSO you may wish to instruct:
"I NOW command that my four lower bodies – the physical, emotional, mental and spiritual – fully manifest into this physical reality, the perfect image and Divine qualities of my I AM Presence or God Self."

Multiplicity

Multiplicity is the natural evolution and companion of re-imaging. When one successfully utilizes re-imaging – evident by both physical and emotional change – one realizes that one can have any aspect of the multitude of characters and images we possess, in conscious 'residence' at any time.

For example, I know that there is an aspect of myself that is tuned, strong and fit. It is the me I feel when I am regularly exercising and caring for the physical vehicle.

I also have an aspect that can be a workaholic, too 'busy' to sleep or exercise. Sometimes after a few weeks of busy-ness and ignoring the body, I can feel tired, less energetic, even listless. When this feeling, or recognition, comes to me I simply DECIDE TO BE – and command forth – the warrior woman, fit and strong. An energy shifts within me and that's exactly how I feel. Instant energy 'pick me up' or state change.

Our cells will release any aspect of ourselves we command forth. I can be limited or limitless. Strong or weak. Energised or energyless. The physical body responds to these commands automatically. Like shape shifting practiced by the Shaman.

Similarly we can command forth characters for various roles. The lover, where you have re-imaged yourself to be your version of the most glorious lover; the warrior or shaman empowered to operate in physical reality joyously; the healer or one in service; whatever you require. Just call it forth and BE IT FULLY FOCUSED IN EACH NOW MOMENT.

With multiplicity you can also split your energy fields and send your healer/warrior/shaman self off to other realms while you attend to physical acts in your day-to-day reality. Splitting energy through our focused intention is about learning to bilocate and operate simultaneously and consciously through time and we talk about this in my book *In Resonance*.

Transmutation – To Eat or not to Eat
The Pranic Journey continued

October 1997:

It's interesting to watch how when certain aspects of life are destined to be, they simply blossom. Four years ago when I began my conscious journey of pranic nourishment, I had no idea that I could be aiding in the pioneering of a small but potent movement in Western culture. At the time it was just another natural step in my personal journey of refinement. Now it is an option well established in both New Zealand and Australia, and also in various new age circles in Asia, Europe and the USA. To keep the information clear and focused, I was guided to write this book and I constantly get the feeling that being sustained by the divine spark within is the way of a very 'civilised' future and will soon be commonplace for many choosing a more simplified and refined expression in life.

What this article expands upon is the "what then?" After a being has proven to themselves that they can be completed pranically nourished, and no longer need to eat, then what? Energetically our global societies still heavily support the socialization around and the emotional dependence on food, and this new movement of pranic nourishers is not yet large enough to pose a threat to McDonalds or the restaurant trade generally. But what about the day to day realities of those involved?

We know from our research and follow-up work that most individuals return to light eating, at least for social occasions, and sometimes just for the pleasure of taste itself. Personally, as mentioned previously, after two years or so on light broths now and then, and generally only having three glasses of liquid per day, with no vitamins or minerals, I was led into the game of conscious transmutation.

One day I decided to indulge socially with coffee and a little bit of cheesecake, for emotional body reasons, and I ended up with excruciating stomach pains. For my body it was like dropping a chemical bomb into an extremely purified system. My reaction was that I needed to either never have anything toxic or begin the journey of conscious transmutation. This was a journey of changing the vibration of any substance so that it harmonized positively with my own. Coffee and cheesecake seemed like a pleasurable way to start! And so I let go once more of ideas of what was nutritionally sound, as I knew prana was nourishing me, and I focused on taste sensation and transmutation.

It's interesting that what many think tastes great is also often said to be 'bad' nutritionally, and is generally advised to be taken in moderation. When taken in small amounts upon a basis of fresh live food, the body readily deals with any toxicity and the waste is carried out easily amongst the roughage through normal elimination. There is a basic understanding that the human mind daily recreates the physical body by choice of quality thinking and feeling and quality feeding or by toxic thinking which also then releases toxic emotions which may then guide us to indulge in toxic feeding patterns.

The Ascended Ones, in their guidance of my pranic nourishment journey, had shared that the only reason many lightworkers were healthy, was because they believed and expected that by choosing to eat nutritionally balanced foods, take supplements and do exercise they would create health. And so it did. But was it their unequivocal belief or the actual food substance ingested? In my research I've swayed to the theory that it was their expectation, as I know of many stories of Indian yogis who took poison and transmuted it without effect.

Our minds are so powerful they can attract and sustain a multitude of realities. In his "Nature of Reality" discussion, Dr. Deepak Chopra shares "the human body is a physical machine that has somehow learned to think, that it's the dance of molecules that creates the epi-phenomena of consciousness, thoughts, feelings and emotions, desires, concepts, ideas, philosophies, dogma, religion … somehow these molecules move around and we get this epi-phenomena called thought. We have physical machines that have learned to think."

Perhaps on another level there was pure thought which then created the vehicle to house one aspect of its own consciousness. If that is so, then surely this same pure thought can self-heal, reconstruct, alter, re-image and sustain the vehicle it has created.

Science proves that our body is a complex machine of billions of cells intricately connected and now even many of the staunchest traditionalists seem to recognise the mind/body connection. Dr. Chopra goes on to say in the same article "that how we have learned to view the human body has not been correct, that the human body is a dynamic bundle of energy, information and intelligence that constantly is renewing itself and is in exchange with the larger field of energy, information and intelligence that we call the universe". He says that it is "fundamentally the movement of consciousness which expresses itself" as the processes of eating, breathing, digestion, metabolism and elimination. And if we could see this consciousness at work we "would see how effortlessly, how easily you can change your body and in fact are doing so all the time".

According to Deepak, with every breath we breathe in, and then out, there are ten to the power of twenty-two atoms. So we are in a constant state of flux and change and what we are creating is a direct result of our intention and awareness. In three weeks a quadrillion atoms – ten to the power of fifteen atoms – have gone through the body of every other species on this planet. Each of us breathing in and breathing out. Ninety-eight per cent of our atoms we replace yearly. So the shelf life of a physical body is shorter than the data stored in our cells, and yet it is the data – emotional body sound waves and mental body light rays – that determine whether our cells degenerate or regenerate.

As Deepak shares "scientists are beginning to see that it is not thoughts which are the products of molecules but in fact molecules are structured out of fluctuations of information in a field of infinite information. That it is consciousness which is the phenomena and matter which is the epi-phenomena. It is consciousness which conceives, governs, constructs and actually becomes physical matter." Thoughts create molecules called neuropeptides. Messages are transmitted chemically – mental body, emotional body, then physical body. Or even mental body directly into the physical body.

This is the core understanding for transmutation.

The immune cell is the circulating nervous system, it is programmed to fight disease, to recognise carcinogens and transmute them. Receptors for neuropeptides are found throughout the body. Chemical signals through neuropeptides to receptors is the body's true language – the signal type reflects the thought – positive or negative, limited or limitless. What the above understanding leads us to believe is that we as masters of the vehicle, because of how the vehicle is structured, have the complete power through mind mastery to transform, to transmute, to self-heal, and even re-image the physical vehicle. And we are only as limited as we believe ourselves to be.

So before I get the nutritionists reacting negatively to what I am suggesting, please be aware that before I began this part of my journey, I was literally a food purist on a very balanced vegetarian diet for over twenty years. A regular meditator, a regular exerciser, I had established through this a very powerful spirit/mind/body connection. I am now simply taking this understanding to a more refined level which happily is now being supported by the neuropeptide understanding.

Even our 'gut instinct' idea comes from the reality that our stomach also has the peptides and makes the same chemicals as the brain when it thinks. A thought releases chemicals transmitted via neuropeptides into their receptors in each organ which also becomes the basis of how we can self-heal the body totally or each organ individually. Because the thinking mechanisms in the organs have not evolved to the stage of self-doubt, all that is commanded into them, they think they have the capacity to do. So perhaps the miracle of spontaneous remission is triggered by an intense will to live then laying that will down into the cells via neuropeptides, and so healing sets in. According to Deepak, what science is discovering is that every cell thinks and is interconnected chemically to every other cell.

One of the most powerful healing agents to be manufactured in our bodies and boost the immune system are interleukins and interferons which are released by the emotionally impacting feelings of joy. When we are in panic or fear we release degrees of cortisol adrenaline which destroys the immune system. Simplistically, the mental body interprets reality. This interpretation triggers an emotional response. The type and depth of emotional response triggers chemical pulses – neuropeptides to receptors – within the physical body, thus creating either harmony or disease.

Lately, I tend to liken the physical body to a dog. First you must begin a conscious relationship with it, see it as the vehicle to allow you to exist more deeply in physical reality. Once you have made the connection with the body consciousness, then you can begin to program it to create a mutually empowering relationship. Similarly, once you have established a level of communication/trust with a dog, you can then begin to have it respond happily to your command and in return it serves you and even teaches you sometimes quite beautifully. Sometimes when training a dog (our physical body) new tricks – like pranic nourishment and transmutation – there is a time lag between old limiting habitual patterns ceasing and new empowering ones beginning.

So for me in the last two years I have pushed the body to extreme by sleeping an average of 2-3 hours a night (I used to require 8-10), and once a week, and sometimes more, ingesting toxic substances for flavour and pleasure hits with no regard to their nutritional value. And I have learned that one can be perfectly nourished from prana – as my recent haemaview (blood) analysis confirmed, yet still have a certain level of toxicity as a L.I.S.T.E.N. diagnosis may show. Intuitively I realised that I had reached a point to give the dog a rest from learning party tricks and to give it a bit of tender loving care. For me it simply meant to rest a little more, and take flavourful mouthfuls of non-irritating substances such as a juice rather than a coffee perhaps when being social.

Many pranic nourishers, who maybe snack once a week, have developed an amazing pure and refined system while those who exist on prana and water only have no food substance toxicity to deal with. Those who enjoy the pleasure of the odd mouthful can either choose non-irritating, that is more natural substances, or play the game of conscious transmutation. Both the game of pranic nourishment and conscious transmutation gives us access to our own inherent creative power and also expands our consciousness to recognise the limitless nature of our being. As the German philosopher Nietzsche said, "We live on the presumption that we think when it is equally possible that we are being thought".

March 2006:
People often ask me how to transmute all substances that they ingest into a frequency more suitable for their bodies and we cover this in detail in the book *The Food of Gods* using digestive grids and specific programming or via irradiating food substances with light, intention and prayer.

August 2012 Update:
After being asked so many times what led me to begin this unexpected journey into living purely on prana, I was guided to write the following book.

Breatharian Pathways – *Memories & Motivations*. In this book Jasmuheen finally shares her memories and motivations around her public work with living on prana. From her times with Jesus, and the disciple Luke, to her times in Cathar country and being starved to death during the inquisition, to the life of an woman in India whose great loss revealed the Breatharian way; to dealing with Sadhus and sages in India modern day – all of this and much more Jasmuheen shares in this book as well as finally revealing the details of some of her most spectacular media trials as she continues to educate the world into this phenomena. She writes: "Is it too much to believe that there is a wise and loving force behind creation? Or that great love brought creation into being, that great love breathes us and gives us life and that great love can heal and guide, as so many have attested? Knowing this, is it too difficult to believe that this wise and loving force that exists within and around us, can also nourish our physical bodies with their breakfast, lunch and dinners?". Click here for more on this.

Chapter 22

The Balance of Being

November 1996:
The previous article focused on how it is possible to be pranically nourished and also transmute toxic feeding so the body can thrive. It dealt basically with the mind/body neuropeptides/receptors connections. Regarding the emotional body we now enter into a discussion of pheromones on a physically evidenced level.

Various experiments, including ones at Stanford University, USA, with mice, have concluded that plants and animals communicate through pheromones. According to Dr. Chopra, this research had led to an openness to the idea that "those pheromones in fact may also be the molecular substrate of our emotions". It appears that the new dynamics of neurobiology are beginning to understand the esoteric idea of the interconnectness of all life forms and their own individual spirit/mind/emotion/body harmony.

Experiments have meant that now "it's known that in fact for every single emotion that we have there is a counterpart, a molecular event that happens not only inside our body but in fact we release these pheromones as information substrates into the environment". Hence, how we intuitively pick up tension in a room, or suppressed anger in a person. So perhaps our sixth sense of intuition also triggers the release of these pheromones giving us feelings of peace or discomfort.

Dr. Chopra continues to share that the most ancient of texts, the Veda, says "that if you can remember who you are you will suddenly recognise that you, in fact, are the creator". The Veda says, "as is the atom, so is the universe; as is the microcosm so is the macrocosm; as is the human body, so is the cosmic body; as is the human mind, so is the cosmic mind". He goes on to call the cosmic mind a "non local field of information with self-referral cybernetic feedback loops". He shares "our bodies are literally the music of nature. We have here a symphony which is part of a symphony that has been there forever." The Veda says "behind the mask of mortality is the quantum mechanical body, that subtle causal body … was never born and it never dies".

Healing and pranic nourishment are then about BEing in balance and moving beyond the restrictions of our denser bodies. On a quantum level we are literally systems of energy. Anyone who has researched quantum physics and/or Deepak Chopra's work PLUS had experiences through meditation of energy, know this to be factual whether Western science and medicine are able to yet confirm this conclusively at all or not.

On an esoteric and quantum level it is about the harmonics of sound waves and light rays. A subtle blend of energy mix, applied both individually and collectively. Balance is about finding the right personal energy mix within our spiritual, mental, emotional and physical bodies. For me living on light and pranic nourishment was an easy transition for the physical body and it was very harmonious about the remembrance* and daily living of this. However after a few years my emotional body was slightly out of balance and savouring flavour for emotional pleasure now and then brought it into balance. Then my physical body became slightly out of balance due to toxicity and so the mental body energy was increased for transmutation to bring the physical body into balance once more. Energy is fluid, what is balance for one may not be balance for another as we all have a pre-determined perfect resonance. Once the mind/body connection is established we become aware very quickly when we are out of balance.

Formulating or finding the right energy mix to create the life we want is like baking a cake. The type and dosage of ingredients determines the type and flavour of the cake. A friend of mine recently described himself as non-monogamous. He travels a lot and likes the idea of a 'girl in every port', the thrill of the chase, this wooing etc. fed his emotional body. Other friends, male and female, have decided they enjoy a deep and meaningful monogamous relationship with one partner. They share that to them now, because their focus and attention is on their blueprint, an intimate relationship is the icing on the cake. Potent and yummy when on, but not contributing a huge proportion of an already yummy cake. For my 'non monogamous' male friend, exciting and different relationships form his cake and the rest of his life is the icing; and he is happy in his creation. This is a perfect example of finding the right energy mix and focus to bring balance to our individual lives yet also how we are all so different with what we personally may feel actually brings us into pleasurable balance.

The idea of being in mastery is being in mastery of our energy fields – our spiritual/mental/emotional body mix, the health of our all our bodies. There are countless methods to consciously tune ourselves to express our mastery. Powerful tuning comes from consciously choosing to have quality thoughts, quality emotions, and quality feeding every moment of the day. Also tools from meditation and reprogramming to recapitulation, where we redefine our response to memories and change their energy impact. As Deepak shares, "we link stimuli to certain memories and every time we're exposed to these stimuli, we reinvent the universe and ourselves according to the memories … it's estimated that the average human has sixty thousand thoughts a day … what is disconcerting is the ninety per cent of the thoughts you have today are the ones you had yesterday", and that these often limiting thoughts are constantly producing biochemical responses and loop patterns of behaviour.

Individually we become what we think, collectively we become what we see and witness. "If you want to recreate the world then look at it with fresh eyes" (Lord Shiva). A person's whole reality will change if instead of viewing the world from a point of looking for lack, discord and disharmony and differences, they simply look for divine perfection and ask to be in perfect synchronistic balance with the force of creation – divine consciousness.

Bliss is being happy for no reason.

A tuned individual is a blissful individual.

So perfect health is also perfect power. By this we mean the power to regenerate the body, to cease the ageing process, to keep the physical body in an immortal state to house our immortal souls. Physical immortality is simply freedom of choice, to be here joyously while we fulfill our part in the divine blueprint. When this contract is complete we can then take the body up into light or drop it as we are guided at the time.

If self-healing and self-regeneration and re-imaging and immortality stretch our minds and makes us wonder if we truly are powerful enough to do all that, then enjoy the following discourse given by Jesus to onlookers after he successfully brought a dead man back to life …

Excerpt from *The Life and Teachings of the Masters of the Far East:*
"When we stand one with the sum of all intelligence, and recognise ourselves as an actual part of that intelligence, and know conclusively that this is the great principle, God, we shall soon find ourselves conscious of the fact that all intelligence throughout the whole cosmic universe is working with us. We also realise quickly that the intelligence of all great genius, as well as the little mentality of the single cell of the body, is working with us in perfect harmony and accord. This is the One Great Intelligent Cosmic Mind that we are positively allied with. Indeed we are that very mind; we are the self-consciousness of the universe. The instant we feel this very thing nothing can keep us from our Godhead."

The Luscious Lifestyles Tuning Program

Update April 2001:

So much has happened over the last 5 years since the living on light phenomena hit the global stage. With over 10,000 individuals now allowing the Divine to feed them, plus many more in the Qigong community who exist in the state of Bigu, the idea that the Divine cannot just love, guide and heal us, but also feed us, is slowly being accepted.

As the ability to live on light is completely related to a person's daily lifestyle, the actual 21-day initiation has become passé as more and more holistic living practitioners find themselves eating light. Our research has found that the long term practice of meditation, prayer, programming, vegetarian diet, exercise, service, silence in nature and the use of Mantras and devotional songs, expand a person's consciousness, thus allowing them to exist in the zone of the Divine where so much more than normal reality is possible. We call this 8 point program the Luscious Lifestyles Program – or L.L.P. – and it is basically designed to tune people into the frequency where living on light is no longer a miracle but easily possible as it changes a personas resonance and allows them to magnetize more cosmic particles.

In 1996, shortly before this book was published in the German language, a young man went into a coma after the process, was admitted to hospital, woke up and was on the road to recovery when he had an epileptic fit, fell over and hit his head on the back of the bed and died.

As I have already mentioned, two years later an Australian woman refused to stop the initiation even though her caregiver recommended she do so. She also fell into a coma and was subsequently taken off life support by her family, when the doctors found her to have internal damage from dehydration and other issues. Her caregiver and his wife were later jailed for negligence.

In late 1999, another Australian woman living in Scotland died when she chose to ignore the guidelines in this book, stopped eating and drinking, travelled for a few days, and ended up collapsing from exhaustion and dying from exposure to the elements.

While I have had no dealing with any parties involved, and I was fully investigated and exonerated by police still the blame of their deaths landed on my doorstep as some in the world felt that the living on light reality is impossible and unsafe. The fact that in 1999, 280,000 Americans died from over-eating is to them, irrelevant. The fact that after alcohol and tobacco, meat eating is the third biggest killer in the Western world is also to many irrelevant.

Yet to me every human being must take responsibility for their own life and act accordingly. If we live a healthy lifestyle through food choices we can live longer, and prana is a food choice—not a common one yet, but however it is a valid and healthy one and thousands now attest to this.

Regardless of whether living on light and being nourished by prana is socially acceptable or not, the fact remains for thousands it is now a preferable lifestyle and pretending that it is not possible so that non-believers can feel more comfortable in their reality, is not going to happen.

For those wishing to be nourished by the Divine I can only urge you to prepare as well as possible by following the Get Fit for Prana guidelines as follows.

Also I must stress again that the 21-day initiation does not necessarily guarantee that the Divine will feed you, for only your daily practice of the Luscious Lifestyles Program can do that. We also recommend that you only do the 21-day process if it makes heart your truly sing. Like many ancient spiritual initiations, the 21-day process is designed to test your trust and faith, and unless you have clear inner guidance with your Divine One Within, your DOW, I personally recommend that you do not do it and wait until you do trust this inner voice 100 per cent. You also need to have a very strong mind/body connection where you can listen to all the subtle signals and nuances that the body constantly displays in communicating with its Master.

These days I tend to recommend the German's approach to living on light, as it is long term and sensible and does not involve any difficult initiation. In this reality, for example, they set themselves a 5 year plan to slowly prepare their physical, emotional and mental bodies, while also conditioning their family and friends to this new intended reality. For example, year 1 – no more meat; year 2 – become a vegan, no more dairy products; year 3 – raw food only; year 4 – fruit only; year 5 – juices only; year 6 – prana only. During this 5 year period, they also plan to exercise and meditate regularly and become as finely tuned as possible, allowing them to expand their consciousness to live permanently in the Divine airwaves.

While the personal and global benefits of pranic nourishment are obvious, living on light is still not a sociably acceptable lifestyle and many light eaters choose to be very selective regarding who they share this information with. Also as you can't hide the fact that you do not eat from family and friends, you need to realise that to many, living free from the need for food as we know it is an absolutely impossible reality, yet to those who have experienced the power of the Divine, miracles happen daily.

Living on light and the 21-day process will not offer a quick fix to health or life problems, nor is it an easy road to enlightenment. Only what we fill each moment of our day with can determine this and while this reality attracts spiritual warriors who accept themselves as their own Masters, we can only ask that you treat yourself and this initiation with the utmost responsibility and respect. Once again we stress, do not do this 21-day initiation process unless it really speaks to every fibre of your being and makes your heart truly sing, for this is not an initiation that will guarantee living on light. It is an initiation that will allow you to dance on a deeper level with your Divine Self and provided you are physically, emotionally, mentally and spiritually fit then you, like many thousands of others, may experience the true gifts of this initiation on many, many levels.

Remember that this is the path of self-mastery, and unless you have complete 100 percent trust in your Divine inner voice, and good clear communication with your body, then once more we recommend you take the less controversial path for living on light – the 5 year plan. The main focus needs to be on our lifestyle so that we may be in the correct frequency where this is possible. This slower approach is detailed in *The Food of Gods* book released in 2003.

The L.L.P. 8 STEP Program includes the following points:

1. Daily Meditation; 2. Prayer; 3. Programming; 4. A Light Vegetarian diet; 5. Exercise; 6. Service; 7. Time in silence in nature; 8. Use of mantras, chanting & devotional song.

It is a combination of these points and practices that tune a person to the Divine love pranic feeding channel.

Get Fit for Prana

If you wish to undergo the 21-day process, and have researched all you can on the matter, then the next step is to ask yourself:

Are you …

Physically fit and able to do at least one solid hour of exercise each day without problem? I recommend a cross training program for strength, grace, flexibility and stamina such as: - weight lifting, walking, yoga, isometrics, swimming, dance, martial arts etc

Have you been a vegetarian for at least a few years?

Prior to the process are you prepared to become vegan for 6 months, then raw food, then liquids for another 6 months before beginning the 21-day process?

Have you done all you can do to detox your physical body system?

Over the years have you learnt to listen to the voice of your body and treat it like a temple?

Emotionally fit – do you have positive relationships with family and friends, do you feel content in life and happy with who you are? Have you worked through your personal agendas and are now wishing to only serve and have your life here make a positive difference to the planet?

Have you sat down and asked yourself why you wish to do this 21-day process and completed the questionnaire in chapter 14?

Mentally fit – do you KNOW and experience that you create your own reality? Do you exercise mind mastery and thus feel the benefits of applied positive thoughts and programming in manifestation?

Do you have a strong mind body connection?

Spiritually fit – have you been meditating regularly enough to feel the presence of the Divine One Within (DOW) you and have you experienced the benefits of daily meditation in your life?

Have you learnt to listen to and trust the voice of the Divine Within you as it guides you in life?

Lastly did your heart really sing when it discovered information about this process – to the point where you just 'know' it is for you?

Do you realise that the 21-day process will not 'fix all your problems' and that the opposite may occur where all your problems are highlighted and can appear to be worse?

Unless you can say 'yes' to all of the above, we recommend that you wait to do the 21-day process. Remember it is a high-level initiation and the success of being nourished continually from prana after the process is totally dependent on the above issues. The continuation of this lifestyle choice takes daily discipline, commitment and courage.

Over the last 5 years in my research, I have heard so many stories on individuals who were physically fit from exercise, raw food diets etc who were not able to be sustained by prana even though they underwent the process exactly as outlined in this book. I have also met many who were very spiritually fit and had a long history of meditation but encountered many difficulties as they were not physically fit. I have met many who were physically fit and had meditated for many years but who didn't apply mind mastery in their lives and hence were unconvinced that they create their own reality.

Only in some cases do people who are not fit on all levels receive amazing healing from undergoing the process and yes, while some have been healed, others have experienced their problems becoming worse. Why it works for some and not others seems to be a matter of divine grace.

While we understand that the type of person attracted to this is often very strong and not the type who needs to be 'told what to do', we do stress that all who undergo this exercise common sense and caution and listen to their body and their DOW every step of the way. Hence we offer the above questions to ensure that you are well prepared and may enjoy this journey without unnecessary problems.

Medical Research

April 2002:
As time goes by, more and more information on being nourished by prana is being presented to the world. I include the below article in this update to add another wonderful layer of understanding to this journey – Jasmuheen

In India in February 2002, I finally met with Dr. Sudhir Shah and his team who had been monitoring a Jain man, Hira Ratan Manek who lived on sunlight and water for 411 days. This is their findings. Dr. Shah admitted to being extremely sceptical at first but also open to discover more.

The Hypothesis: on Prolonged Fasting with Dr. Sudhir Shah

This is unique. You will agree that such a prolonged continuous Jain fasting for religious (the spreading of Ahimsa and other high mottos) and scientific purposes (to create awareness about Sun-energy) and also aimed at a solution of four-way human crisis (Physical, Mental, food and neurological) under scrupulous daily medical supervision is unheard of. It's just fantastic, and absolutely amazing, but this is not a myth. It's not happening in Himalayas or distant jungles. It is happening in Ahmedabad, Gujarat (India) in the continuous presence of public and under strict medical check and supervision by an expert doctor team.

There is no reason to be sceptical. One may personally come, check, and scrutinize. We doctors have done all these months and fellow men have been staying with him all throughout. And also several visitors see him throughout the day and night. Mr. Hira Ratan Manek has successfully completed a 411 day fast on 14th February 2001. It started on 1st January 2000. He was on total fasting as per Jainism. He was consuming boiled water daily only between 11 a.m. to 4 p.m. no other liquids and no other food. No I\V or I\M injections. He was completely kept isolated while under strict observation.

Medical check-up commenced a few days before the fasting program and continued until today. It consists of a daily written record of pulse, blood pressure, respiration, temperature, water intake, urine output, weight etc. and relevant haematological and biochemical (basic and few advanced) tests periodically i.e. monthly or fortnightly. ECGs are taken regularly, Ultra Sonography, EEG, C.T. Scan and M.R.I. Brain have been taken at the end of one year and a team consisting of general practitioner doctors, physicians, surgeons, cardiologists, endocrinologist and a neurologist have been examining HRM regularly and periodically from the first day of fasting. Except for a weight loss of 19 kgs (which is now stable with no further weight loss for 3 months), a slight reduction of pulse rate and B.P. and definite reduction of respiratory rate (from 18 it is now 10/minute) amazingly, there is no medical abnormality. Even the brain and mental capacities are absolutely normal. There are hardly any findings. He stopped passing stool after the 16th day of fasting and urine output is maintained at around 600 to 800 c.c. His blood sugar is 60 to 90. There is no acetone. All rest parameters are normal.

It is just amazing. Isn't it? But how do we hypothesize it? How does science look at it? As per science, under normal circumstances of prolonging starvation, (under accidental situation or extraordinary situation,) human being loses weight fast. First fat is utilised, and ketones appear in urine in first week. Then the proteins are burnt. Before that, the person becomes dull, lethargic and irritable, his logic reasoning fails and vital parameters fall and within 8 to 10 weeks, as per science the physical existence will be challenged. Here there is no such ill effect. How do we explain this? How does his energy mathematics works? How he is still so intact with normal intellect and normal mental function? Though so far there is no solid thesis (as this is the first event in the world under medical supervision), there has to be some logical, scientific hypothesis. It explains quite a bit, but also leaves few questions unanswered, for all of us to further analyse. It also opens, at the same time, several new avenues for the coming time to work upon it. (e.g. issue of obesity).

This hypothesis has four basic steps to explain energy-metabolic mathematics. i.e. (1) Reducing calorie requirement by chronic adaptation. (2) Deriving basic energy from cosmic source-chiefly, 'sun energy'. (3) Utilising the energy in an efficient way and recycling the same in his body. (4) Genetically or phenotypically a different body disposition.

(1) Chronic Adaptation Syndrome: As the body and the mind adapts to chronic stress in a healthier way, as compared to acute stress, similarly the body's adaptation must be different to chronic fasting (beyond 30 days) as compared to acute fasting (e.g. 3 to 15 days). Nobody knows which is the exact point where the body adapts chronically, but 30 days sounds like a reasonable time though it may vary individually. This is some kind of hibernation, so to say. The routine calorie mathematics sounds logical and quite applicable to acute fasting where fats break up first, ketones appear in urine and weight loss starts; muscle mass reduces and vital functions and mental capacity may start slowing down. Thus in acute fasting, energy dissipated must come from stored sources in the body to match 1:1 ratio of calorie consumption against utilisation. In chronic adaptation; the metabolism of the body must slow down. The body needs are reduced to the minimum. This is possible by decreasing the regulation of the cellular and receptor function. Therein thus altering the energy metabolism to the lowest possible. Oxygen and water are supplied to cells as basic things. At this stage, the hunger centre will become depressed and the satiety centre will be activated. So there will not be any feeling of hunger or food craving. It may be possible for such an individual to do a routine activity with a very low amount of energy or calories e.g. 500-600 calories, to sustain cellular metabolism.

(2) Deriving Energy from Cosmic source – Solar Energy: Whatever low amount of energy, that is required, must come from some source. He is only on boiled water – which as per science is having hardly any caloric value, or does it really supply some energy? Most

likely, he is drawing energy from cosmic energy – Cosmic Sources. Hence more correctly it is energy mathematics rather than calorie mathematics; a concept worth understanding.

Out of all cosmic sources, the SUN is the most powerful and readily available source and has been used for energy, by sages and Rishis since ancient time, including lord Mahavir, Tibetan lamas and other Rishes. Again, how the SUN energy is received. The Brain and the mind are the most powerful recipients in human body. The retina and the pineal gland (the third eye or the seat of soul as per Rene Descartes) are equipped with photoreceptor cells and may be considered photosensitive organs. As the plant kingdom thrives on chlorophyll and photosynthesis, directly dependant on the Sun, similarly some photosynthesis must be taking place when we hypothesize Sun energy.

Through complex ways and distinct pathways this energy must enter the body. There is a pathway from the retinas, to the hypothalamus, called the retinohypothalamic tract. This brings information about the dark and light cycles to suprachiasmatic nucleus (SCN) of the hypothalamus. From the SCN, impulses along the nerve travel via the pineal nerve (Sympathetic nervous system) to the pineal gland. These impulses inhibit the production of Melatonin. When these impulses stop (at night or in the dark, when the light no longer stimulates the hypothalamus) pineal inhibition ceases, and Melatonin is released. The pineal gland (or the third eye) is therefore a photosensitive organ and an important timekeeper for the human body. The unexplored process of energy synthesis and transformation from the sun energy perhaps partly occurs here.

While going through the details of recent scientific literature and also comparing it with ancient Indian spiritual texts, as well as Western occult and new age, the following things are apparent. The activation of the pineal gland is the key step in the psychic, spiritual and energy transformation processes. Here in this gland, energy processing and re-distribution occurs. Pineal gland is the commander of all endocrine glands, therefore controlling the humeral system. It also regulates the circadian rhythm, sleep wake cycle and it also slows down the ageing process. It has psychic properties and is the seat of soul or mind – so called the third eye. It is the Agna (Ajna) chakra of tantric system. Its activation can be done with prolonged yoga and meditation techniques or through practice of solar energy. The later does not use classic yoga steps. Pineal also inhibits growth and metastasis of some tumours. It has a stimulatory effect on the immune system. In birds and other animals, it has a magnetic material and is therefore the navigation centre in birds.

Scientists are looking at the magnetic, navigatory properties of the pineal gland in humans. So pineal activation and charging through solar energy is the vital step and that is the doorway of the energy highway. This may be Kundalini Shakti activation, in other words. Normal Pineal gland measures 6 x 8 mm in human body. As per C.T. Scan & MRI Scan reports of Mr. Hira Ratan Manek it is 8 x 11 mm (enlarged!). This may indirectly support the important role of the pineal gland in energy transformation. However it may be mentioned, that an anatomically enlarged gland does not necessarily always mean hyper function.

Ever since mankind has started ignoring the psychically and Spiritually equipped pineal gland it has fallen on merely physical-material plane and endless pains have fallen on mankind. Mankind must now relearn to activate the pineal and the other psycho-spiritual bodies either through cosmic energy dynamics or through the practice of Rajyoga or the Tantric ways or other such practices. Kundalini Shakti is said to be activated through these and happiness and bliss with peace are bound to follow. This light energy may be transformed into electrical, magnetic or chemical energies in the body. Once processed, this energy must be transported and must be stored somewhere. Actually the ultimate form of all energy is light. Energy and light can be transformed into matter and back again to energy. The hypothalamus is the commander of the autonomic nervous system and the Pineal gland is in proximity to the autonomic nervous system, so it is logical that new energy transportation may either activate this system or it may use this system as vehicle.

Parasympathetic nerves and its hormones and chemicals may be more useful than the sympathetic system. As the sympathetic system increases the body needs (e.g. thinking, fighting stress, excitement etc.), the parasympathetic system is known to reduce the energy needs. It keeps the person serene and at mental peace and alters the metabolic requirements to a lower state and puts it to sleep. There may be other hormones or chemicals too. The role of the temporal lobe and limbic system may also be important. It may work as a regulator if not receptor and may be psychically involved in directing the energy in proper pathways. Deep into the limbic systems or in the parts of the medulla oblongata, this energy may ultimately be stored and from time to time, may be recalled, charged or recycled. The medulla oblongata has all vital centres and therefore can be proposed as a storer of vital energy.

Thus there are energy receivers or receptors, processors analysers, transformers, storers etc to explain the energy logistics. As this form of energy mathematics is different from what we conventionally are used to in the form of food and calorie mathematics; we will call this micro-food or mind utilisation food (Manobhakshi Aahar {Ttu¼ûte ytnth). Here, we have talked about the Sun energy, but one may use any source from the cosmos, i.e. air, water, plants, earth etc. This may be called Surya vigyan, but equally there is Chandra vigyan and Vanaspati vigyan as mentioned in our ancient texts.

Also apart from the retina and pineal gland, skin and other senses may be responsible for receiving the energy. In short, this opens up tremendous possibilities. This micro-food can solve the food crisis on Earth and in fact is the only possible food in present context for somebody who wants to be a long-term space traveller or planet traveller. Amazing! It is time to note, that our routine food is not the only source to sustain the body. The role of mind: Whatever said, in this step (i.e. the step II of deriving the energy from the sun and transforming it in body), the mind may play the crucial role. It is well known that the mind has an enormous capacity, the soul has even further or infinite capabilities. Through Sun Tratak and Meditation, tremendous capacities are born which will bring tranquillity to the mind and also slow down the metabolism, as mentioned in step 1.

The mind can do everything including so-called miracles. It can revitalise the body, it can heal diseases, it can know things in advance and it can manipulate the laws of physics. It's unclear till this date whether the mind is a separate entity or the pineal gland itself. The faith and blessings from Yogis and Gurus have their own roles sustaining one's self in adverse situations. On religious days, under high spirits and a cultivated atmosphere, a few people surprisingly do unusual things like walking on fire or piercing pointed swords through their bodies without damaging themselves. If similarly, someone fasts, these phenomena may help to pull him/her through the period of physiological problems until one enters chronic adaptation phase.

(3) Energy Economy in efficient ways and re-cycling the energy in his own body: Those, who are chronically deprived of energy, learn to utilise the available energy in more efficient ways – so that even at the low energy state body metabolism and vital functions including nervous system do not suffer. This is quite logical and one can imagine this happening in the individuals caught in natural calamities, or those left alone in the sea or survivors of high altitudes after plane crash etc. managing to live for several days or weeks, without food. Also, one can hypothesize that these people may be recycling the energy in their own bodies. This may be done, through complex mechanisms, involving neural and humeral organs. Solar energy, dissipated through the body, may get absorbed into the Earth and while walking bare footed on the soil or standing in the sun, may help absorb this energy through the skin of the toes and the soles of the feet as Shri Hira Ratan Manek does regularly and always preaches to do so to recycle the energy. This may be related to the principals of acupressure or reflexology.

(4) Gene typically or phenotypically a different body predisposition: We should also examine this aspect carefully, as this leaves scope for an important discussion – whether each and every individual can use sun energy and if so, so efficiently? Only time can answer this. But it is possible that each individual has a different genetic code and also each body has different physical capabilities. Hence, one may be able to receive this Solar energy more readily, can transform and store it in a better way and also can utilise more efficiently and even recycle it – while another person may not be able to do it to the same extent. Hence experiments must be taken up, if possible, on a randomized base upon volunteers with control population. However, leaving this component aside for the time being is possible that many people can do this experiment very successfully under supervision. A prior body check-up and particularly a retinal-ophthalmic check-up is mandatory and under strict medical guidance, a graded time bound experiment upon volunteers may be taken up.

If this theory can be generalised, then it can change the destiny of mankind. First of all, the food crisis will be solved. Through activation of this supreme energy in the body then transforming it in electrical, chemical then magnetic forms, a person can not only become free of diseases but they can gain positive health with a vibrant aura. If his lustre can impress enemies then the enmity may dissolve. With the improvement of mental and intellectual capacities, one may be able to use brain-power up to 90 to 100 %, as against to 3 - 10% as we normally do. There will be reign of peace and prosperity. As there is no food, the bad thoughts and ill feelings will be stopped, so eternal peace is bound to follow.

This will also question the routine common calorie mathematics. By this, there is a challenge to the routine calorie based science. Its limitations are highlighted, at the same time the complex issues of obesity and malnutrition can be readily explained through the concept of solar energy. It is possible that obese people, though not eating excess food, still receive energy from cosmic sources explaining their obesity. The concept of cosmic energy can be used thus for a total uplift of mankind at physical, mental, intellectual, supramental and Spiritual levels. Extensive scientific research work therefore should be immediately taken up by appropriate authorities, including bio-scientists and medical personnel, who can then answer all these issues.

(Ref. case study of Mr. Hira Ratan Manek: 411 day fast: 375 day fast completed on 9-1-2001.)

Dr. Sudhir V. Shah M.D., D.M. Neurophysician 206-8, Sangini Complex, Nr. Parimal Crossing, Ellisbridge, Ahmedabad-380 006. Ph: (c) 079-646 70 52 (R) 079-662 17 42. Hon. Neurologist: H.E. The Governor of Gujarat, India. President: Assoc. of Physician of A'bad. (97-98) Hon. Asst. Prof. of neurology: Sheth K.M School of PGMR Smt. N.H.L. M.M College Hon. Neurologist: V.S.Hospital, Ahmedabad. Jivraj Mehta Smarak Hospital
    I acknowledge suggestions and help received for this hypothesis... From: (1) Dr. Navneet Shah M.D. FICA (U.S.A) Physician Endocrinologist (C) 6425566. (2) Dr. Gargey Sutaria (M.D.) and Dr. Kalpesh Shah (M.D.) Radiologist Usmanpura C.T. Scan Centre. Clinical Assistant: Dr. Nalin Gheewala M.D. Physician. Dr. K.K. Shah M.S. Surgeon. Dr. Viresh Patel M.D. Physician. Dr. P.G. Shah M.B.B.S. Family Physician. Dr. P.D. Doshi M.B.B.S. Family Physician.

Note 2012: - Dr Sudhir and Hira Ratan Manek, both also feature prominently in the movie "*In The Beginning There Was Light*".

Additions March 2006:

Personal Calibration and Testing methods for safely fulfilling the freedom agenda:
Post-script with Jasmuheen – January 2005 – from the e-book *The Law of Love*
http://www.selfempowermentacademy.com.au/htm/cia-education.asp#law

In 2002 a book called *Power vs. Force* was released and read with great interest. In it the author David Hawkins, a psychiatrist and spiritual teacher, shared his research findings on a simple method to calibrate levels of human consciousness and the various spiritual paths that many of us undertake plus much more. An in-depth twenty-year study using the applied science of behavioural kinesiology, I highly recommend this book.

Excited by the possibilities that his calibration system offered as far as a way of checking our freedom models, I began to apply it during my October/November 2004 tour. Quickly recognising that we can use this system as a base to move into levels perhaps unexplored by David Hawkins, during this tour I took advantage of testing and confirming my findings with hundreds of special test subjects from four different countries – France, Italy, Germany and Switzerland.

In order to understand what I'm about to share in this post-script, it is important for you to read and understand what David Hawkins is talking about in his *Power vs. Force* book, nonetheless I will provide a brief synopsis here so that its relevance to our own findings is a little easier to understand.

Hawkins sees the potential of kinesiology as "the 'wormhole' between two universes – the physical, and the mind and spirit – an interface between dimensions … a tool to recover that lost connection with the higher reality and demonstrate it for all to see."

Founded by Dr. George Goodheart and given wider application by Dr. John Diamond, Behavioural Kinesiology is the well-established science of muscle testing the body where a positive stimulus provokes a strong muscle response while a negative stimulus provokes a weak response.

Using Diamond's system, Hawkins developed "a calibrated scale of consciousness, in which the log of whole numbers from 1 to 1,000 determines the degree of power of all possible levels of human awareness." In this model 200 represents emotions of positive stimulus where muscle response remains strong and below 200 is where muscle response weakens as emotions anger, fear, guilt or shame, begin to influence the body.

200 is the energy of truth and integrity, 310 is the calibration for hope and optimism, 400 is the energy of reason and wisdom, 500 is the energy of love, 540 of joy, 600 is perfect peace and bliss and 700 to 1000 represents even higher levels of enlightenment.

Hawkins shares: "The individual human mind is like a computer terminal connected to a giant database. The database is human consciousness itself, of which our own cognizance is merely an individual expression, but with its roots in the common consciousness of all mankind. This database is the realm of genius; because to be human is to participate in the database, everyone, by virtue of his birth, has access to genius. The unlimited information contained in the database has now been shown to be readily available to anyone in a few seconds, at any time in any place. This is indeed an astonishing discovery, bearing the power to change lives, both individually and collectively, to a degree never yet anticipated.

"The database transcends time, space, and all limitations of individual consciousness. This distinguishes it as a unique tool for future research, and opens as yet undreamed-of areas for possible investigation." He is of course talking about accessing the universal field of intelligence which is within and around us all.

Applying the Kinesiology principle and test results re the freedom agenda:
When I start to download a book from universal mind, information that is needed to be incorporated is always given to me, particularly when the research is beneficial to my findings. Consequently I experienced great joy when I read David Hawkins's work as I realised that I was finally able to provide a safety check for the freedom model, particularly for someone who tests yes as per the questions asked meditation 4 in Chapter 16.

For example, among the hundreds of people that we tested in the countries mentioned:
- 80% tested yes that it is part of their blueprint to create a disease free life.
- 70% tested yes that it was part of their blueprint to learn how to be free from taking nutrition through food and access it through feeding from the divine nourishment flow within.
- 18% tested yes for setting up the reality of being free from the need for fluid, this lifetime, by again allowing that divinely nutritional source of prana within them to hydrate their body quite perfectly without the need for external fluids.
- 40% tested yes that it was part of their pre-agreed service blueprint to demonstrate physical immortality;
- 15% tested yes for pre-agreeing to learn, and demonstrate, the art of dematerialization and rematerialization and
- 70% tested yes for developing the ability to stop the ageing process.

As you can see from these figures the type of people that are attracted to the freedom agenda and the workshops that I do are a very particular group of a very specific calibration. Hence having a model that can ascertain our calibration level before we enter into the release of these types of limitation adds a very beneficial layer.

What I would like to offer therefore is the use of David Hawkins's work as one layer, in a three layer testing system, some of which we have already touched on previously in the sacred support systems chapter.

A THREE LEVEL CONFIRMATION SYSTEM

This three layer testing system is outlined as followed:
DOW – Divine One Within – our inner voice. This must always be our first method of testing in that it is the only reliable source of confirmation that is completely incorruptible. This requires us to establish a clear line of communication between ourselves and our divine nature – whether we call this our DOW, Monad or Atman or whatever. This level of communication comes via our sixth and seventh senses of intuition and knowing and needs

to be, in my opinion, our first barometer of guidance in everything that we do in life; particularly in accessing and manifesting our pre-agreements. Our DOW is the only thing that all humanity has in common, It is pure, It gives us life, It breathes us, loves us and guides us to evolve into our perfection. Learning to listen to It and trust Its guidance is a basic part of self mastery and self knowledge.

The second level of testing is to use the art of kinesiology to gain information confirmation using muscle responses in the body. Kinesiology, as many trained in this field know, has its limitations because it depends on how it is used and how strongly people's muscles test. It also depends on the calibration purity of the one being tested, the one doing the testing and the questions being asked. Reading David's book on this subject will provide a deeper understanding. I also recommend that when we use kinesiology that we ask the Divine One Within to confirm data, using the muscle testing system through the body, rather than asking the body's consciousness itself.

The third level of testing that is a wonderful support system for us as we journey through the freedom agenda, is to ask to receive clear confirmation from the universal field of intelligence which is all around us. This goes back to the story of people who, looking for answers, walk into a book shop, find that a book falls off the top shelf and hits them on the head, then spirals around and falls at their feet open and the right way up and when they pick this book up, there is the answer to the very question that they had been thinking about. This is one way that the universal field of intelligence responds to our telepathic thought patterns when we have a strong desire for further knowledge, particularly when the knowledge that we are seeking is supporting our own evolutionary path in a positive way and is also beneficial for the world.

So these three levels of testing 1) accessing and listening to the divine voice within then 2) confirming its guidance or your query through muscle testing with kinesiology and c) asking for further confirmation from the universal field. These are three wonderful ways to provide a very clear system of guidance and a safety mechanism for human beings who are ready, willing, able and who are preprogrammed to display 'freedom from human limitation' to the degrees that we have discussed in this book.

When people go through the testing program in Chapter 16 to ascertain their pre-agreements, and if they receive a clear yes, then they will find that the universe will provide them with all the support that they need to fulfill this. There are many different ways to move into this agenda and setting the intention that we fill our preagreed agendas with joy and ease and Grace, allows the universal field to deliver whatever information and tools that we need to do this. Also as time goes by and the calibration of the mass morphonogenic field changes, then the way to attain and demonstrate these freedoms will become easier.

We have often had people receive an answer of 'no' during the meditation even though their own inner feeling was that these freedoms were something that they would like to embrace. Receiving a 'no' from the testing mechanism simply means that it is not part of your 'preprogrammed' blueprint, however as a being of free-will you may choose to exhibit these freedoms anyway as a side issue along with your main service agenda.

We also had people test the following using the David Hawkins "Power vs. Force" system, and I recommend that you may like to look at these yourself in more detail. These are:
- The testing of your birth calibration.
- The testing of your current calibration.
- The testing of your home field calibration – which will allow you to see how supportive your home field environment is for you to move into these agendas.
- The testing of your work field calibration.
- The testing of your current biological age plus
- the testing of the biological age your body is happy to support you into demonstrating.

From these tests we also found some interesting things. Firstly it is imperative that if someone tests 'yes' for a fluid free agenda then we can only recommend that they let go of fluid when the bio-systems calibration can support this in health and safety.

By first checking if it is in your blueprint and then checking, after intensive preparation using the methods discussed in *The Food of Gods* and *The Law of Love* books, when/if the bio-system is ready and able to sustain this, we then have a safe system to advise us. To attempt to do this without the support of the right calibration is only asking for potential physical trouble.

Other points to note regarding testing calibration levels:

Calibration limits: While David Hawkins shared in his book that most people in general society rarely move more than 5 calibration points per lifetime; this is not true for the spiritual student who lives a lifestyle that allows them to download and radiate more of their Divine essence or their DOW power; for this essence is able to create instant change provided that our bio-system can handle it.

Another anomaly with David Hawkins's system is a process that I call weaving.

Field Weaving: This relates to a discovery I made when I wanted to test my youngest daughter's calibration. The first thing I did was to check with her own divine force if it was okay for me to be given this data to which I quickly received a 'yes'. However when testing her calibration using muscle testing on my body I kept getting some very strange readings which intuitively I felt could not be right. Switching to Erik's body, who was testing with me, we realised that because I had an emotional attachment to her, sometimes the readings can be incorrect, but more than that we also realised that because I have been consciously weaving my energy through her energy fields to support her these last few years, by the conscious weaving of my field with hers, then her calibration was changing, because of how I calibrate, and so we had to look at the question differently. Using Erik's body to check, we procured a truer reading which we then confirmed using additional methodology.

Interestingly enough the calibration was still quite high even though at this time she does no meditation or yoga or the practices that I recommend in *The Food of Gods* book, however what this particular being does have is an incredibly open, loving, caring and compassionate heart. She is someone who has a huge network of friends and is always there for others. This in itself will bring a human being into wonderful calibration levels and can sometimes compensate for a lifestyle that maybe not as supportive of the physical bio-system as it could be.

The process of weaving is also very interesting because it can allow conscious access to other beings of great light and great love. For example, when we connect strongly through the doorways of love and devotion, to Mother Mary or to any of the other Holy Ones, that opens up an energetic path through our will and intention, for us to connect to their energy field, which then can weave back through into ours as we are all one and connected.

The recognition of this type of connection and possibility allows the weaving to begin and also is a way of fine tuning our calibration and strengthening it quite quickly. For people who do play with these realities, who are not living the sort of metaphysical lifestyle that we recommend in our previous manuals, then David Hawkins sharing that most people will only move 5 points in their calibration per lifetime is truth.

Personal Calibration Requirements for the Law of Love Freedom Agenda:
When originally tested, via two test subjects using kinesiology and David Hawkins's system, and confirming this via an additional two sources using the pendulum and inner plane Divine One Within confirmation, thus using a triple blind test with metaphysical tools – we originally found the following regarding the freedom models. These calibrations were then confirmed by approximately 500 test subjects and this is what we have noted:

In order to establish a disease free existence where there is no physical, emotional, mental and spiritual disease a human bio-system needs a personal calibration of 635.

The creation of an ageing free system where the ageing process is literally stopped a human bio-system needs a minimum calibration of 637, which is interesting as this is very close to the calibration of a disease free existence.

In order to safely exist on purely a pranic flow for nourishment and no longer need to take physical food a human bio-system needs to calibrate at 668.

In order to safely exist with the fluid free existence a human bio-system needs to calibrate at 777.

The calibration for physical immortality for a human bio-system is 909

and the calibration for successful dematerialization and rematerialization is 1367.

I then asked for the calibration of classic miracles; to really witness the flow of Grace in such a powerful way, that the majority of people would deem it a miracle, the field around it needs to calibrate at around 1450.

For the last two calibrations, which are over Hawkins's 0-1000 scale, these are possible due to field weaving and coming into the consciousness of pure Oneness.

I do recognise in these results that we have been given, that as the general morphonogenic field of the mass of humanity changes, then the hundredth monkey system kicks in to change these calibration levels. According to Hawkins, while 78% of people calibrate at less than 200, mass consciousness as a whole registers at 207 due the process of entrainment where 22% of people of higher calibration are dominating the field enough to shift it into the level of truth and integrity en mass.

Another thing that we asked the bio-systems of the groups was to ask the body consciousness at what weight, in kilograms, that their body would stabilize at, once they entered in the food free and then later the fluid free existence. I felt that by asking the body consciousness this question this is another wonderful way to affirm our readiness. For example, a few years ago when I checked where my body weight would stabilize at with a fluid free existence I was told 45kgs. For me intellectually and emotionally I rejected this simply because I felt that it was not good for me to look so skeletal, and perhaps the health that I was seeking would not be maintainable, and so I held off on my decision to go onto a fluid free existence. When testing this same question this year, I was told that my body can now sustain a fluid free existence at 51kgs because my calibration has changed over the last few years. This is a lot more acceptable for me and therefore makes the movement into this level of freedom far more attractive.

Hence if you get a confirmation from your body of a weight that you feel is unacceptable to you then the advice is to wait and increase your personal calibration levels before going into this additional level of freedom.

The quickest way, as we all know, to increase calibration levels is simply to love a lot in life, for love is one of the most powerful feeding mechanisms that we have to match our calibration levels with our DOW because the divine essence is a being of pure and limitless love.

As we mentioned in earlier chapters, setting the home field calibration and refining it, is something that is easily done through the art of Feng Shui, and also through how life is conducted within the home field. It is important to have a field calibration in your home of a minimum of 200 which is, as David Hawkins has shared, the beginning levels of operating in truth and integrity. The higher the home field calibration then obviously the more supportive the environment is for you to move into and maintain these levels of the freedom agenda.

When Hawkins's book was first published in 1995, his research shared that only 4% of the world's population calibrated at over 500, while in 2004 it is now 6%; and in 1995 only 1 in 10 million calibrated at over 600. Nonetheless a person calibrating at 300 has the enough DOW power radiation to energetically influence 90,000 people; at a calibration of 700 we can counterbalance the energy of 700 million. These figures confirm that if all we do is refine our personal calibration levels to radiate maximum DOW power, this in itself is a valuable service, for not only does it deliver us naturally into the freedom agenda but it will also allow our presence here to positively influence the world.

♥ Namaste – Jasmuheen

2012 Update: Please note that I much prefer the Breath Test as we outlined in Chapter 14.

March 2006 Summary:
In conclusion to this update I would like to add the Questions and Answers from Chapter 7 of *The Prana Program* ...

Q & A's on the 21-day process,
Sceptics & The Media

THE PRANA PROGRAM AND THE 21-day PROCESS
(Excerpt from *The Prana Program* e-book)

Q: In your first book on the prana program, you describe not just your personal experience with this conversion but also a specific initiation now known as the 21-day process. Briefly, what was the 21-day process initiation about?
A: It was a spiritual initiation that increased our internal light quotient and personal calibration levels and as a consequence delivered to some people the gift of being able to be free from the need to take physical food. For some it recalibrated us into deeper levels of the Divine Love channel so that we could receive other esoteric gifts.

Q: What motivated you to do the 21-day process?
A: At that time my only interest was in my personal ascension and path of enlightenment. If someone had said, "do this initiation and you won't need to take physical food anymore", it would not have interested me. Living purely on prana for physical nourishment was a small by-product of a much bigger personal, spiritual journey, that is still unfolding. To me enlightenment is a journey not a destination, as we can always increase our capacity to attract and radiate more light.

Q: What were the benefits you gained from undergoing the 21-day initiation?
A: This is hard to say as my general lifestyle at the time kept me in the channels where many gifts came so it's hard to separate them. However I believe the 21-day process accelerated and expanded my capacity for things such as being constantly in the flow of Grace, experiencing constant synchronicity, inter-dimensional telepathy, clairsentience and also the prana as nourishment reality.

Q: What are its problems or challenges?
A: If a person is unprepared and not listening to their inner voice there can be many problems with the 21-day process, from extreme weight loss to even loss of their life. An athlete must train to compete with ease in a marathon and it is similar with the 21-day initiation – people need to be physically, emotionally, mentally and spiritually fit so that they have the right calibration levels.

Q: You constantly share that you prefer the conversion process detailed in The Food of Gods book, why?

A: It is a slower and safer system of conversion that promotes easier integration within the physical, emotional and mental bodies. It eliminates many of the problems that people had with the 21-day process.

Q: Such as?
A: The 21-day process is a fast track program that switches people too quickly from one reality to another. There is not much social/family/emotional body adjustment time so it can be a shock to the bio-system on these levels. A gradual process of refinement seems to lessen this and be more permanent.

Q: Would everyone doing the 21-day process be aiming to connect with the higher or ascended aspect of their divine nature?
A: No. 83% of people surveyed throughout the globe, said they did the 21-day process because it just felt right; 72% did it to experience their God – the DOW. 19% did it for health reasons and 12% for dietary reasons and 5% out of curiosity! But I say to people: "If you don't believe in God, or the U.F.I.*, then if you stop eating what do you think is going to feed you?" To do this one needs to know they create their own reality and also have mind mastery such as "I expect prana, the God force, to feed me", and so it does as the U.F.I. mirrors and supports our beliefs.
* U.F.I. = Universal Field of infinite love and Intelligence.

Q: In your first book on this the steps that people needed to undertake to prepare for the program were quite simple, but in your later books the instructions have become more detailed e.g. vegetarian for several years, vegan for six months and raw food and liquid for a further six months. Why is this?
A: I came from a background of over 20 years of physical fitness, vegetarian diet, meditation etc and I just assumed that anybody who would be attracted to this process would have naturally had that sort of background as well. For the untuned person the prana only program is a very extreme thing to do and one obviously needs to be well prepared for it to be as successful as it can be and to get the most out of it. So the new methods deal with more prolonged preparation and we now recommend that people convert their bodies into pranic nourishment via the program offered in the book The Food of Gods and also understand the cosmic particle hydration and feeding reality that we cover in The Law of Love manual with its emphasis also on heart energy.

Succinctly on just a dietary level if you wish to be a lot healthier and even be free from the need to eat food, then you first: -
- Become a vegetarian.
- Then become a vegan and cease consuming all animal products.
- Then move on to raw food, then go to fruits.
- Then liquids, then prana.

The more gradually you make this dietary transition, the easier it will be to let go of your emotional body's addiction to the pleasure gained from eating a wide variety of foods.

Simultaneously a person needs to tune themselves mentally and emotionally. But dietary refinement alone will not attract enough cosmic particles to you to remain healthy on a prana only regime.

Remember The Prana Program is not about eating or not eating, it's about establishing a very strong connection with the Divine One Within – our DOW. A very small by-product of this is that It will feed us if we choose not to take nourishment from food any more but without this connection what will feed us? This is definitely not about a new non-physical food diet.

Q: Do you feel now that the guidelines in the first book were wrong or misleading?
A: Not wrong; but I assumed people would be a little more discerning and I assumed and trusted that people understood the true message of the book and would be self responsible and well prepared.

Q: Could you describe what the true message of your first book is?
A: Its basic message is that it is possible to be nourished on *all* levels by another source of nutrition and that the Divine One Within us can do this if we choose to allow it to. Our message is also about the need for humankind to take responsibility for everything that is happening in their life right now, because their choices are affecting the planet. There is a lot we can all do to make our transition through this new millennium a joyous one for all while utilising resources more effectively. The first book was really the journey of my personal experience with this reality field and the realisation that it is possible although I didn't understand the science of it and how. All I knew was that I was given the gift of this as a by-product of the 21-day initiation.

Q: So presumably only a few people would have the mind mastery and the physical fitness to go through the 21-day process discussed in your first book?
A: Or the desire. Still there are enough out there to create a global shift around this. A funny thing happens when people get information that's right for their blueprint – their heart sings. By asking, we can trigger a 'data download' of the blueprint as to why we're truly here. So if the information in the books on this subject doesn't make your heart sing, don't do it as it's not part your blueprint. If you decide to do it then you need to ask for help from the Divine One Within, so that the transition is one of joy and ease and grace, and then you need to clean up your diet, get fit, look at your emotions around food, and prepare your family. *ONLY* your DOW can provide the perfect conversion procedure for you and only your DOW can reveal to you your blueprint.

Q: You then took this "prana as nourishment" discussion to the Global stage with Book 2 in the Divine Nutrition series. What was its focus?
A: In book two *Ambassadors of Light – World Health, World Hunger Project*; we have more information regarding our research projects and we also emphasize again the need for fitness and preparation. Every edition that we have released we have added more information as we ourselves have been exposed to more and in this book we also applied it

to Global programs such as resource redistribution, global environmental impact and other more political issues.

Q: You say in your additional material that not all people improve their health with the 21-day process and in fact some people's condition deteriorates?
A: It affects everyone differently although 91% of people surveyed said they found the 21-day process beneficial and 66% said their health improved. The initiation is about a redirection of energy and there are many gifts that happen to people through the 21-day process that are nothing to do with prana as an ongoing source of physical nourishment. I have noticed that the gifts people receive are dependent upon the purity of their intention.

Q: Did you put restrictions on who can do the 21-day process initiation, to make it safe?
A: You can't do that – it's out there, like a runaway train as the first book in the Divine Nutrition series is now in 17 languages, nonetheless we have released regular updates and guidelines, one being "Get fit for Prana". We have also given out a checklist of what we want people to do and we keep updating and disseminating our research and recommendations. I take the view that people are intelligent and do use their discernment. Also we have the greatest teacher and guide with this which is the Divine One Within and It has our best interests at heart. Who am I to tell people what they can or can't do – particularly the sort of people who are pre-programmed to do this? But we can offer guidelines and improve our models with subsequent texts as we have continually done through our writings in the free online magazine <u>The ELRAANIS Voice</u> and now in this compendium.

Q: Can people who are sick do the 21-day process?
A: I hear about lots of miraculous healings occurring through increasing the pranic flow and yet many of these people are not fit on all levels yet still have found great benefit in doing this. Why The Prana Program heals some and not others we don't know but we do know that the fitter we are on all levels, the safer the 21-day process is. Still I personally recommend that everyone apply *The Food of Gods* conversion program instead.

THE PRANA PROGRAM – SCEPTICS AND THE MEDIA

Q: In 2000 you were awarded the IgNobel Prize for Literature by Harvard University for the Pranic Nourishment book, what was your response to this?
A: German philosopher, Arthur Schopenhauer said: "All truth passes through three stages. First, it is ridiculed. Second, it is violently opposed. Third, it is accepted as being self-evident." So good holistic education programs that focus on human potential and combine ancient Eastern tradition will alleviate this. Having said this, my personal reaction to the news of the IgNobel Prize was lots of laughter as I'm sure the award was issued in good humour based on the seemingly incredulous nature of our reality.

Q: How do you now deal with sceptics?

A: Light-heartedly and with humour plus a dose of re-educational data. Things are rarely as they seem. For example, my favourite physical exercise lately is barefoot backward beach walking. Some who see me do this each day may think, "There goes that strange lady in the cowboy hat with no sunglasses, walking backwards again. I wonder if she's eccentric or does it for a reason?"

The hat shields my face from the hot Australian sun, yet wearing no sunglasses (which is unusual in our climate) allows me to absorb more prana directly into the brain through the eyes. Walking barefoot means I can feed off ground prana and walking backwards rebalances my whole internal energy flow and energizes and exercises the body in a different way.

Similarly people say: "That's rubbish everyone has to eat, she's a liar". What they have not understood – due to lack of educational exposure – is all the benefits we discuss in this book, so you need to treat scepticism respectfully and lightly and humour always helps.

Q: Speaking of sceptics and doubt, you've been criticized for not doing empirical tests to prove your claims that prana nourishes you. Is this something you would be prepared to do?
A: I have done lots of allopathic and alternate testing to satisfy myself that it is possible as my body has remained healthy and I have shared the outcomes of this with the world. I have also worked with and been tested by doctors in Germany, India and more recently Russia. Due to the time I have needed to fulfill my own blueprints, I have not been prepared to interfere with my work schedule and get tested every time someone asks me to prove this. I also know that in time, as more people discover this, then prana power will prove itself and become a very common lifestyle choice for many – just as vegetarianism is today. Time is a good leveller in fields of controversy.

Q: As a leading proponent in the world for the Divine Nutrition paradigm, and as someone who has had to deal with all the natural scepticism regarding the pranic nourishment reality, what else do you see as the future of this?
A: Like many yogis and shaman, I have been blessed with the ability to glimpse – from time to time – into our future and I have witnessed that due to its personal and global benefits, the 'prana as nourishment' reality is being Divinely supported and will not go away. I have seen a world where the slaughter of any life – human or animal – is no longer part of our reality and is seen as something belonging to our more barbaric, unenlightened past. In this 'new' world, there is love, honour and respect for all life and people have been educated as to how to create and maintain physical, emotional, mental and spiritual fitness. In this world we exist in rainbow cities of crystalline light that radiate with love and wisdom and health and happiness.

The question is how do we get there?

What steps do we need to take to evolve into this new world?

The answer is simply a matter of the expansion of our consciousness which happens when we adopt a more holistic lifestyle that is designed to change our brain wave patterns and activate our higher sensibilities.

While scepticism is healthy, ignorance and fear come from lack of education which is why it is crucial for those in the 'frontlines' of this new paradigm, to always act as masters. Part of this mastery entails being able to hold and radiate the vibration of love in all situations regardless of what is happening.

Q: How has the media dealt with this reality in the West?
A: Generally it has been very supportive although in my personal experience the mainstream media has often been more focused on sensationalism than responsible educational reportage. Also while I appreciate the fact that they wish to present two viewpoints, asking someone who is completely ignorant as to the prana field, questions about its possibilities, so that the media can offer an objective view is very strange to me. We have done over a decade of experiential research with thousands on this and to ask us questions and then check it with a medical practitioner who often hasn't even heard of prana, who operates in Beta field mentality, all of this is also very nonsensical to me. It's like asking a mathematician to comment on the complexities of writing a symphony of music – different field of education and creativity.

Q: At the start of the millennium you virtually retired from dealing with global mainstream media regarding education with The Prana Program. Why?
A: Firstly we had completed the anchoring of this reality in the morphogenetic field by imprinting nearly one sixth of Earth's population with the reality of this possibility. This gave me the luxury of being able to be a lot more selective and only deal with open and positive media of integrity. Most proponents of this program retire from mainstream media after a while as the sensationalistic stand the media often adopt can be a little disconcerting. Secondly it was time for me to begin another level of my own service blueprint.

Q: As media spokesperson you now have spoken – directly or indirectly – to over 1 billion people about Divine Nutrition since 1997, what has been your greatest learning in dealing with a disbelieving and sceptical media?
A: Most of what I have learnt regarding dealing with the mainstream sceptical media I outlined in the document on Responsible Reporting at: -
http://www.jasmuheen.com/wp-content/uploads/Article-DNP-Responsible-Reporting.pdf

I have personally learnt greater humility and also that when we stand in a truth, that is a real experience for us, then it doesn't matter what people say. I have also learnt the benefits and importance of good research and thorough knowledge – both intellectual and experiential – of a subject. Lastly I experienced a reconfirmation that research that is beneficial for the world is not necessarily promoted if it clashes with more dominant money or power agendas. The economic, environmental and medical changes that will eventually occur through the adoption of The Prana Program are revolutionary and so can only come via a change in human consciousness where win/win/win resolutions are supported.

Q: Why have you persisted in being vocal with The Prana Program?

A: Because the benefits that The Prana Program offers to our world are too amazing and positive to ignore. I have also persisted in dealing with selective media as I believe it is one of our most powerful tools for speeding up global education and releasing the world from both fear and ignorance paradigms – assuming of course that it is used for the highest good and in integrity.

Q: *Can you share more on your own blueprint regarding anchoring The Prana Program in this world?*
A: This answer is now shared below in our April, 2012 media update.

Summary:
For me the best preparation process is to experiment and experience and then choose what allows you to feel and function best.

For example, I discovered in my early teens that my body's energy levels were greatly improved when I exercised regularly and had a light mainly raw-food diet. Later when I began meditation and yoga my bio-system functioned even better and the benefits were obvious. The process of physical, emotional, mental and spiritual refinement can bring incredible rewards that come through time, dedication and interest based on personal experimentation and via learning to listen to our inner voice and also the needs and voice of the physical body.

End of Book 1

2012 Update

22nd April 2012 – Media Update and deaths with the 21 day process ...

In Brazil I received the news that a Swiss woman died in January 2011 after being inspired by the movie *In the Beginning there was Light*, to do the 21 day process. Apparently she passed through the complete initiation okay but was later found dead by her adult children. An autopsy revealed she died of starvation and a further investigation revealed that she was very committed and conscious of this choice and determined to do this, regardless of the fact that we no longer support this process and have not done so since the late 1990's.

Four people have died in association with the 21 day process, since 1993 over a period of 19 years. With 40,000 now safely transitioned, our statistics are phenomenal compared to the fact that millions die each year from hunger related diseases and medical misdiagnosis. However statistics don't help those grieving for the loss of loved ones and any death can hinder our education program into this field of possibility which so many still don't understand.

And yet we can feel the impact of our work as the media response to this news release has been minimal compared to a decade ago. With so many names and people now to target – of other people now being nourished by prana – some articles did not mention me at all, preferring to focus on Prahlad Jani and others in the *In the Beginning there was Light* movie.

Preparing a press release in response – if required – is such a sensitive matter. Condolences to loved ones coupled with the gentle reminder that this research will go on regardless, due to the potential benefits it can bring to our world and the individual benefits it has already brought to so many; all of this requires a delicate diplomacy, a sensitivity of recognition of all who hurt when someone they love moves on.

This is what eventually came through for release:

Response from Jasmuheen at the Embassy of Peace re the 2011 death of a Swiss woman associated with the living on light breatharian process and the movie "*In the Beginning There Was Light*"...

Firstly we wish again to express our sincere condolences to the families of the four people who have died over the last 19 years in association with this. Regardless of the facts around how and why each death occurred, to lose a well loved friend or family member is extremely sad for all concerned.

Perhaps in a perfect world we would not lose our loved ones or the hundreds of thousands of children and adults who die each year from both hunger related and obesity related diseases. Nor would we lose the many that die each year from suicide, disease, medical malpractice and/or medical misdiagnosis. Research into solutions for all of this is ongoing in many fields including our own at the Embassy of Peace.

Until solutions can be found and until this perfect world can be created we all must deal with these issues every day.

I recognise that many in our media and society are still not educated into the full understanding of this alternative stream of nourishment called Prana as while it is well known in India it is still relatively unknown in the West. However as can be seen in the well made insightful and educational documentary "*In the Beginning There Was Light*" by Austrian filmmaker P.A. Straubinger, there are now many people from all walks of life and spiritual beliefs who have safely developed this unusual ability. For example the Russian breatharian Zinaida Baranova, Indian yogi Prahlad Jani, the Swiss biochemist Dr Michael Werner, the well known Solar Gazer Hira Ratan Manek who has been involved in extensive medical research, myself, plus countless Qigong practitioners as shown in the movie.

In this movie the list of doctors and scientists involved in assessing this phenomenon is impressive.

IN THE BEGINNING THERE WAS LIGHT:- Screened at Cannes Film Festival in the South of France in 2010, this documentary has also been shown in major movie cinemas globally. Filmed over a 6 year period, this documentary shows the quantum aspects of living on prana and has many detailed interviews with people such as:- Dieter Hochegger, Prof. Dr. Wolfgang Marktl, Prof. Dr. Anton Luger, Univ. Doz. Dr. Ingrid Kiefer, Dr. Ruediger Dahlke, Jasmuheen, Walter "Omsa" Rohrmoser, Dr. Michael Werner, Mataji Prahlad Jani, Dr. Sudhir Shah, Dr. V.N. Shah, Dr. Urmann Ohruv, Dr. Sanjay Metha, Hira Ratan Manek, Yuan Limin, You Xuande, Dr. TCM Qi Duan Li, Prof Dr. Gernot Pauser, Zinaida Baranova, Prof. Dr. Gerhard Hacker, Prof. Dr. Fritz-Albert Popp, PhD Dean Radin, Prof. Dr. Brian

Josephson, Prof. Dr. Amit Goswani, Prof. Dr. Rupert Sheldrake, Dr. Jakob Bösch, Prof. Dr. Robert Jahn.

All those who are able to live on Prana as a physical body source of nourishment are involved in their own way in creating a world that uses resources more wisely while also researching their own human potential. While our methods may seem unconventional they are still valid as we seek to find alternate ways of nourishing our world.

In our book *The Prana Program*, we shared that my role with this was as follows:-

Discover The Prana Program's gifts and live it all experientially thus proving to myself beyond a doubt its infinite possibilities as outlined in all of our books.

Research all that I could on the subject, write about it and offer my research to the world in a pragmatic and simple way as possible. This included researching and simplifying data in the ancient and hidden mystery schools, and personally undergoing various training.

Be a bridge regarding The Prana Program between the Eastern understanding, and my own experience of prana, and introduce the benefits of increasing the pranic flow as widely as possible to the West.

Find and support other proponents of this – Hira Ratan Manek, Zinaida Baranova, the Bigu states in the Qigong networks –and introduce their methodologies through our networks.

Be a media spokesperson for The Prana Program and via holistic education principles utilise the media to anchor The Prana Program reality in the morphogenetic field.

Set up communications systems to share our research en mass as per my constant touring, books and websites.

Introduce The Prana Program and its benefits through political networks, and formulate an effective program to combine and share our research with existing aid and resource redistribution programs via the United Nations and others.

Over the last decade we have achieved points 1 to 7 and have been well supported in so many ways. It was not my role to give a year or two of my time – as Hira Ratan Manek the solar gazer has done – to personally be involved with extensive medical and scientific testing. Yet it has been my role to act as a reporter and share the results of Hira's testing which has essentially proven the same thing – that a person can access enough prana, as an alternate form of nourishment so that they are free from the need to take physical food.

Despite all of this since the late 1990's I have been discouraging people in using the 21 day process as while thousands have safely utilised this deeply spiritual initiation, it has proven dangerous for those unprepared and to some who have chosen not to follow the guidelines in our *Living on Light* book (also called *Pranic Nourishment*.)

Over the years we have developed a safer, slower method to experience and access this ancient yogic alternative stream of nourishment so that the people of our world have more freedom of choice. This safe method is outlined in our book *The Food of Gods* and it must be noted that this is a spiritual journey and not a diet. People who stop eating food will die unless they have tuned themselves via their lifestyle to the Prana channels.

Our research manual *The Prana Program* provides a potential solution to world hunger.

Facts – Food for Thought - our world:-
- From Poverty.com website:- About 25,000 people die every day of hunger or hunger-related causes, according to the United Nations.
  Think Quest data: -
- In the Asian, African and Latin American countries, well over 500 million people are living in what the World Bank has called "absolute poverty";
- Every year 15 million children die of hunger;
- For the price of one missile, a school full of hungry children could eat lunch every day for 5 years;
- Throughout the 1990's more than 100 million children died from illness and starvation. Those 100 million deaths could be prevented for the price of ten Stealth bombers, or what the world spends on its military in two days!
- The World Health Organization estimates that one-third of the world is well-fed, one-third is under-fed one-third is starving. One in twelve people worldwide is malnourished, including 160 million children under the age of 5.
- Hunger in Global Economy; Nearly one in four people, 1.3 billion – a majority of humanity – live on less than $1 per day, while the world's 358 billionaires have assets exceeding the combined annual incomes of countries with 45 percent of the world's people.
- UNICEF; 3 billion people in the world today struggle to survive on US$2/day;
- In the U.S. hunger and race are related. In 1991 46% of African-American children were chronically hungry, and 40% of Latino children were chronically hungry compared to 16% of white children;
- One out of every eight children under the age of twelve in the U.S. goes to bed hungry every night; Half of all children under five years of age in South Asia and one third of those in sub-Saharan Africa are malnourished;
- To satisfy the world's sanitation and food requirements would cost only US$13 billion- what the people of the United States and the European Union spend on perfume each year.

In light of all that we have just stated, we invite the global media to publish this response in entirety rather than promote sensationalism via misinformation regarding this unusual lifestyle that more than 40,000 have successfully chosen thus freeing themselves on dependence on global food resources.

Due to the many benefits this research provides especially its impact on our environment, on global warming, plus our more efficient resource usage and the marked improvement on health and happiness levels (that come to all who increase their chi or Prana levels) our research into this field will continue. In the long term we trust our responsible education programs into how this is possible will be supported by the media so that the global benefits we envisage can come to pass. Remember we once believed that the earth was flat and just because we may not understand how something can be possible does not mean it isn't.

Due to the fact I am now travelling with the work of The Embassy of Peace, I will be unavailable for further commentary. - Jasmuheen for the Embassy of Peace

It was this 2011 death that prompted me to search again within and decide to withdraw the previous copy of this book from the German market, add more updated data and offer instead this new updated version.

OUR ESSENCE
AS A SOURCE OF COSMIC MICRO-FOOD
Excerpt from *BEing Essence* at
http://www.jasmuheen.com/products-page/other-books/3781-2/

As we move into a higher dimension of expression, which is a result of BEing more imbued with our Essence, we find that It can also provide us with a type of physical body nourishment that I have come to call *Cosmic Micro-food*.

Due to the beneficial effects that our research has found, that this can have on both our health and our environment, we will include some of the basics of this here on a bigger picture level.

To me, one of the most fulfilling journeys a soul can make while anchored in the plane of duality, is awareness of and full reconnection and perfect union with their I AM Essence.

Yet unity consciousness allows us to feel-sense that Essence as being everywhere, the very fabric of creation, the baseline frequency of life.

Apart from being able to nourish us physically via its cosmic micro-food flow, it also aligns us to a rhythm of such peace and contentment, that we find ourselves forever transformed.

Its gifts are endless.

Its ability to love, guide, heal and nourish us completely, is natural yet profound. It reveals itself in Its own way, in Its own time, when the energy streams can match It within us and around us, and yet we are never separate from It, It is always there, just Its volume alters, the strength or subtlety with which It flows.

All of this we can control by understanding the science of pranic living, which is the science of being Essence.

While we have already written five books on the being-physically-nourished-by-prana reality which share much more detail about this; the key to being able to be free from the need to take physical food and fluid, is to be anchored in the versions of ourselves that are most imbued with Essence.

This makes the Breatharian reality a spiritual journey and not a diet, for this intake of cosmic micro food comes from direct access to our Essence and its multi-dimensional nature.

Everyone has a version of themselves that has this freedom. We all have multi-dimensional, inter-dimensional versions that are already the true Breatharian, versions that exist without form as a flow of intelligent loving consciousness.

We all have versions of ourselves that are also so light-filled yet still in form, that prana as Essence, is the natural source of nourishment.

It is impossible to live without physical food or fluid intake if all we focus on is our personality self with its beta brain function living in a dual-natured world.

Yet a breatharian is said to be a breather of God and God as Essence breathes us all. As we shift identification to our Essence nature, feel It, experience all Its gifts including the choice of where we wish to take our physical body nourishment from, then we find that not only is our Essence as a God-like force, breathing us, but that we are in Essence the pure I AM that some call God.

Our Baseline Essence
Resource of Nourishment (Living on Light) - a quick summary

Our Essence is our life force which is pure prana.

To understand how we can utilise our Baseline Essence (B.E.) as an internal resource, we need to understand its composition, i.e. what our B.E. contains.

As an energy source, our B.E. holds all the building blocks of life and all creation has the same baseline Essence woven through it.

For example, a cotton shirt cannot be made until the cotton has been sown as seeds, then grown, harvested and woven, and from this fabric many types of garments can be made. Our baseline is like the cloth, a weave that runs through all.

Similarly the fabric of creation can be woven in many different ways. Some is woven into universes, galaxies, solar system, planets, human and other life forms.

How the B.E. expresses Itself, and Its very existence in everything, then becomes the common denominator of all as It is in all.

As the supporting fabric of creation, our Baseline Essence has every vitamin, mineral, element, chemical, electro-magnetic pulse potential and much more than a human body could need to utilise.

Therefore feeding our body and living purely on prana – or our Baseline Essence - is not about *creating* an alternate source of nourishment.

Instead we just need to tap into what is *already* in our Baseline Essence, and allow it to do what it has always known how to do even though we have forgotten this.

Merging our awareness and aligning our bio-system back with our B.E. brings many additional gifts apart from our Its ability to physically nourish us.

We tap into our B.E. in many different ways, yet the process begins by our acknowledgement of our B.E. as an internal resource that we all can access.

Acknowledgement of our B.E. is easier also when it is not just an idea but a tangible experience.

Experiencing our B.E. comes from matching frequencies with it, which we do via the Luscious Lifestyle Program that also emphasises Baseline Essence identification and conscious alignment.

Due to the Universal Law of Resonance, our B.E. also grows via our focus upon it.

Our B.E. contains a field of infinite intelligence. In this field is the innate knowing of how to keep a life-form alive and healthy on all levels.

In fact, our B.E. holds pre-programmed data flows on how to access anything we need to be self-sustaining and feel whole and complete.

Thus it is the perfect teacher.

Our steps then so far are:- attitudes of acknowledgement, allowance, and lifestyle alignment on a day to day basis.

Allowance requires a mindset shift, holding the awareness that we only eat for pleasure not for need as we know our Baseline Essence can feed us.

While food is wonderful to consume, it is nice to know we do not need it and to have a greater choice in how we wish to be nourished.

Next we need to lovingly invite our physical body system to open to receive a perfect blend of nourishment from all healthy sources including Cosmic Micro-food (or Chi, as prana) which is also our Baseline Essence.

We can also lovingly instruct our complete bio-system to open to our Essence as a source of perfect nutrition.

We can intend this to occur within our physical, emotional, mental and spiritual systems.

We can further ask our intelligent B.E. for us to be so well nourished on all levels, that we exist with Grace and ease in the rhythm of health, happiness, harmony and mutual enhancement with all.

This program of intention allows us to be a self-sustaining mechanism on all levels not just physically.

Next we need to learn to talk to and listen to the physical body. Stop eating out of habit. Eat only when and if you are hungry while you hold firm in the knowledge of what your B.E. can do for you.

Begin to eat less and eat more live and light foods. Go from 3 meals per day to 2 then 2 meals a day to 1. Put less on your plate – eat only until you are no longer hungry and not until you are full, as research has shown that this is better for you.

Via meditation, tune to your body consciousness and ask it what it wants you to eat, rather than what you think it needs.

Learn the B.E. Guidance breath test technique that we have already shared and use it to check your prana percentage on a regular basis and improve this percentage via your lifestyle. (This breath Test system is available in our <u>Being Essence booklet</u>.)

Using this method make the statement …

"Prana now provides more than 50% of my physical body nourishment!"

If the breath confirms this, then check using the same statement for more than 60% and so on until you ascertain your exact prana percentage.

Anytime you get a no response with the breath test, then drop the percentage amount you are checking, down as maybe your prana % is 40%, or even 49% for example.

If you get a yes to 50% then you can safely reduce your physical food intake by that % amount.

However if you do this, you must also hold the intention that:

"All my vitamins, all my minerals and everything I need to be a healthy, self regenerating, self sustaining system comes directly to me from prana as my Essence."

Full conversion to living purely on prana and our B.E. cannot be attempted until this level reads 100% and your complete bio-system is hooked in.

Note: while your mental and physical systems can often handle a quick conversion, the emotional body system can take much longer.

Conversion rates vary within our own bio-system, as well as person to person, as each is unique.

The embodiment of certain virtues is also important as a mode of accessing a stronger flow of Essence energy to the degree that a pure, pranic flow can feed us.

Use the B.E. Guidance System to assess your required virtue components for an easy transition. Which ones need more attention and development?

With sincere hearted intention, ask your Baseline Essence to guide you into this experience of nourishment organically, in the rhythm of joy, ease and Grace, in the right way and time for you.

Know and trust that your B.E. is your perfect energy resource of love, wisdom and true nourishment, by using meditation to experience what your Essence really is!

Be more conscious of the Divine Resource within and use It to free you from, or lessen, your dependence on the world's food resources.

TREAT YOUR BODY WITH LOVE AND CARE.

For a more detailed guidance system on this please read
The Food of Gods & also *The Prana Program*
And also *BEing Essence*.

For details on how and why Jasmuheen became involved in this reality please read her *Memories & Motivations – Breatharian Pathways* book.

All these books can be downloaded from her website at
http://www.jasmuheen.com/products-page/living-on-light/

Also go to http://www.jasmuheen.com/living-on-light/

On this page you will find our research on pranic living. There are books to read on this subject, CD's with meditations to increase your prana flow plus free videos. We trust that these will answer your questions on this matter. Pranic Living is Peace Path 11 of the 12 Pathways of Peace which form part of Jasmuheen's global service agenda.

Also see:

'In the Beginning There Was Light' movie data; Cannes film festival promo; Official film website for Peter Straubinger; 'In the Beginning There Was Light' – Trailer; Film Trailer on YouTube.

NEW! In depth interview with Jasmuheen – Parts 1 to 5 on the 21 day process and more – released September 2011. Click here for more.

Jasmuheen's Background

Ambassador of Peace, founder – Embassy of Peace, international lecturer & Online Course facilitator.
Artist & Sacred Art Retreat facilitator; film-maker & musician.
Author & metaphysical researcher of 35 books in 18 languages plus Jasmuheen's guided meditations for improving health & happiness. Also enjoy her Successful Living tips in the Our Selves page of our sister site the C.I.A.
Jasmuheen's Background; Darkroom Training facilitator.
Researcher into Pranic Living plus living on light and the breatharian agenda.
President of the Global Congress of Spiritual Scientists – Bangalore, India; Self Empowerment Academy founder & Cosmic Internet Academy facilitator.

Jasmuheen's main service agenda is the raising of consciousness to co-create a healthy, harmonious world.

www.jasmuheen.com

http://www.youtube.com/jasmuheen
http://www.facebook.com/pages/Jasmuheen/187152512352

Jasmuheen's Background Timeline
with her work with Pranic Living

Jasmuheen writes: "I am an Ambassador of Peace. My focus is to feed the children of our world the nourishment that they need. While a child dies every 2 seconds we cannot say that we live in a civilised world. Some may say that this is due to lack of both correct resource distribution and holistic education. Yes it is true that since the early 1970's, I have been experientially researching ancient, alternate nourishment sources that can feed us all – on physical, emotional, mental and spiritual levels – so that we can co-create a peace-filled, healthy and harmonised world. Yes it is true that there is a free, limitless inner resource that can unhook us from our dependence of our world's resources and release us from many perceived human limitations. I call the more recent research we have done on this resource, The Prana Program."

1993 – Began to live purely on prana after undergoing a specific spiritual initiation.
1993 – Began a 17 year intense experiential research study on the nourishment from prana phenomena.
1995 – Wrote & released the book *Pranic Nourishment* also known as *Living on Light*.
1995-1998 – Toured globally to share research on this reality.
1996 – Began a massive re-education program – via the Global Media – regarding prana as nourishment/resource stream.
1996-2004 – Talked about Divine Nutrition to > 900 million via the global media.

1997 – Began to set up various scientific research projects for Living on Light

1998-1999 – Wrote and published *Ambassadors of Light – World Health World Hunger Project*.

1999 – Began contacting World Governments & speaking with select ministers regarding solutions to eliminate world Hunger and Health issues.

2002-2003 – Wrote *The Food of Gods* as a safer, more gentle alternative for people to convert to pranic nourishment.

2003 – World Tour to promote "Divine Nutrition and The Madonna Frequency Planetary Peace Project".

2004 – Wrote *The Law of Love* with its focus on true breatharianism techniques, then toured with "The Law of Love and Its Fabulous Frequency of Freedom" agenda.

2005 – Began work on *The Prana Program* manual with its Prana Program Project specifically for eliminating hunger issues in Third World Countries.

2005 – Presented THE PRANA PROGRAM to the Society for Conscious Living at the United Nations Building in Vienna – Nov. 2005 & later at the UN in New York.

2006 – International tour with THE PRANA PROGRAM.

2006 – Filmed the documentary "*In The Beginning There was Light*" with Peter Straubinger – released at Cannes film festival in 2010.

2007 – Launched THE EMBASSY OF PEACE on 07-07-07 & began training programs for Ambassadors of Peace & Diplomats of Love.

2008 – Appointed President of the Global Congress of Spiritual Scientists Pyramid valley, Bangalore India. Began to implement The Prana Program in India.

2010 – Attended Kumbh Mela, Haridwar, India, to discuss pranic living with Indian's top Swamis & Yogis.

2010 – Toured with the Harmonics of the Heavenly Heart & Pranic Living Agenda & began to write/download the *Pathways of Peace Pragmatics* book.

2011 – Wrote and released her new book *Breatharian Pathways – Memories & Motivations* & also delivered the Pathways of Peace tour with its 12 Paths of Peace.

Jasmuheen is now focused on THE PATHWAYS OF PEACE and providing free education on her YouTube Channel – http://youtube.com/jasmuheen

During the past decade Jasmuheen has filmed countless documentaries for education into the pranic nourishment reality. See below videos.

RELEVANT YOUTUBE VIDEOS regarding living on light & pranic nourishment:-
Alternate nourishment sources for efficient personal & global resource usage.
Jasmuheen's interview with SupremeMasterTV – Part 1, Part 2, Part 3, Part 4, Part 5
Jasmuheen on her background with Pranic Nourishment
Pathways of Peace YouTube Video with Jasmuheen on her journey with her work.
Pranic Living – insight into what this is really about plus The Western Breatharian – introduction.
Jasmuheen at Raw Spirit Festival discussing the 8 point Luscious Lifestyles Program for pranic living.

Sensible Transitions for living on prana plus testing our prana percentage plus The Breath test – in English & Portuguese. A way of receiving pure inner guidance and answers.
Breatharian & Prana – Living on Light YouTube playlists;
The Global Picture:- Jasmuheen on prana & the world's resources; The Prana Program – introduction video to series on eliminating world hunger. These are also listed below.
Doing it:- Link to brief meditations - free on YouTube plus the Love Breath meditation to increase internal pranic flow.
Heart Talk – Higher Dreaming - Pranic Living with Jasmuheen - In this video Jasmuheen speaks from her heart about Earth's rising – here now – higher dreaming, enjoying oneness, united heart rhythms, divine delusions and pranic living.
Jasmuheen in Belgium 2008 with Paul Codde commenting on the new children and their expectations of higher standards.
Interview with Jasmuheen – Bridging Heaven & Earth plus Interview with Paula Gloria – Jasmuheen in New York.
Interdimensional Energy Field Science video playlist; also see all the videos in our Personal Harmonization Programs playlist – these are designed to increase personal & global harmony, health & happiness levels.
Living on Light – Nourishment from Source
Media Insights:- Jasmuheen & 60 Minutes; Skeptics & The Media - The German philosopher, Arthur Schopenhauer said: "All truth passes through three stages. First, it is ridiculed. Second, it is violently opposed. Third, it is accepted as being self-evident." Schopenhauer, like leading prana researcher Jasmuheen was a student of the Vedas, from which the very first information about prana has come. Prana is the energy behind the breath, it is also the energy that allows the divine to dance so evidently within the universe.

~Jasmuheen's books are now in 18 languages~

BOOKS - A selection of JASMUHEEN'S research manuals can be purchased from http://www.jasmuheen.com/products-page/

1. THE ENCHANTED KINGDOM Trilogy - 3 books in one.
2. QUEEN OF THE MATRIX - Fiddlers of the Fields with Jasmuheen (book 1 in the Enchanted Kingdom Trilogy)
3. KING OF HEARTS - The Field of Love - with Jasmuheen (book 2 in the Enchanted Kingdom Trilogy)
4. ELYSIUM - Shamballa's Sacred Symphony with Jasmuheen (book 3 in the Enchanted Kingdom Trilogy)
5. The Food of Gods
6. The Law of Love & Its Fabulous Frequency of Freedom
7. THE PRANA PROGRAM - Effective & Enjoyable Evolution
8. PRANIC NOURISHMENT - Nutrition for the New Millennium
9. Ambassadors of Light : World Health World Hunger Project
10. The Bliss of Brazil & The Second Coming

11. In Resonance
12. Divine Radiance - On the Road with the Masters of Magic
13. HARMONIOUS HEALING & The Immortal's Way
14. Darkroom Diary Downloads & The Freedom of The Immortal's Way
15. Cosmic Colleagues – Messages from the Masters
16. Biofields & Bliss Trilogy
17. Four Body Fitness : Biofields & Bliss
18. Co-creating Paradise
19. 'The Madonna Frequency' Planetary Peace Program
20. Meditation Magic
21. Sacred Scenes & Visionary Verse
22. Cruising Into Paradise
23. Embassy of Peace Programs
24. Breatharian Pathways - Memories & Motivations
25. Pathways of Peace
26. Being Essence

Coming soon – Pathways of Peace – book & CD
plus Cosmic Wanders – book 4 in the Enchanted Kingdom series

LINKS of interest:-
MAILING LISTS: Be kept up to date with the Self Empowerment Academy and the Cosmic Internet Academy's research and activities, then we have various mailing lists that you can freely subscribe to - so please go to http://www.selfempowermentacademy.com.au/htm/contact.asp and leave your details.
Follow JASMUHEEN on **TWITTER** and read JASMUHEEN'S **BLOG**; Jasmuheen's personal website – www.jasmuheen.com
EMBASSY OF PEACE: http://www.selfempowermentacademy.com.au/htm/Embassy-Peace.asp & at http://www.jasmuheen.com/what.asp .
FREE e-book on Embassy Programs & Projects go to:- http://www.selfempowermentacademy.com.au/htm/files/e-books-free/EMBASSY-TOTAL-PROGRAM-2009-web.pdf

OTHER INTERESTING LINKS:

For more data on Jasmuheen's Darkroom Retreats, Sacred Art Retreats and **tour schedule** go to: http://www.jasmuheen.com/htm/tour-retreats.asp
PRANIC LIVING:- http://www.jasmuheen.com/htm/Pranic-Living.asp - free data, books, CD's, DVD's, articles re Living on Light (Pranic Nourishment)
EDUCATIONAL E-BOOKS, **CD'S** & **DVD'S**: http://www.jasmuheen.com/htm/who-author.asp.
Books printed in paperback can be ordered and mailed to you via http://www.lulu.com/spotlight/jasmuheen

E-books can also be purchased via Amazon at http://www.amazon.com/author/jasmuheen

VIDEOS: For a large selection of free, brief videos by Jasmuheen go to: http://youtube.com/jasmuheen

GUIDED MEDITATIONS are available as MP3 downloads at http://www.itunes.com/jasmuheen

Pranic Nourishment
with Jasmuheen - 2012 edition

"Pranic Nourishment, also called Living on Light, is Jasmuheen's fourth book of metaphysical interest.
It is a fascinating story of her personal journey into being physically sustained purely by Light. It also touches on physical immortality, spirituality and
sexuality, new millennium relationships and mind mastery utilising the powerful programming of Dimensional Biofield Science.

Pranic Nourishment offers another, more positive, option in this time of world starvation and poverty that currently faces our Third World countries
and even more recently some Western countries.
A solution for Global Hunger issues is outlined in detail in her book "The Prana Program".

Pioneering new yet ancient pathways, many are
now exploring the option of neither being a meat eater, a vegetarian, a vegan,
a fruitarian but rather a 'liquidarian' or an individual sustained
and nourished purely by the Light of their own
Divine nature. To many this freedom of choice,
of dependency upon the world's food resources,
is another level of personal mastery.

Formerly a 'state of being' reserved for, or
attributed to, the Holy men, Saints or Sages
of the East; the process described in this text
offers a practical and spiritual alternative for
those wishing to practically begin to embrace
physical immortality, cease or reverse the aging process or 'live on Light'
and be nourished instead by cosmic-micro food or prana.

Please note that the 21 day process, as described in this book, can be dangerous for the unprepared.
This is a spiritual journey of self mastery, not a diet.

Ⓞeating
90

Made in the USA
Lexington, KY
25 July 2013